Profiles in Cognitive Aging

Profiles in Cognitive Aging

DOUGLAS H. POWELL

in collaboration with Dean K. Whitla

Harvard University Press

Cambridge, Massachusetts
London, England
1994

Test development and normative data copyright © 1993, 1994 by the Risk Management
Foundation of the Harvard Medical Institutions, Inc.

This book has been printed on acid-free paper, and its binding materials have been chosen for
strength and durability.

Library of Congress Cataloging-in-Publication Data

Powell, Douglas H.
    Profiles in cognitive aging / Douglas H. Powell in collaboration
with Dean K. Whitla.
        p. cm.
    Includes bibliographical references and indexes.
    ISBN 0–674–71331–1 (alk. paper)
    1. Cognition in old age. 2. Cognition—Age factors. I. Whitla,
Dean K. II. Title.
    [DNLM: 1. Cognition—in old age. WT 150 P882p 1994]
BF724.85.C64P68 1994
155.67—dc20
DNLM/DLC
for Library of Congress   94–18126
                          CIP

To my teachers, at Lawrence University and at Harvard,
who have made so much difference in my life

Contents

Preface

This book presents our findings about patterns of cognitive aging in the later adult years. It is a product of the close collaboration of more than a dozen colleagues who worked with me to develop a new computerized test for assessing cognitive functions. In the pages ahead we will share with the reader what we have learned about which abilities are best preserved in the later years and which ones decline earliest and most rapidly. We will see how factors such as gender, years of education, and health influence those patterns. We will also describe models for assessing mild cognitive impairment, normal cognitive aging, and optimal cognitive aging.

The core consulting group for this project consisted of experts in neuropsychology and neurology as well as research design, quantitative methods, and computer technology. Our work resulted in the creation of *MicroCog: The Assessment of Cognitive Functioning,* which was published last year. The focus of this book is not so much the development of MicroCog but rather what we have learned about the process of cognitive aging. With this unique sample of physicians and normal volunteers, we had a rare opportunity to understand to what extent education and occupation might influence the retention or loss of particular intellectual skills.

Because of the increased interest in cognitive aging over the past decade (the two divisions of the American Psychological Association that have grown most rapidly in the last ten years are Gerontology and Neuropsychology), because the results of longitudinal research, some of which was begun nearly four decades ago, are now bearing fruit, and because of the development of new quantitative methods for aggregating research, some of our "discoveries" have turned out not to be so new today. Rather they have confirmed reports that have appeared during the past five years while our investigations have been in progress. For instance, the low correlation between physical health and cognitive abilities found among our older volunteers has been reported by others. The finding that verbal memory after delay is not the first ability to decline with age is another example. That our data independently confirm these recent reports, which run counter to previous theory, may contribute building blocks for new models of cognitive aging.

Two other areas we have explored in which the reports of others have not been plentiful are the development of empirical models for normal cognitive aging and optimal cognitive aging. Because of my own longstanding interest in defining normalcy and understanding normal human development, these two topics have been especially interesting. With age-based mandatory retirement now outlawed for most occupations, and growing numbers of older individuals physically and mentally able to continue to work beyond the age of sixty-five, it will be important to have empirical standards for normal cognitive aging that differentiate this state from mild cognitive impairment. The proposed model is flexible and can be adjusted to meet the requirements of selection questions. Our interest in optimal cognitive aging grew out of the observation that a significant minority of the volunteers in our sample who were in the eighth to ninth decades of their lives scored well above the average for individuals in their prime, and we explored some of the characteristics of this group of high scorers.

The foundation blocks from which a project such as this grows are the creative efforts of hundreds of other researchers, many of whom are cited in this volume. An equal number, whose work covers much of the same ground, just as easily could have been acknowledged. There are two investigators whose work merits special mention: K. Warner Schaie and Timothy A. Salthouse. Schaie was among the very first to see the value of studying the cognitive aging process longitudinally. His visionary project, the Seattle Longitudinal Study, begun in 1956, has produced extensive findings about the nature of cognitive aging. These rich data from the Seattle study have been analyzed and compared by generations of social scientists and are likely to continue to excite researchers in the future. Our findings have benefited greatly because we were able to examine them in the context of Schaie's work.

No less important to our understanding of cognitive aging has been Salthouse's prolific work. For more than a decade, he has been producing extensive reanalyses and integrations of the research in cognitive aging carried out by others. During this period he and his colleagues at the Georgia Institute of Technology have also produced extensive research of their own, especially in the areas of disuse, working memory, and processing speed. When we have encountered puzzling findings, such as patterns of relative decline or stability across decades or the relationship between health and cognition, it has been helpful to be able to refer to Salthouse's comprehensive works.

This project grew out of the creative vision of the Board of Directors of the Controlled Risk Management Insurance Company, Ltd. (CRICO) and the Risk Management Foundation of the Harvard teaching hospitals (RMF). It was this small group of individuals who in 1986 saw the potential need for a way to screen older professionals who are now entitled to continue working beyond what until January 1, 1994, was a normal retirement age. CRICO/RMF provided most of the funding for the project. A NIA Small Business Innovative Research grant provided support for the concurrent construct validity study.

The vision of the CRICO/RMF Board of Directors was complemented by the enthusiasm and creativity of the consulting group who conceived and nurtured earlier versions of MicroCog through its developmental years. They were neuropsychologists Edith F. Kaplan, Ph.D., Sandra Weintraub, Ph.D., and Helene S. Porte, Ed.D.; psychiatrist Randolph Catlin, M.D., neurologist H. Harris Funkenstein, M.D., and clinical psychologist Babette Whipple, Ph.D.; research design and quantitative methods experts Dean K. Whitla, Ph.D., James H. Ware, Ph.D., and John Harrington; project administrator Patricia A. Horgan; and Frank B. Bernstein, who served double duty as a creator of the initial software for MicroCog and a person all of us came to depend on for statistical analyses. Kirk Daffner, M.D., and Theodore Bililies, Ph.D., joined the consulting group toward the end of the project and made substantive contributions. Dr. Ware left before the end of the project because he was called to be Dean of Students at the Harvard School of Public Health. Dr. Funkenstein, formally a Chief of Neurology at Brigham and Women's Hospital in Boston, died in an ocean swimming accident, something he loved doing, prior to the publication of the test. His tragic death was a grave loss for us all. His memory, however, lives on in his contribution to MicroCog and to this book.

This undertaking would have been impossible without the remarkably accommodating spirit of numerous individuals and organizations. This spirit created an atmosphere of congeniality and trust, adaptation to stress, and tolerance for the unexpected. We experienced this pleasant working atmosphere in our dealings with CRICO/RMF. It was also apparent within the consulting group, the medical schools of the Universities of Miami, South

Florida, and Florida, in the county medical organizations throughout Florida, at the School of Aerospace Medicine, at Beth Israel Hospital and Brigham and Women's Hospital, at the Emory-Wesley Woods Center for Aging, at the Florida Geriatric Research Program, at the North Cambridge Senior Center and the Brockton Veteran's Administration Medical Center, and most especially among the hundreds of individuals who volunteered to take earlier versions of MicroCog.

Thanks go to the following people at CRICO/RMF: Alison Anderson, Anne Blotner, Diane Falter Butera, Daniel Creasey, Judy Foley, Jock Hoffman, James Holzer, Helen Kuzenevich, Mark Lindsay, Janice Lynch, John McCarthy, Kim McLeon, James Moore, Bridget Poole, Katie Quinn, Lynnette Robinson, Elizabeth Romo, Kathy Schlachter, John Swift, Lynn Volk, Sheila Vorgeas, and Judy Wells.

We also express appreciation to Professor Stephen Bradley and his committee for their oversight and suggestions. Professors John Pratt, Frederick Mosteller, Robert Rosenthal, and Donald Rubin, as well as reviewers from the journal *Psychology and Aging,* provided us with valuable critical comments on our statistical analyses.

Without the unfailing interest, encouragement, backing, and physical support of Dr. Warren Wacker and many of his staff at the Harvard University Health Services, this project would have been impossible to begin and continue. Key among the UHS staff who provided us needed help were Drs. Sholem Postel, Michael Carty, and Charles Weingarten; also Mary Kocyk, Carlyle Flash, Janet Cooper, Mary Lawton, Piero Pisani, and Norma Somers. Special appreciation goes to John Ketterer and the physical therapy staff for allowing us to use their facilities for the weekend pilot testing of retired Harvard faculty.

Very special appreciation is extended to four Florida physicians: Dr. James B. Perry, past president of the Florida Medical Association; Dr. David Challoner, Vice President for Health Affairs, University of Florida Medical Center; Dr. Bernard Fogel, Dean of the University of Miami School of Medicine; and Dr. William Hale, Director of the Florida Geriatric Research Program. Key executives at the Florida medical schools and at the county medical societies in Florida supported our efforts to test physicians at their facilities: Sue Ellen Apte, Arthur Auer, Thomas Clark, William Coletti, Peggy Davenport, Tad Fisher, Jane Icely, Sarah Puga, Dr. Robert Rubin, Joan Runnels, William Stafford, Elsie Trask, Theresa Van Norman, and Anne Wilke. Thanks also go to Vito Culicchia for moving and setting up the equipment from site to site and to Elizabeth Ann Evans for coordinating much of the Florida testing.

Testing in Texas at the School of Aerospace Medicine, Brooks Air Force Base in San Antonio, was made possible by the invaluable support of Colonels J. G. Davis, James Raddin, and John Bishop. Others at Brooks Air Force Base who lent significant assistance were Colonel Alfred Cheng, Lieutenant Colonel Allen Parmet, and Doctors Bryce Hartman and John Patterson.

We are indebted to the Tandy Corporation, which donated computers and other necessary equipment, provided emergency assistance, and at times stored the equipment for us to use at each site for testing participants. We would like to thank Bernard Appel, Robert Meyers, and James Mc-Grody at corporate headquarters in Fort Worth, Texas; Ted Badger, John Butler, Ernest Hamilton, Lee Lomax, Joseph Malouf, Edward Roy, Alan Schneider, and Walter Whitacre in Florida; George Ricks, George Simpson, and Selwyn Polit in San Antonio, who supported us with equipment and on-site help; and Alan Lyscars, who unfailingly met our needs in Massachusetts.

We appreciate the day-to-day backing of Virginia Powell and her staff at Powell Associates: Angela Adinolfi, Belinda Chu, Maura Kelly, Jane King, Kathleen O'Leary, Teresa Osborn, Maryjane Quinn, and Elaine Watson. They offered invaluable assistance in so many ways throughout the entire project. Special thanks go to Norman Littell for the endless hours spent recovering references in the Harvard library system.

We are grateful to Dr. Robert Green, Dr. Joanne Green, Joan Harrison, and their group at the Wesley Woods Center for Aging for their willingness to carry out validation studies. Gratitude also goes to Professors Robin Morris at Georgia State University and Theodore Millon at the University of Miami for allowing us to recruit their graduate students to help with the testing.

Special thanks go to the staff at the Florida Geriatric Research Program for allowing us to test at their facilities, to test members of their program, and for their invaluable work with the concurrent construct validation study. We wish to acknowledge Doctor William Hale, Linda Smiley, Jeanette Hale, Patricia Bennett, Dorothy Hatfield, Lois Johnson, and Agnes (Toni) Kovak. Our appreciation is also extended to Dr. Lewis Wurgaft, the principal investigator of the research, Doctors Cynthia Cimino and Mark Golden at the University of South Florida, and the graduate students who assisted us with testing: George Behner, Jill Cattarin, Sylvia Johnson, and

Stacy Tantliss. Thanks also go to Dr. Charles Spielberger for his valuable contribution of a research version of the State-Trait Personality Inventory to our study.

We express our gratitude to Doctors Mitchell Rabkin, Richard Nesson, and Eugene Braunwald, as well as Nick Johnson, Kristians Veinbergs, and all the staff at Beth Israel Hospital and Brigham and Women's Hospital for allowing us to use their facilities for testing and to recruit their interns and residents. Special appreciation is extended to Helene Corry, Coordinator of the North Cambridge Senior Center, and her staff, and the staff at the Council on Aging in Cambridge for all their support and assistance. Thanks also go to all the volunteers at the Senior Center who were willing to take the test twice for our test-retest study.

Without the willingness of staff members at the field sites to work long days, nights, and weeks to test nearly 2,000 individuals under, at times, extraordinarily challenging circumstances, the project would never have been completed. We salute you: Marc Caggiano, Bonnie Carlson, Michelle Cochran, Daniel Donnelly, Mel Eldridge, Dora Fienberg, Rob Godsall, Lisa Graham, Danette Hahn, Daniel Hampton, Tricia Jones, Lori Lackman, Lawrence Passman, James Pates, Clint Patterson, Debbie Rogell, Kimberly Shaw, Stephen Sinclair, Keith Vandercook, and Patricia Wick.

Several people deserve special mention. The first of these is C. Lee Birk, M.D., who first encouraged me to write this book. Several members of the consulting group contributed substantially to portions of this manuscript. Patricia Horgan was the administrator of the project from start to finish in Cambridge and Boston, all over Florida, and in Atlanta and San Antonio. Without her management, energy, negotiation skills, willingness to learn new material and master unfamiliar techniques in a very brief time and to volunteer for the toughest jobs, this project could not have been completed. Doctors Kaplan, Porte, and Weintraub wrote earlier drafts of a theoretical basis for MicroCog. Dr. Weintraub also wrote the section of Chapter 8 on suggestions for cases where a screening test score falls below a minimum threshold for normal cognitive functioning. Dr. Whipple made many of the "rough places plain" in the manuscript. Dr. Dean K. Whitla, whose unexpected new responsibilities at Harvard precluded his being a coauthor as we had originally planned, made significant contributions throughout the book, especially to the portions of Chapter 3 concerning reliability and factor analyses, as well as contributing ideas to the chapters on normal cognitive aging and optimal cognitive aging. Frank B. Bernstein compiled most of the statistical data and carried out the computations that provided the bases for nearly all of the tables and figures. It should be said, however, that I wrote the final drafts of every chapter, and the responsibility for the content of the book and the opinions expressed is mine alone.

Finally, we acknowledge our deep gratitude to the many volunteers who participated in this work. Many of these individuals contributed precious time snatched with difficulty from a busy schedule, and a large number traveled a considerable distance to the testing sites. Their gift of time and effort enabled this work to be completed.

D.H.P.
Naples, Florida
April 1994

Profiles in Cognitive Aging

1

Introduction: Understanding Cognitive Aging

Sooner or later almost all adults worry about whether we are "losing it" cognitively. Not long after 40, we may begin to notice occasional mental lapses—forgetting a friend's name, a familiar phone number, or the word for the thing we use to turn over pancakes. By age 60 these name/number/word-finding difficulties accelerate, along with problems recalling a detail of something that happened this morning, why we have opened the refrigerator door, or whether we parked our car to the right or left of the supermarket's front door. Nearly everyone who has had these moments of forgetfulness and disorientation wonders whether these are "normal" declines, passing episodes, or whether they signify the onset of Alzheimer's disease or something equally ominous.

These questions are now in the forefront of science and medicine. The U.S. Congress has designated the 1990s as the "decade of the brain." Funding for research on understanding aging and ameliorating its effects is at a higher level than ever before. In 1985 the National Institute of Aging, a division of the National Institutes of Health (NIH), had a budget of $144,527,000. For 1994 Congress approved $420,303,000 to support research areas such as the biology of aging, the psychological, cultural, social, and economic factors affecting the process of growing old, the maintenance of health and effective functioning in the later years, the neuroscience of aging, and investigation of the differences between normal age-related changes in physiological and cognitive functions and Alzheimer's disease and related dementias of aging.[1]

This last area—understanding the differences among normal, optimal, and impaired cognition among older women and men—may be a more important issue today than at any other time in history. The reasons are demographic, legislative, physical/psychological, and economic. Demographically, senior citizens are more numerous than ever before. Legislatively, mandatory retirement is largely a thing of the past. Physically and psychologically, the elderly are more likely to enjoy the challenges and satisfactions that life has for them. Economically, this society and its citizens shortly will have a reciprocal need for work to continue beyond age 65.

Demographic Patterns

Today, more older people live in the United States and the rest of the world than at any other time. At the beginning of the twentieth century, the average American would not live to see a fiftieth birthday. When the twenty-first century begins, the average life expectancy will be about 80 for women and 76 for men. In 1990 there were more people 55 and over than there were teenagers in the United States. The 85-plus group, presently numbering over 3 million, is the fastest-growing segment of the population. By the year 2000 one American in seven will be over 65; twenty-five years later the proportion will be one in five.[2]

Population growth among the aging is not unique to the United States. Successful efforts to reduce fertility and mortality in East Asian countries have created demographic changes paralleling those in America. By the year 2025, the population of those 65 and over in Japan will double. In the People's Republic of China and Latin America, this percentage will triple. A near quadrupling is projected for Korea, Singapore, and Malaysia.[3] Population projections for other parts of the world follow these trends, though the rate of increase is less. In Europe and Africa the growth rate for these older age groups is 46 percent and 26 percent respectively.[4]

These demographics play out in everyday life. Shopping malls have created more numerous parking places for the handicapped, most of whom are elderly. Curbs with ramps built into them at crosswalks accommodate arthritic walkers as well as wheelchairs. At airports, wheelchairs in growing numbers await the arrival of older travelers who are physically frail yet adventurous in spirit. A church service program in a New England town says, "All who are able may stand during the hymns."

The statistics showing a dramatic lengthening of life expectancy over the twentieth century may be slightly deceptive with respect to older adults. Although life span has been growing dramatically for infants, it has been creeping up more slowly for adults. In the United States, the life span for a baby girl in 1900 was about 48 years; by 1960 it rose to 73; and in the year 2000 the average female newborn will live to age 80. In other words, during the twentieth century there has been a 67% increase in the longevity of female infants. For male infants, the improvement in life span is 59% over the twentieth century.

What has happened during the same period to 65-year-olds? Figure 1.1 plots the average life remaining at birth and at age 65 for the twentieth century by gender. The increase in life expectancy during the twentieth century will be the same for the 65-year-old woman (66%) as for the female infant. We can see that the improvement curves are less spectacular for older males. In 1900, the average 65-year-old man had about 11.5 years remaining; in 1960 he could expect to live 13 years longer; and by 2000 he can

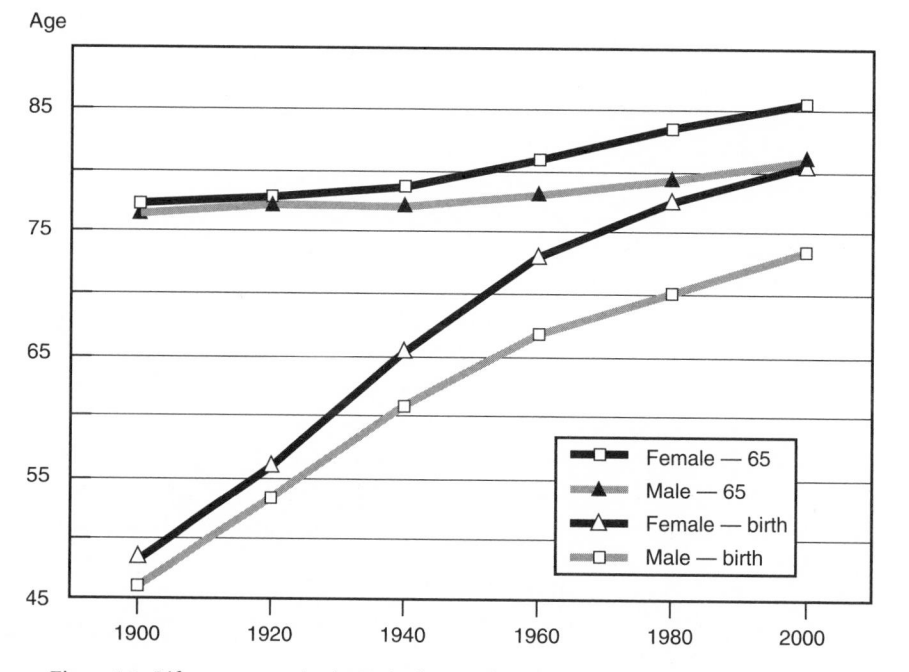

Figure 1.1 Life expectancy in the United States for all races, at birth and age 65. *Sources: Vital Statistics of the United States, vol. II: Mortality, 1988,* section 6, p. 13; G. Spencer, *Projections of the Population of the United States by Age, Sex, and Race: 1988–2080* (Washington, D.C.: Bureau of the Census, 1989), table B-5, p. 153.

anticipate 16 more birthdays. This is a more modest improvement of 37% in the life span during this century—surely not insignificant, but less than that of females.

Legislative Changes

Compelling a worker to retire because of age is prohibited in the United States by Public Law 99-592 as of January 1, 1994. This law, banning age-based mandatory retirement, made two exceptions: public safety officers and tenured faculty. The law did not apply to the former group—firefighters, police, and corrections officers—because of the importance of their occupations with respect to public well-being. The exemption was based on the logic that age so adversely affects physical and mental capabilities that public safety officers could no longer perform their jobs competently. Therefore, public safety would be put at risk. Two conditions were thought to potentially compromise the effectiveness of these workers: either sudden physical incapacitation by a serious medical event such as a stroke or heart attack, or what might be called an "accumulated deficit," in which a particular cognitive skill, such as memory, deteriorates over a period of time to the point where an individual can no longer carry out a safety procedure properly. Therefore, Congress felt that age-based mandatory retirement should be retained for this group.

An exception was also made for college professors because of four primary concerns: faculties would become clogged with older faculty members who were no longer mentally competent; less room would be available for new teachers and researchers with fresh ideas and current training; fewer openings would exist for minorities and women; and budgets would skyrocket because of the inability of colleges and universities to replace older professors with less expensive younger ones.[5]

As part of the new legislation, Congress directed that studies should be carried out prior to the effective date of the law to assess the potential impact of eliminating mandatory retirement for these two groups. For the public safety officers, the Secretary of Labor and the Equal Employment Opportunity Commission (EEOC) had the responsibility for determining whether valid physical and mental tests can be used to assess the competence of police officers and firefighters to perform their jobs beyond the normal retirement age. For tenured faculty, the law required the EEOC to enter into an agreement with the National Academy of Sciences to form a committee to carry out a study of the potential impact on institutions of higher education of eliminating mandatory retirement.

The EEOC contracted with the Center for Behavioral Sciences at Pennsylvania State University to study the question of whether age-based retirement for public safety officers was appropriate. Their task was to determine if accurate standardized measures were available that could be shown to be valid predictors of job performance, and then to recommend the course of action that might compare chronological age with test performance. Landy and his colleagues[6] approached this challenging task by reviewing numerous sources of information: scientific journals, technical reports, data sets on fitness, illness, and injury, and the expertise of their research team. They produced an extensive report and bibliography which supported the following conclusion: "We believe that age is a poor predictor of individual capacity and limitations. Further, we believe that the public safety is seldom at substantial risk from ineffective performance of a single public safety officer. Thus, we cannot recommend the retention of chronological age as a criterion for mandatory retirement decisions."[7]

This conclusion was based on two primary findings. First, Landy and his research team confirmed the data-based judgments of others[8] that enormous variability exists among older adult workers. Many individuals well into their sixties easily match their younger colleagues on tests of physical and cognitive vigor. Second, they believe it is crucial to distinguish between "chronological age" and "functional age." They then recommended that existing tests of physical and mental ability be used to make decisions about the retention of public safety officers rather than an arbitrary mandatory retirement age.

The National Academy of Sciences also recommended against a compulsory age ceiling for tenured faculty, though for different reasons. They reached their conclusion by a complex process that involved inviting college presidents and senior faculty from 58 institutions of higher learning to identify issues related to mandatory retirement; intensive case studies of 17 colleges and universities; surveying the potential impact of uncapping the age requirement for retirement for 8,382 faculty members; and studying retirement patterns of institutions that have no age ceiling. The study reached two major conclusions: first, "at most colleges and universities few tenured faculty would continue working past age 70 if mandatory retirement is eliminated"; and second, "at some research universities a high proportion of faculty would choose to work past 70 if mandatory retirement is eliminated."[9] In other words, this survey concluded that uncapping the age ceiling for mandatory retirement would be unlikely to burden most colleges and universities with older professors who would block the infusion of necessary new blood.

These projections were confirmed independently by Rees and Smith, who studied retirement patterns at 14 private liberal arts colleges and 19 public universities.[10] Some had no age cap for retirement, and some required mandatory retirement. The investigators discovered no appreciable differences between the average retirement ages at capped and uncapped public universities. The only difference was that faculty tended to work 1.45 years longer at research-based universities. Among liberal arts colleges, the professors teaching longer were those at the more elite institutions whose students had higher SAT scores.

It is also likely that teaching load influences how long faculty members work beyond normal retirement age. Professors at research universities and more prestigious colleges generally are called upon to teach fewer classes and to instruct fewer students than faculty at larger state universities and private institutions. To teach one course in the fall to bright undergraduates and perhaps a seminar in the spring on his own research to a dozen graduate students might not seem so daunting for a 72-year-old professor. By contrast, his mid-50s counterpart in a community college, worn out from teaching three different classes each term for 25 years, may be looking for an early exit.

Physical and Psychological Factors

Although the total life expectancy of the 65-year-old has expanded by only a few years since 1900, little doubt exists that the physical vigor of many present-day 55-, 65-, 75-, and even 85-year-olds is superior to that of their parents and grandparents at the same age. The quality of life especially for the "youngest old," those from about 60 to 75, surpasses that of their parents.[11] A large number remain vigorous physically and mentally, are comfortable financially, and, if retired, devote leisure time to personally fulfilling activities such as travel, study, gardening, sports, service to others, and politics. A significant minority of this young-old group continue to work full or part time. Much of this improvement has to do with an understanding of the benefits of eating more healthfully—reducing the amount of fat, cholesterol, and calories in our diets. Adults of all ages know about the value of stopping smoking and moderating the intake of alcohol and caffeine. Exercise is a priority for many.

Many of those older people who exercise continue to compete at what would have been an astonishing level of proficiency two generations ago. One uncomplicated index of the proficiency of today's physically fit older athletes is comparative times for distance running. For instance, the U.S. records for male and female 65-year-olds for 10 kilometers (6.2 miles) are 35:62 and 46:18 respectively; for 75-year-olds, 43:24 and 53:40. Anyone who has ever tried running 6.2 miles will find the times of these older runners astonishingly fast.

Figure 1.2 shows the percentage decline from age 35 expected among male and female competitive runners from ages 40 to 80. These statistics, compiled by the *National Masters News*[12] and by the World Association of Veteran Athletes on the basis of hundreds of masters races, equate the per-

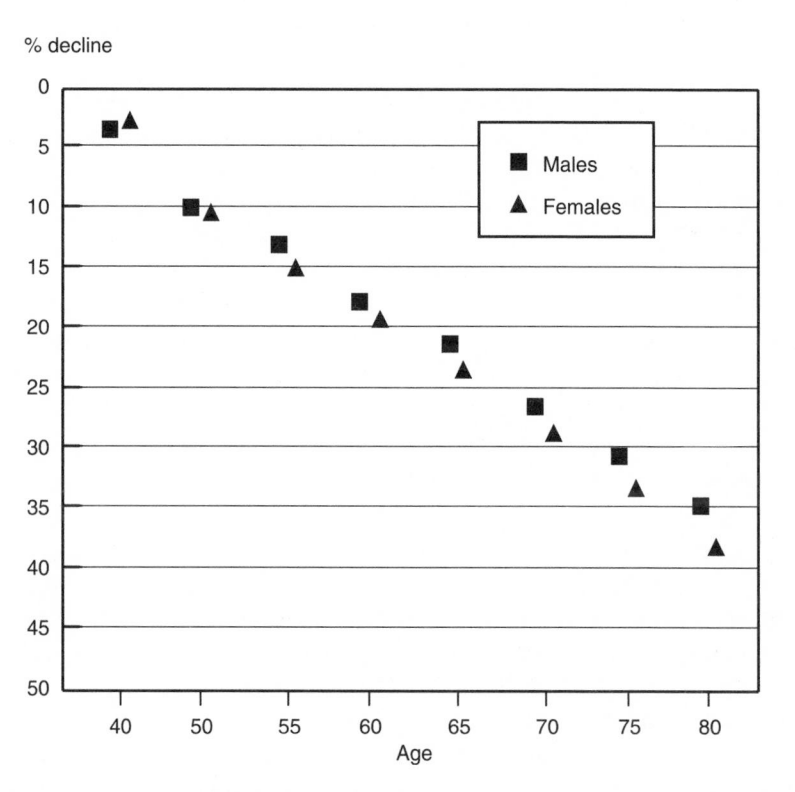

Figure 1.2 Percentage decline in time from age 35 for running 10K (6.2 miles), by age group and gender. *Source: Masters Age-Graded Tables: 1990 Edition* (Van Nuys, Calif.: National Masters News), pp. 24–25.

formance of older runners with those at younger ages. It can be seen that the percentage differences between 40-year-olds and those who are 35 are small: 3.3% and 3.0% respectively. At 60, the gap is 17.3% and 19.1%, and at 75 the differences are 30.5% and 33.6%.

Not all senior citizens are distance runners. Doubtless a large number exercise infrequently and enjoy eating and drinking what they please. But there is a growing subset of healthy, more physically and intellectually vigorous older people who have a continuing need to enjoy the challenges and satisfactions available to them. Larger numbers than ever before are enrolled in colleges and universities, in volunteer work, and in employment.

The need to obtain the satisfactions derived from working may remain well beyond age 65 or may reappear after a first retirement. For example, a previously burned-out senior automotive executive, reinvigorated by a two-year retirement, may discover that he misses making something happen as he did when he was on the job. In particular, he longs for the satisfaction that accompanied a sense of competence,[13] the sense of agency that used to come from executing a business plan. Though he has no desire to return to Detroit, he may look for a small business in which to invest. Finally, he joins a younger man and begins a successful waste oil recycling company, which he continues to manage for 15 more years.

Another motive for returning to work is that, in Freud's words, having a job, more than any other activity, gives us a place in society.[14] Some retirees find that they greatly miss this sense of having a position in the world. A former college English teacher returns to the faculty of a small private school because it provides her with a role to fill, a function to carry out, and a sense of being of value to an institution, which brings a personal remuneration beyond the paycheck.

A need for social belonging prods some to return to the workplace. Maslow makes the point that everyone has a fundamental need for acceptance from others.[15] For many, retirement brings growing isolation. Family members are busy with their active lives; old friends have scattered and new ones are hard to make. A year after retiring from a medical practice in New Jersey, a woman now living in a small Florida town decides to work half-time on the staff of a senior center because she misses being part of a community of working people.

Finally, many people find that their psychological adjustment is linked to their having a job. This is not so surprising: studies of men in their prime who have lost their jobs often discover dramatically negative psychological effects.[16] Other evidence across a broad spectrum of people shows that many people prefer working to retirement. In the early 1950s, 400 men from ages 21 to 65 in occupations ranging from unskilled jobs to professional and managerial positions were asked: "If by some chance you had inherited enough money to live comfortably, do you think you would work anyway or not?" 80% said they would continue to work. In a similar study conducted 25 years later, the number was 72%. The reasons that were given for continuing to work in the earlier study support the idea that employment is related to mental health. Many commented that if they didn't work they would feel lost, bored, or wouldn't know what to do with their time. Some said they would have difficulty keeping out of trouble, or would go crazy.[17]

Most people returning to work after their first retirement find employment in lower-level positions than they had previously. Some cannot find comparable jobs; others do not want the stress of their previous careers. One example is a former vice president of a bank who now works as a gate keeper, 20 hours a week, at a condominium complex in Arizona. Another is a woman who sold her business and fills in as a hostess at a friend's restaurant three nights a week. A third is a retired USAF officer who bags groceries part time at a store down the street in order to have something to do.

The desire to do something productive, to have a place in society, and to be part of a group is independent of age. Many older workers know that the satisfactions deriving from being employed cannot be taken for granted. This may partially explain why older people have fewer absences, are more satisfied with their work, feel less stress on the job, and have fewer accidents than younger employees.[18]

Economic Considerations

There shortly will be a growing mutual need for the citizens of the United States to continue to work past age 65. If the American economy is to continue to expand in the first quarter of the twenty-first century, it will need the services of its senior citizens to work longer than before. This may be difficult to believe in the present economic climate, where recent college graduates are unable to find work and their parents worry about keeping their jobs as organizations downsize. However, fewer young people are entering the work force today. In 1990, about 1.3 million young people aged 18–24 started full-time employment, as compared with approximately 3 million just over a decade before.[19] This reduction in the number of young people going to work is a direct result of what has been called the "baby bust" generation. They follow the "baby boomers," born in the 1946–1964 period. In the years 1965–1977, the birth pools were substantially smaller than in the two prior decades: on average, there was about a three percent decline in infant births each year. The trough of the baby-bust generation was the period 1973–1977, when about 3.2 million births occurred yearly. This compares with 4.2 million ten years before.

Because the baby-boom generation will be in their working prime until beyond the end of the first decade of the twenty-first century, and because all of the baby-bust generation will have entered employment by then, the turn of the century will find the average U.S. worker closer to 40 than 30. In 1980, for example, the median age was 34.3; in 1988 it rose to 35.9; and it is anticipated to be 39.3 by the year 2000.[20] For these reasons, the economy will need to continue to employ those who pass their sixty-fifth birthday.[21]

The prediction that the turn of the century will bring with it an oversupply of jobs because of the baby-bust years 1965–1977 is subject to four caveats that influence both supply and demand. On the supply side, the first caveat concerns immigration: it is possible that legal and illegal immigration could go a long way toward filling the necessary pool of workers. Population projections to the year 2000, however, anticipate little change in the number of documented and undocumented immigrants entering the United States. A census bureau forecaster predicts that net immigration will actually decline from about 600,000 in 1988 to 500,000 in 1998.[22]

A second supply-side factor that could influence the need for older workers concerns education and training. To what extent will new workers, especially those preparing for management or professional responsibility, possess skills equal to those aging workers they would normally replace? Recent studies show this to be a serious concern. A study by the Educational Testing Service of 3,600 Americans aged 21–25 found that most were unable to understand a newspaper article at a level much beyond a minimal degree of proficiency.[23] A later assessment of the math and science knowledge of 13-year-olds in the United States found the American students to be in the lowest group when compared with youngsters from Korea, Canada, Spain, and Ireland. These data heighten the concern that young people entering the labor force may not be sufficiently prepared to handle the more demanding jobs.

The third caveat is related to demand. Will advances in technology diminish the need for new workers? Numerous occupations require fewer people today than a quarter of a century ago. Voice-mail has taken the place of switchboard operators and answering services. Robotics has reduced the need for people on the assembly line. More sophisticated flight controls have resulted in the elimination of one pilot from the cockpit in most commercial jets.

The fourth issue concerns economic questions. Will the U.S. economy continue to grow throughout the final decade of the twentieth century as it has in the previous ten years? Can the economy, which has done a remarkable job absorbing a large supply of baby boomers during the 1970s and 1980s, continue to absorb new workers, even a diminished supply, in the next ten years? Present projections suggest that the U.S. economy will recover from the recession that has marked the early portion of the 1990s. The Bureau of Labor Statistics has projected three alternative economic scenarios for the year 2000: slow, moderate, and high growth projections.[24] These forecasts take into account fiscal policy, monetary policy, energy supplies, consumer spending, and the assumption that no man-made, historical, or natural catastrophes will occur. A moderate growth assumption projects an increase of just over 18 million jobs before the turn of the century. Although this is substantially lower than the 28 million jobs added in the previous decade, the share of the work force occupied by those 55 and over is still expected to increase.[25]

A second economic reason why older Americans will have to work longer in the twenty-first century is that social security benefits will begin at a later age and may be reduced. When the social security law was originally enacted in 1935, the average life expectancy of a 65-year-old American was about 77, as Figure 1.1 shows. In the year 2000 it will be approximately 83, a 50% increase in longevity. So far, the longer life span of retirees has not presented a problem because the funds have been adequate to cover the payments. In 1993, these payments totaled 309 billion dollars to 41 million individuals, about 20% of the national budget.

Contrary to what many people think, the social security benefits paid to retirees are not the invested return from the social security paid in during their working lives. The benefits come from employers' contributions to and the payroll deductions into FICA/Medicare of those presently working. In 1950, there were about sixteen workers paying into social security to fund one retiree. In 1990, the ratio was three to one. In the first third of the twenty-first century, it will be closer to two to one.[26]

As a result of the growing longevity of seniors and the presence of fewer workers to pay for social security benefits, the age for retirement has been gradually increasing. For those born prior to 1942, the age of retirement was set at 65; for those born between 1943 and 1959, the average retirement age is 66; and for those born after 1960, it is 67. If this curve is projected another half-century, it is estimated that for those born after 1977, the retirement age will be 68. By about 2010, newborns may look forward to working until age 70.

This situation presents complex political problems. Summarizing opinions on the subject, Murray noted that while everyone agrees on allowing seniors greater opportunities and incentives to remain in the labor market, it is equally true that the elderly lobby—for example, the American Association of Retired Persons (AARP)—strongly resists advancing the eligibility age for either social security or Medicare. Moreover, many business groups support AARP in opposing age changes particularly in Medicare because they fear that if Medicare stops covering 65-year-old employees, they will have to pick up the tab. "But," Murray concludes, "eventually government policy will have to be brought into line with the facts of life. People are leading longer and healthier lives. There is no reason they will not lead more productive lives as well."[27]

Economic needs presently may be causing older Americans to return to work after a first retirement. In addition to the psychological reasons for continuing to work, it is possible that the combination of earlier retirement and increased life expectancy may have resulted in a miscalculation as to the money required to maintain a desired standard of living, prompting a return to work. The trend toward early retirement has grown in the past two decades. In 1970, 83% of those aged 55–64 were working; in 1980, the proportion was 72.1%. The percentages will dip further to about 68% by the turn of the century.[28] Whatever the reason, both men and women are returning to the work force for a second career in larger numbers than ever before.[29] From 1972 to 1980, there was a 58% increase in the number of men over 55 who returned to work following retirement, with a similar percentage for women. Recent data from the Department of Labor show that these patterns continued through the 1980s. Since 1985 the percentage of people over 65 at work has grown: in 1985 10.8% of those aged 65 and over were in the labor force, whereas in 1988 11.5% of those seniors had jobs.[30]

Age-Related Variability

Changing laws to eliminate mandatory retirement resolves one problem but exposes another: namely, the increasing variability in most human physiological and intellectual functions.[31] Typically, studies of age-related changes have concentrated their attention on what are called "measures of central tendency"—averages or mean scores. The mean scores of 45- and 55-year-old subjects are compared to the average performance in groups of 65- and 75-year-olds. To no one's surprise, the average scores drop with age. Overlooked in many of these investigations is the extent to which individuals in each of these age groups may vary among themselves as they age. Although it is undeniably true that overall scores on nearly all cognitive scales follow a downward trend by advancing decade, it is also a fact that many older individuals retain a remarkably high degree of intellectual vitality. Their retention of these abilities, while many in their age cohort are declining, accounts for this growing age-related variability. A research study by Benton, Eslinger, and Damasio[32] illustrates this point: they found that 33% of octogenarians they tested performed as well as a group of younger adults on 11 separate cognitive tests. This and other evidence suggests that the portrait of linear decline based on group mean scores may oversimplify what happens to individuals in a census decade. While the average score on a test of vital capacity tells a man what is typical for his age, it is the range of variability that gives him a sense of what the possibilities may be.

In the cognitive domain especially, a far more useful statistic when speaking of older people is variability rather than average performance. Figure 1.3 shows the relative changes in total average score on MicroCog: Assessment of Cognitive Functioning, the test we created to measure cognitive functioning. It can be seen that those at age 70 score about 18% lower than those who are 40. But this group is 60% more variable (as measured by the standard deviation) than the younger subjects. In other words, the increase in variability is more than three times the average cognitive decline. A further look at the figure shows that at every decade beginning with 50-year-olds, the dispersion is far greater than the mean decrease in total score.

Growing age-related variability is not specific to this test. Nelson and Dannefer examined 185 studies in the biological, cognitive, psychological, and social domains to see how variability behaved in relation to age.[33] To their surprise, they discovered that only 43% of the gerontological studies even bothered to report variance, focusing instead on average changes. In 14 studies on the cognitive domain, where reports of dispersion were provided, 79% found that age-group variance increased with age. In longitudinal studies, which followed the same group of subjects over time, 83% reported growing age-related variability.

% change

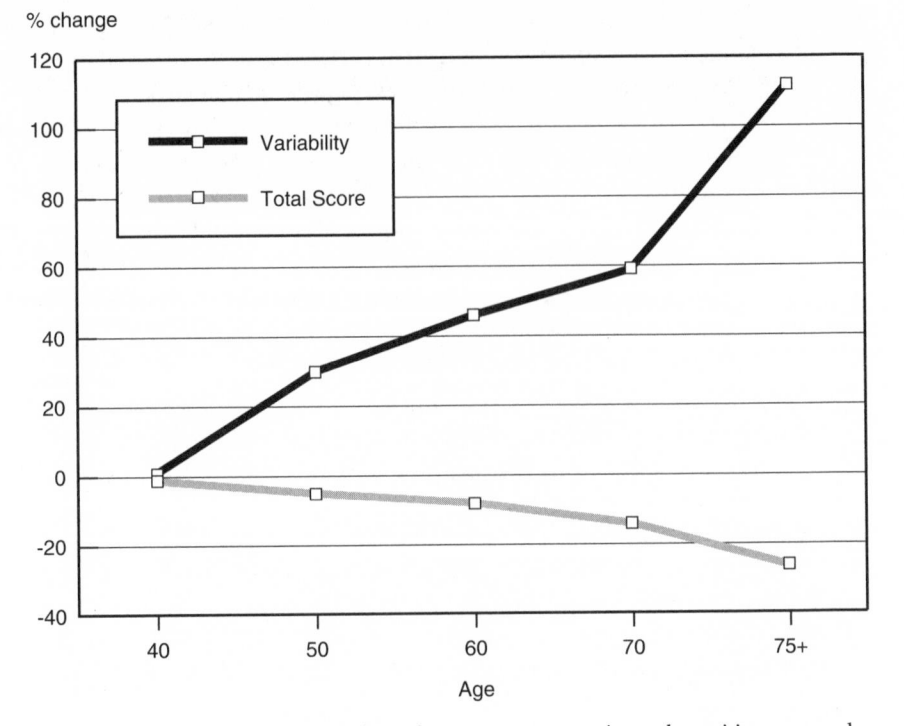

Figure 1.3 Percentage of change from the age 35–44 group in total cognitive score and variability among 1,002 physicians.

Alzheimer's Disease

If the 1990s are the "decade of the brain," it also could be said that the 1980s were the decade in which Alzheimer's disease (AD) emerged as a recognizable threat to all of those in their late prime. In 1980 the Alzheimer's Disease and Related Disorders Association was founded. In that entire year, the *New York Times* mentioned Alzheimer's disease or dementia in only 13 articles. A decade later, these terms were the topic of 212 separate reports in that same newspaper. Similar proportional growth of reports of AD and dementia during this decade occurred in the *Washington Post* and the *Los Angeles Times*.[34] Today it is difficult to pick up the Sunday paper or a periodical without coming upon some reference to Alzheimer's disease.

Alzheimer's disease was first described by the German psychiatrist Aloïs Alzheimer in 1907. His first case was a 50-year-old German woman who exhibited rapid loss of memory, deterioration in language skills, and behavioral changes characteristic of senile dementia over a five-year period before her death. Autopsy revealed abnormal brain structures in the hippocampus and neocortex, which are now referred to as neurofibrillary tangles (NFT) and neuritic or senile plaques (SP).

As Alzheimer's case demonstrated, the age of onset differentiated this disease from senile dementia or chronic brain syndrome associated with senile brain disease.[35] Textbooks in the mid-1950s stated that the onset of this condition must occur prior to age 55.[36] The age of onset has been slowly advancing as Alzheimer's disease has become of greater interest, and as a result, it is losing its focus as a dementia of late middle age. The Alzheimer's Disease and Related Disorders Association now says that AD can begin as early as age 40 or as late as 90.[37]

The Diagnostic and Statistical Manual of Mental Disorders, Third Edition, Revised (DSM-III-R, published in 1980) differentiates between dementia itself and AD.[38] Dementia is characterized by impairments in memory, abstract thinking, judgment, and other higher cortical functions, along with substantial personality changes. These are sufficiently severe to compromise social and occupational functioning. Dementia may arise from a number of causes other than AD, including head trauma, encephalitis, tumors, strokes, hypothyroidism, and Acquired Immune Deficiency Syndrome (AIDS). Depending on the cause, the degree of structural damage to the brain, and the effectiveness of treatment, the dementia may be arrested or even reversed.

AD, called "Primary Dementia of the Alzheimer Type" in the DSM-III-R, is a specific type of dementia. A differentiation is made between pre-senile (prior to age 65) and senile (age 65 and over) onset.[39] Its essential features, shown in Table 1.1, include a progressive deterioration of intellectual functions along with personality and behavioral changes. Traumatic, physical, or psychological causes for the condition exclude the diagnosis. At autopsy, microscopic examination of brain tissue typically shows the NFTs and SPs along with degeneration of particular neurons. Present evidence indicates that the numbers of NFTs and SPs advance continuously and lawfully with increasing age.[40] In other words, normally functioning middle-aged adults may have visible plaques and tangles in their brains upon autopsy, though not in the numbers found in older individuals.

At what point the frequency of NFTs and SPs is correlated with AD has not yet been determined. There is evidence to suggest that *where* the NFTs and SPs occur in the brain is associated with the clinical manifestations of AD. Summarizing a decade of research, Katzman has argued that AD is a

Table 1.1 Criteria for clinical diagnosis of Alzheimer's disease

I.   The criteria for the clinical diagnosis of probable Alzheimer's disease include:
      Dementia established by clinical examination and documented by the Mini-
        Mental Test, Blessed Dementia Scale, or some similar examination, and con-
        firmed by neuropsychological tests;
      Deficits in two or more areas of cognition;
      Progressive worsening of memory and other cognitive functions;
      No disturbance of consciousness;
      Onset between ages 40 and 90, most often after age 65; and
      Absence of systemic disorders or other brain diseases that in and of themselves
        could account for the progressive deficits in memory and cognition.

II.   The diagnosis of probable Alzheimer's disease is supported by:
      Progressive deterioration of specific cognitive functions such as language
        (aphasia), motor skills (apraxia), and perception (agnosia);
      Impaired activities of daily living and altered patterns of behavior;
      Family history of similar disorders, particularly if confirmed neuropatho-
        logically; and
      Laboratory results of:
          Normal lumbar puncture as evaluated by standard techniques,
          Normal pattern or nonspecific changes in EEG, such as increased slow-wave
            activity, and
          Evidence of cerebral atrophy on CT with progression documented by serial
            observation.

III. Other clinical features consistent with the diagnosis of probable Alzheimer's dis-
        ease, after exclusion of causes of dementia other than Alzheimer's disease,
        include:
      Plateaus in the course of progression of the illness;
      Associated symptoms of depression, insomnia, incontinence, delusions, illu-
        sions, hallucinations, catastrophic verbal, emotional, or physical outbursts,
        sexual disorders, and weight loss;
      Other neurological abnormalities in some patients, especially with more ad-
        vanced disease and including motor signs such as increased muscle tone,
        myoclonus, or gait disorder;
      Seizures in advanced disease; and
      CT normal for age.

IV.   Features that make the diagnosis of Alzheimer's disease uncertain or unlikely
        include:
      Sudden apoplectic onset;
      Focal neurological findings such as hemiparesis, sensory loss, visual field deficits,
        and incoordination early in the course of the illness; and
      Seizures or gait disturbances at the onset or very early in the course of the illness.

Table 1.1 (continued)

V. Clinical diagnosis of possible Alzheimer's disease:

May be made on the basis of the dementia syndrome, in the absence of other neurological, psychiatric, or systemic disorders sufficient to cause dementia, and in the presence of variations in the onset, in the presentation, or in the clinical course;

May be made in the presence of a second systemic or brain disorder sufficient to produce dementia, which is not considered to be *the* cause of the dementia; and

Should be used in research studies when a single, gradually progressive severe cognitive deficit is identified in the absence of other identifiable cause.

VI. Criteria for diagnosis of definite Alzheimer's disease are:

The clinical criteria for probable Alzheimer's disease and

Histopathologic evidence obtained from a biopsy or autopsy.

VII. Classification of Alzheimer's disease for research purposes should specify features that may differentiate subtypes of the disorder, such as:

Familial occurrence;

Onset before age 65;

Presence of trisomy-21; and

Coexistence of other relevant conditions such as Parkinson's disease.

Source: G. McKhann et al., "Clinical Diagnosis of Alzheimer's Disease: Report of the NINCDS-ADRDA Workgroup under the Auspices of the Department of Health and Human Services Task Force on Alzheimer's Disease," *Journal of Neurology,* 34 (1984): 939–944.

highly specific biological process resulting in characteristic pathological changes in portions of the brain called the amygdala and the hippocampus. In addition to the high incidence of NFTs and SPs, there is selective loss of neurons in these parts of the brain, which are critical to association and memory. The surrounding nerve cells in the cortex are often normal.[41]

A problem with much of this type of research has been the absence of detailed documentation that the individuals whose brains were studied were, in fact, either normal or exhibiting signs of AD. A research team from the Washington University of St. Louis Memory and Aging Project partially resolved this dilemma.[42] Older subjects had been recruited into this project beginning in 1979 and had been assessed at one- to two-year intervals. The process included interviews with the individuals, interviews with informed collateral sources (for example, spouses or children), physical and neurological evaluations, and a battery of neuropsychological tests. On the basis of these data, the researchers staged each subject on their Clinical Dementia Rating (CDR) scale. Inevitably, some of the subjects died. The brains of ten documented mild AD subjects and four who were assessed as normal during their lifetime were studied post-mortem. The clinicopathological studies found NFTs and SPs in the neocortex of the AD subjects, but they were essentially absent from the brains of the normal subjects. Although the small number of highly selected subjects limits the generalizations that can be made from this research, these findings are consistent with the notion that AD is a condition distinct from normal aging.

Experts distinguish between Alzheimer's disease and senile dementia of the Alzheimer type (SDAT). The former, AD, can be diagnosed only by brain autopsy in which the presence of NFTs and SPs is confirmed. SDAT refers to those conditions in which the dementia is confirmed by clinical assessment, neuropsychological testing, imaging techniques, and laboratory studies but not by autopsy evidence. Since AD is the most common term, we will use it to denote both AD and SDAT.

Criteria agreed upon by the National Institute of Neurological and Communicative Diseases and Stroke and by the Alzheimer's Disease and Related Disorders Association are presented in Table 1.1. These standards conform to the latest diagnostic criteria in the DSM-III-R for the disease. The committee has identified criteria that distinguish among possible, probable, and definite Alzheimer's disease, and as the table shows, the diagnosis is easier to make when the impairment is more severe. Probable or definite Alzheimer's disease is characterized by deficits documented by neuropsychological testing in two or more areas of cognition (memory, motor skills, or language), a gradual progressive deterioration, and impaired social or occupational functioning; in addition, it may be associated with depression, insomnia, emotional outbursts, or apathy. Contraindications of probable or definite Alzheimer's disease include loss of consciousness, systemic diseases, focal neurological findings, and serious psychiatric disorders. In other words, Alzheimer's disease occurs in individuals who are otherwise healthy with no clear-cut neurological symptoms that would be apparent on imaging techniques or EEGs.

The present population of those afflicted with Alzheimer's disease and other dementing illnesses is estimated to be more than 3 million. The prevalence of these conditions depends greatly on the criteria used to diagnose them. It is generally agreed that the percentages of those afflicted with moderate and severe forms of AD are less than 1% for those 64 and under, 2–3% in the 65–74 decade, and 10–20% in the 75–84 age group. Beyond age 85 the rates vary from 20% to 70%, depending upon which standards are applied. We will discuss this topic in greater detail in Chapter 7.

Differentiating individuals with AD from those with the decline in cognitive functioning associated with normative aging is one of the most challenging tasks confronting clinicians and researchers in gerontology today. A particular problem in diagnosing AD is that individuals afflicted with this illness are often free of other serious physical complaints,[43] especially if they are in the early stages of Alzheimer's disease. As a result, older women and men with incipient AD may not attract medical attention because they are otherwise healthy.

Problems of Accurate Assessment

All those who live into their eighth, ninth, or tenth decade have a growing need for scientifically sound methods of assessing cognitive functioning, just as they presently benefit from regular physical checkups. Unfortunately, current tests of intellectual and neuropsychological functioning are not as well developed as physical tests. Existing measures have three primary deficiencies with respect to being able to differentiate those with normal cognitive aging from those who may be impaired. First, many of the best tests do not provide norms beyond age 65 or 75. For example, two of the most widely used IQ tests (the WAIS-R and the Stanford-Binet 4th Edition) do not provide normative data beyond the age of 74. The same normative problems occur with some of the most venerable neuropsychological measures, such as the Wisconsin Card Sorting Test, the Shipley-Hartford Institute of Learning Scale, and the Wechsler Memory Scale–Revised.[44] When norms are available, the number of subjects may be so small as to seriously limit their utility for nonimpaired populations.[45]

The second deficiency is that many cognitive screening tests are relatively easy and have low ceilings. This means they are more effective in diagnosing those who are severely impaired than those whose intellectual functioning may be only mildly compromised.

A third limitation is that test scores tend to be confounded by education. This results in a "false positive" problem for those with fewer years of schooling, who may be normal but wrongly classified as impaired.[46] It also can result in a "false negative" problem where well-educated individuals may be misread as being normal because their impaired cognition is masked by a higher level of knowledge to begin with or because they are more practiced at test-taking.

Our research grew out of what we perceived to be these limitations of existing cognitive scales for assessing normal, well-educated individuals.

Our intention was to develop a cognitive test that not only would be sensitive to mild cognitive impairment among seniors, but also would be able to differentiate optimal agers from those functioning in the more normal range. Along the way, we observed significant patterns of intellectual functioning that discriminated among those who were aging normally in the cognitive domain, those who were showing notable impairment, and those whose intellectual vigor continued at an optimal level, and we devised provisional empirical criteria that distinguish these groups from one another.

Overview of the Issues

In this book we address the following issues in the field of cognitive aging and discuss them in light of our research:

When does cognitive decline begin? A notable absence in the literature on cognitive aging has been data on the trajectory of intellectual functioning in the middle adult years. In Chapter 4, we will trace age-related changes across the life span in both overall intellectual functioning and specific abilities. We will note that among our subjects deterioration in selected areas can be detected as early as age 40, while other cognitive domains hold up remarkably well.

What skills do we lose first as we grow older, and what abilities are normally retained the longest? It has been widely reported that memory is the first casualty in the cognitive aging process. Recent reports indicate that other abilities, such as visuospatial functioning or reasoning, may also show impairment. In contrast, some skills such as attention are largely preserved during the aging process. We will address these topics in Chapter 4.

Do women and men differ in the way they age cognitively? There is some evidence that groups of adolescent women and men differ in certain skills. For example, it has been reported that females outperform males on verbal tasks while males are superior on math and visuospatial problems. Do these differences persist into the later years? Or do the sexes grow closer together as they age? In Chapter 6 we will examine differences in the measured skills of groups separated by gender and matched for educational experience.

How much do health and other functions influence the retention of intellectual vigor? It has been said that physical health and cognitive functioning are highly correlated. Other researchers have not confirmed this presumption. In Chapter 5 we will consider the impact on intellectual vitality of medical conditions and medical histories as well as psychological states and fatigue.

Does continuing to "use it" prevent us from "losing it"? One of the most passionately held views in the field of cognitive aging is that continuing to exercise our mind will prevent us from losing our intellectual powers, or at least will slow the process. But doubters have begun to publish data that raise questions about this cherished truth. In Chapter 5 we shed some light on this subject by comparing groups of physicians who continue to work with those who have retired.

Are normal cognitive aging (NCA) and Alzheimer's disease separate conditions or do they exist on a continuum? Some believe that normal cognitive agers are healthy while those with AD have a disease, much as one has cancer or does not have cancer. Others have found evidence to suggest that NCA and AD exist on a continuum, much the same as with blood pressure. Where one draws the line between normal and pathological is a matter of clinical judgment. We will explore this question in Chapter 7.

Can old dogs be taught new tricks? Are the intellectual losses associated with aging remediable? Or are efforts to retrain older people, especially those who have mild cases of AD, doomed? In Chapter 7 we will examine the impact of various types of cognitive retraining programs on both normal and impaired seniors.

What is normal cognitive aging? A major theoretical problem in the literature on cognitive aging has been the absence of agreement as to what constitutes normal cognitive aging (NCA). Though many have pointed to the need to demarcate the normal condition, about the best that has been done has been to define NCA by exclusion, as the absence of pathology. In Chapter 8 we examine this question in detail and suggest empirical definitions of NCA based on our data.

Is optimal cognitive aging (OCA) possible? Interest in maximizing cognitive functioning in the later years has been growing. It has been pointed out that the increase in the life expectancy of U.S. citizens has not been, for the most part, paralleled by increases in *productive* life expectancy. There has been little systematic thinking about how this condition might be defined or what proportion of individuals in the later years might be identified as optimal cognitive agers. In Chapter 9 we will propose definitions of OCA and will present evidence from the pilot study of the nongenetic correlates of OCA.

What is the nature of wisdom, and do older people possess more of it? A subject of growing interest in gerontology is the nature of wisdom and whether older people possess it in larger measure than younger ones. In Chapter 9 we will review current thinking on the components of wisdom and offer our interpersonally-oriented definition of this quality; we will then examine our data in an attempt to determine the proportion of individuals by age group who possess characteristics related to wisdom.

Before examining in detail the profiles of the groups discussed above, we will present the research basis of our findings in two chapters. In Chapter 2 we describe the creation of our cognitive screening test, MicroCog, which generated much of the data in this book; we also describe the pools of nearly 2,000 subjects between ages 25 and 92 who participated in this project. In Chapter 3 we present the broader statistical characteristics of both Micro-Cog and the subjects by age group. Because many of the conclusions in later chapters about the differences among normative, optimal, and mildly impaired cognitive functioning rest on these test findings, we will present the results of reliability and validity studies that have been completed.

This book is not so much about the development of MicroCog as it is about the discoveries we made along the way about the process of cognitive aging. While we all experienced satisfaction in creating the test, what continued to fuel our interest and enthusiasm throughout the undertaking was what we learned about normal cognitive aging and how this process differed from cognitive impairment. This book is a record of the excitement of our discoveries about cognitive aging as well as the questions and mysteries that remain.

2

MicroCog and the Volunteers

The primary cognitive test used in our studies is a research version of MicroCog: Assessment of Cognitive Functioning, a test that we administered to samples of 1,002 physicians and 581 normals. MicroCog is designed to be administered and scored by a personal computer.[1] This enabled us to obtain test results on a large number of subjects from ages 25 to 92 and to analyze the resulting data quickly and thoroughly.

Computerized cognitive testing is a relative newcomer to the assessment field. Yet the field of neuropsychology seems an especially attractive area for automated testing.[2] Many researchers have pointed out the advantages of computerized cognitive testing,[3] which include standardization of administration; the capacity for multiple simultaneous administrations; speed of scoring; ease of data handling and analysis; precise quantification of reaction times; the ability to include a branching function so the subtest can be given at a level appropriate to a subject's capability; ease in generating alternative forms; provision of rich data for a process analysis of how the subject goes about problem solving; freeing the examiner from the tedium of test administration and scoring; and greatly shortened reporting time. Computers are also useful in tracking the steps of a person's problem-solving strategy. Individuals can arrive at a similar answer by many different routes. The computer can follow the problem-solving path that a subject takes, which may illuminate particular deficits not apparent in a response simply scored "right" or "wrong."[4]

Automated testing is not without disadvantages, however. Primary among them is that it restricts the choice of presentation of item types. For instance, when subjects are asked to recall story content, they must select

23

among the multiple choices presented rather than confronting the more demanding task of free recall. A second disadvantage is the mechanization of the evaluation process, which could be difficult for the elderly or cognitively impaired. Such subjects could become anxious because of inexperience or "computer phobia." In addition, they might find interactions with a machine less stimulating than with a person and therefore would not be motivated to perform optimally.

Reasonable as these doubts initially may appear, research comparing individually administered and computerized versions of the same tests shows that the latter yield similar results and may actually be more "user-friendly." For instance, a series of studies examined the differences in scores on computer-presented and examiner-presented versions of two cognitive tests, the Raven's Progressive Matrices and the Mill Hill Vocabulary Test.[5] With older subjects, it was found that the correlations between the administrations of the two tests were 0.84 and 0.85 respectively. The authors reported that automated tests were well received by all groups, especially the elderly subjects. Although this research awaits empirical confirmation from others, it does correspond with our experience and that of others who have given both computerized and standardized cognitive tests to normal and clinical populations.

A number of automated cognitive tests have emerged in the past decade. A review by Kane and Kay lists 13 computerized screening instruments.[6] Five promising batteries for which prototypes have been developed are the Neurobehavioral Evaluation System,[7] the Alzheimer Disease Assessment Battery,[8] the Everyday Memory Battery,[9] the NYU Computerized Test Battery,[10] and the Cogscreen.[11] The first contains modifications of eight existing tests formatted for computer administration. The second is a more comprehensive, 13-subtest battery. As the name implies, the Everyday Memory Battery assesses tasks that simulate real-life situations. Consisting of 13 subtests and taking about 1.5 hours, this battery asks the subject to recall and dial a 7- or 19-digit number, recognize faces and names, remember items on a grocery list, pair first and last names, recall the placement of objects and story content, and react as quickly as possible in an automobile driving simulation. The NYU battery is a precursor of this test, but is more complex; it includes subtests in language and concept formation. The Cogscreen is a 12-test screening battery originally commissioned to be part of the FAA's recertification process for pilots.

Preliminary studies on each are encouraging. Because of their recency, however, and with the notable exception of the Everyday Memory Battery, all suffer from the lack of published information concerning normative data, statistical properties, factor structure, and validity.

Subtest Construction

The categories of cognitive functions included in the traditional assessment of mental state formed the basic structure of test selection for MicroCog. The subtests initially selected for the pilot testing are shown in Table 2.1. They can be grouped into six a priori categories of cognitive functions: tests of reactivity, attention, verbal memory, visuospatial facility, reasoning, and mental calculation. These subtests are familiar to most working in neuropsychology, neurology, gerontology, clinical and counseling psychology, and related disciplines. They are described in detail elsewhere, along with their theoretical rationale for inclusion.[12]

We gave several of the subtests twice. There were two reasons for this decision. First, we wanted to know whether subjects, especially older individuals, would tire in the course of taking MicroCog and perform at a lower level toward the end of the test. Second, we were interested in the effects of delay and interference on verbal memory, so both a name and address and two stories were presented that required delayed recall later in the testing.

In an effort to make MicroCog as user-friendly as possible, we employed an "eye chart" model for several subtests, namely Tictac 1 and 2 and Numbers Forward and Reversed. If the subject failed an item at a particular level (say, five digits forward), the next problem would be the recall of a four-digit string. Automatic termination of the subtest occurred after three errors.

The sequence of MicroCog and the number of items in each subtest are shown in Table 2.2. The battery takes about an hour to administer. Younger people often complete MicroCog in 45 minutes, while older people may take as long as one and a half hours.

Design of the Software

Simplicity in operation was a major design consideration throughout, in order to minimize the handicap experienced by subjects who had never before used a computer. The usable part of the keyboard was restricted to the

Table 2.1   Initial subtests constituting MicroCog

Tests of reactivity:
Reaction Times 1 and 2: The subject is instructed to respond as rapidly as possible to
   auditory signals, visual signals, and visual signals preceded by an auditory warning
   signal. This subtest is presented twice with different content.

Tests of attention:
Alikes: Pairs of words or numeric sequences are presented for "same" or "different"
   judgments.
Alphabet: A continuous performance test in which letters of the alphabet embedded in
   a random series of letters are to be responded to in sequence.
Wordlist 1: A list of 16 words containing groups of category-related items is presented
   four times. Each time, the subject is instructed to respond to words that are members of one of the four given categories.
Wordlist 2: A list of 36 words including the 16 from Wordlist 1 is presented, and the
   subject must indicate which words were previously shown.

Tests of numeric recall:
Numbers Forward: Digits are presented visually, one at a time in spans up to 9, requiring the subject to recall their correct sequence.
Numbers Reversed: Following the visual presentation of digits in spans up to 9, the subject must recall them in reverse order.

Tests of verbal memory:
Address: A name and address are presented on the screen for the subject to memorize
   for later recognition.
Stories 1 and 2: Immediate Recall: A brief story is presented on the screen to be memorized, immediately followed by six questions requiring multiple-choice recognition
   of several items from the story. Story 2 has different content.
Stories 1 and 2: Delayed Recall: Twelve multiple-choice questions testing delayed recognition of each story's content.

Tests of visuospatial facility:
Tictac 1 and 2: A 3 × 3 block matrix is presented. Three to five squares are briefly illu-
   minated. Immediately after presentation the subject must indicate which blocks contained the squares. This subtest presented twice with different content.
Clocks 1 and 2: Clock faces with the hands indicating the time, but without associated
   hour markings, are presented. Digital choices are offered among which the subject
   must choose the correct time. This subtest presented twice with different content.
Cubes: A three-dimensional array of cubes is presented and the subject must indicate
   how many cubes are shown.

Tests of reasoning:
Analogies: Verbal analogies, to be completed by selecting among three multiple-choice
   alternatives.
Object Match: A test of abstraction and conceptual flexibility based on the "breaking
   set" paradigm.

Tests of mental calculation:
Math: Simple tests of arithmetic (addition, subtraction, multiplication, and division)
   are presented.

Table 2.2 MicroCog subtest sequence

1. Reaction Times 1 (15 items)
2. Address Presentation
3. Clocks 1 (8 items)
4. Analogies (15 items)
5. Story 1: Immediate Recall (6 items)
6. Cubes (4 items)
7. Math (10 items)
8. Tictac 1 (9 items)
9. Numbers Forward (9 items)
10. Wordlist 1 (16 items)
11. Wordlist 2 (16 items)
12. Object Match (24 items)
13. Story 2: Immediate Recall (8 items)
14. Alikes (15 items)
15. Numbers Reversed (9 items)
16. Address Recall (4 items)
17. Tictac 2 (9 items)
18. Story 1: Delayed Recall (12 items)
19. Clocks 2 (8 items)
20. Alphabet (15 items)
21. Story 2: Delayed Recall (12 items)
22. Reaction Times 2 (15 items)

numeric keypad area (0–9), the BACKSPACE and ENTER keys, and the letter P (PAUSE, as described below). A standard for all programs is locking out all other keys, and clearing the keyboard queue immediately before requesting a response, to eliminate the possibility of the subject anticipating a response. All keyboard entries made before a response is requested by the program are not recorded.

With subject comfort in mind, a PAUSE function was built into most subtest programs enabling subjects to take "time out" when they choose. None of the six subtests that require giving an immediate response/recall to an item (for example, Numbers Forward) has a PAUSE function.

Each subtest program has its own instructions and examples where appropriate. Writing subtest instructions and examples clearly and briefly, and presenting them in a logical sequence, had a high priority. When explanations of the test required multiple screen presentations, the goal was to make them understandable on the first reading and thus eliminate the need for scrolling.

Alternate Forms

Two forms of MicroCog have been constructed in English, called Version I and Version II. In addition, a Spanish version has been created. Most of the data has been collected on Version I. Version II has been used in test-retests of reliability. Pilot data have been collected using the Spanish version on a small sample of subjects.

Scoring

The computer format lends itself to many forms of scoring, including accuracy, reaction times, and pattern analysis. Since the quality of response is more crucial than speed of response for this population, and since correlations between accuracy and speed were high for both MicroCog total scores and specific subtests, it was decided that for the purposes of this research only correct responses would be used in the initial studies. The MicroCog total score was calculated by summing the individual raw subtest scores.

Characteristics of the Subjects

The subjects who are the basis of the observations and inferences reported in this book are drawn from two volunteer pools collected as we developed MicroCog. The first was a group of 1,002 physicians of ages 25 to 92. They will be called the "MD" panel. The second pool was a group of 581 women and men of ages 25 to 83 who were selected from among 873 subjects who participated in related research in refining MicroCog. This group was balanced for education. They will be called the "Normal" panel.

At the time of the testing, all subjects were living independently and represented themselves as functioning normally. Not all subjects who were tested initially became part of the MD or Normal panels. Among the MDs, a total of 28 were eliminated because of machine failure (5), because of inability or unwillingness to complete the testing (16), or because their scores were so unusually low as to be considered outliers for reasons unknown (7). In addition, we decided to eliminate 82 younger physicians who were medical house officers and were part of another study on sleep deprivation. Though we included only those who said they had had a full night's sleep in the preceding evenings, we found a significant difference in the variance of this group of house officers compared with the other younger doctors included in this study. We eliminated these subjects with great reluctance;

they will be the subject of a forthcoming report. When we chart patterns of cognitive aging by decade in later chapters, we will use these two groups for comparison purposes.

The MD Panel

Physicians were tested in an effort to examine how MicroCog worked as a test instrument with a well-educated population. The majority of the doctors were recruited in Florida. This geographic area had considerable appeal for two reasons. First, the Palm Beach–Miami corridor and the Tampa–St. Petersburg areas have a greater proportion of people aged 75 and older than other comparable areas in the country. Second, Florida draws residents from many sections of the United States, which means that the resulting databases were less likely to be affected by regional influences. We found that all of the lower 48 states were represented in the licenses held by these physicians.

Invitations to participate in the project went to 18,831 active and retired physicians. The correspondence described MicroCog and the research project, and included a participation form and self-addressed envelope. Of the 2,342 physicians who volunteered or showed interest in participating, 1,246 made appointments for testing. About one-fourth of the appointments were canceled because of various unforeseen circumstances. Eventually, 908 physicians in Florida participated in standardizing MicroCog, roughly a five percent yield from the initial mailing.

Administration of MicroCog took place at eleven different locations in Florida: seven county medical organizations, two university medical schools, a senior citizen friendship center, and a hotel during the annual meeting of the Florida Medical Association. In addition to the Florida sites, tests were given in Texas at the School of Aerospace Medicine in San Antonio, and at two professional offices in Cambridge, Massachusetts. In all, 1,002 doctors were tested in these locations.

The sample, as Table 2.3 shows, consists largely of Caucasians; only 106 doctors identified themselves as members of a minority group. Data obtained from the American Medical Association and the U.S. Census Bureau indicate that whites in this volunteer panel are overrepresented (89.5% versus 82.6% in the United States). Minority groups constitute 17.2% of all doctors according to 1980 census figures, whereas minority groups represent only 10.6% of our sample. The minority populations that are overrepresented in this sample are Hispanics (6.2% versus 4.4% in the United States) and Native Americans (.45% versus .12% in the United States).[13]

Table 2.4 shows the distribution of the MD panel by gender and age

Table 2.3 Characteristics of the MD panel

State	Caucasian	Hispanic	Black	Asian	Native American	Total
Florida	822	64	4	13	5	908
Texas	36	3	4	1	—	44
Massachusetts	38	1	4	7	—	50
TOTAL	896	68	12	21	5	1,002

group. As can be seen, males constitute the largest number of subjects. Only 72 physicians in the final sample of 1,002 were female. For the purposes of the study, it was essential that a large number of older physicians be obtained. Table 2.4 shows that this goal was achieved: data were obtained on 146 physicians who were 75 or older, and 210 in the 65 to 74 age group.

Another characteristic of interest is the doctors' current occupational status. How many of the doctors are retirees? How many are working, but no longer as physicians? Table 2.5 shows their current job status by age group. At the time of testing, 740 physicians (73.9%) were practicing physicians. About 22% of the sample (222) had retired. Almost nine out of ten of the retirees (86.5%) were 65 and older. Yet the majority of physicians 65 to 74 years of age continued their work in medicine.

The value of the MD panel is considerable for studies of cognitive aging. One reason is that they are relatively homogeneous in terms of intellectual ability, education, occupation, and socioeconomic status. Therefore, changes in cognitive patterns over the decades have a higher probability of being a function of natural changes rather than being influenced by differences in young adult IQ level, academic preparation, work experience, or economic resources.

The limitations of the MD panel are equally apparent. The pool is largely male, and its homogeneity of education, occupation, and socioeconomic status raises serious questions about the generalizability of the findings to a

Table 2.4 Age and gender distribution of MD panel

	< 35	35–44	45–54	55–64	65–74	75+	Total
Men	28	178	178	209	197	140	930
Women	12	21	10	10	13	6	72
TOTAL	40	199	188	219	210	146	1,002

Table 2.5 Physicians' current job status by age

	< 35	35–44	45–54	55–64	65–74	75+	Total
Physician							
Full Time	40	194	185	174	93	24	710
Part Time		1		5	14	10	30
Other Work		1		2	3	3	9
Retired/Not Working		1	1	28	88	104	222
No Information		2	2	10	12	5	31
TOTAL	40	199	188	219	210	146	1,002

more diversified population. For this reason a panel of normal volunteers, representing a larger cross section of the United States, was accumulated. This permits cross-checking of the data derived from the MD panel.

The Normal Panel

The Normal panel consisted of 581 individuals, ages 25 to 83, who volunteered to participate in several substudies associated with the development of MicroCog. The largest number of subjects 65 and older were part of a construct validation study carried out in Dunedin, Florida. The majority of other subjects in the older groups were enrolled in the North Cambridge, Massachusetts, Senior Center and were part of the test-retest research on the reliability of MicroCog. The younger subjects were drawn from volunteers from the Risk Management Foundation, who were also part of the reliability research, and from two clinics in the Boston area where they were seen for vocational testing. The ages and education levels of these Normal subjects are shown in Table 2.6. The 581 subjects within five age groups were matched closely for educational level.

The Nature of Volunteer Subjects

The subjects for this investigation were volunteers recruited specifically for these studies. Among behavioral scientists, the suspicion has been growing that individuals who volunteer to be research subjects may not provide a random sample of the populations they represent. Stated differently, those who elect *not* to participate in research studies may differ in important ways

Table 2.6 Characteristics of the Normal panel

	N	Education	
		Mean	S.D.
75+			
Female	40	13.1	3.2
Male	19	13.6	3.9
All	59	13.2	3.4
65–74			
Female	251	13.4	2.4
Male	96	14.2	2.7
All	347	13.6	2.5
55–64			
Female	40	15.4	2.4
Male	11	14.5	3.3
All	51	15.2	2.6
45–54			
Female	24	15.7	2.9
Male	12	15.7	3.1
All	36	15.7	2.9
35–44			
Female	21	15.2	2.9
Male	14	16.4	2.1
All	35	15.7	2.7
< 35			
Female	32	16.3	2.1
Male	21	16.1	2.0
All	53	16.2	2.0

from volunteers. These differences could seriously limit the generalizability of research based on volunteers to the population at large.

In their book *The Volunteer Subject,* Rosenthal and Rosnow summarize studies about how volunteer subjects may differ from non-volunteers.[14] They make the point that if a pool of volunteers differs systematically from the population at large, the resulting bias could cause an inaccurate estimation of a particular population parameter. For instance, do the doctors who volunteer to take MicroCog differ substantively on qualities such as intelligence, level of success, health, or motivation? If so, such differences would cause us to wonder if their scores would be representative of those physicians who elected not to participate in the study.

There are two ways to raise the probability that the volunteers who took MicroCog are representative of their cohort. First, in our recruitment of volunteers we followed many of the suggestions of Rosenthal and Rosnow for reducing volunteer bias,[15] including the following: making the appeal for volunteers as interesting and nonthreatening as possible; stating the theoretical and practical value of the research; making it clear why the target population was important and why volunteering to participate in this research might benefit others; having the request made by a person of high status (for example, a Harvard medical school professor); having someone known to the target population make a separate appeal for volunteers; and reassuring the potential volunteer that no adverse psychological or physical outcome was likely. We were not able to offer financial incentives, as Rosenthal and Rosnow suggest, though we were able to offer both general and personal feedback which might be construed as a form of payback. We also were unable to communicate the normative nature of volunteering, though in some settings we were able to test a large percentage of the total number of potential subjects.

The second way of reducing the effect of volunteer bias is to understand the nature of the volunteer. Table 2.7 summarizes data compiled by Rosenthal and Rosnow on the characteristics of volunteers in a situation that may influence individuals to participate in a research study. Each of these qualities is rated as being supported with high levels ("maximum" or "considerable") of confidence. Clinical observation of our subjects in both the MD and Normal samples suggested that these situational determinants influencing their participation were at work. Most indicated a strong interest in the subject of cognitive aging and viewed this research as important. No data are available concerning whether the subjects thought they would be evaluated favorably. We did not find it necessary to provide a financial incentive to be tested, though the provision for feedback seemed to be much appreciated.

The question remains whether the volunteers in our study differed systematically in ways that bias our data analyses. It seems reasonable to assume that, in spite of our efforts to recruit a representative group of subjects, we may have a select group of volunteers. We think this may be particularly true for the older subjects. If this is the case, it is not altogether clear that this will have an adverse effect on questions such as how

Table 2.7 Factors that influence subjects to volunteer

Situational Determinants
   Greater interest in topic under investigation
   Higher expectation of being evaluated favorably
   Perceive research as important
   More positive feelings about self
   Greater financial incentives

Characteristics
   Better educated
   Higher socioeconomic status
   Higher intelligence
   Greater need for social approval
   More sociable
   Higher need for sensation seeking
   Less conventional
   Less authoritarian

Source: R. Rosenthal and R. L. Rosnow, *The Volunteer Subject* (New York: Wiley, 1975), pp. 195–197.

aging affects cognition. Presuming for the moment that the older participants are relatively more able than their cohort, this could have the effect of diminishing the differences between them and the younger groups. Therefore, if we were to find that 70-year-olds score lower than 60-year-olds on a memory test, we might conclude that these observed differences actually understate the true differences that would be found if it were possible to test a random sample of individuals from these two decades.[16]

Cross-sectional versus Longitudinal Data

The ideal research design for the questions we had in mind would to be to examine a group of individuals in early adulthood and follow them through their lives. This longitudinal model would allow us to measure cognitive changes within each individual that would inevitably occur as a function of age. Presuming that we were also able to rule out other influences such as health, we could be relatively confident in saying that certain mental skills decayed with age or were spared. Most research, however, is conducted using the cross-sectional model. Such studies examine groups of individuals by age groups, such as census decades, and compare the performance of younger subjects with that of older subjects. Although these studies are less expensive, and can be completed within the lifetime of the investigators, they have a number of limitations. The primary drawback is that it cannot be said with confidence that an observed difference between the average scores of a group of 55-year-olds and 65-year-olds on verbal memory is definitely caused by age. While there may be a negative correlation between age and verbal memory in these two groups, it is not the same as studying the same individuals at 55 and again at 65. We cannot be certain that differences in cognitive performance are not related to other subtle differences between the groups.

Even if we make an attempt to match the groups on the basis of factors known to be important correlates of intellectual functioning, such as years of education, socioeconomic status, gender, region, and race, other influences could make comparisons between subjects in different census decades problematic. Consider the cohort effect: there are powerful experiences shared uniquely by a particular group, and not others, which could change the pattern of performance on cognitive or other tests. For example, the 65-year-olds in our samples were all greatly influenced by both the Great Depression and World War II, while the 55-year-olds just missed both. Though it has yet to be demonstrated that the cohort effect has specific influences on intellectual functioning, the possibility has led prominent researchers to argue that people may score differently on cognitive tests because they have shared different generational experiences rather than because they are of different ages.[17]

This is not to say that longitudinal research is without problems. First, the interests of researchers or investigators working fifty years ago may differ greatly from what is studied today. For example, longitudinal research begun in the 1930s focused on the dimensions of health, family relationships, and personality. Far less time was taken to assess intellectual functions because these scientists could not have anticipated today's interests in cognitive aging.[18] Second, there is a major problem of attrition. Many longitudinal studies may lose as much as 80% of their subjects during the period of follow-up. How representative of the original cohort are the members of the group remaining? They often differ systematically in several important ways: they may be more vigorous physically, better educated, more highly motivated, and greater risk takers.[19] Third, there are factors likely to enhance the cognitive performance of those remaining in the study, such as the shared experience of being test subjects, a warm relationship with investigators they have known over decades, and practice effects. All these issues combine to raise questions about the generalizability of longitudinal findings to the cohorts that follow.

7-year T-score
difference

Verbal Meaning

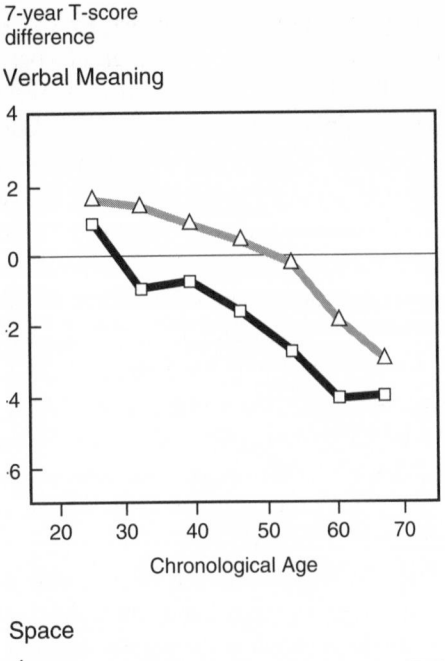

Space

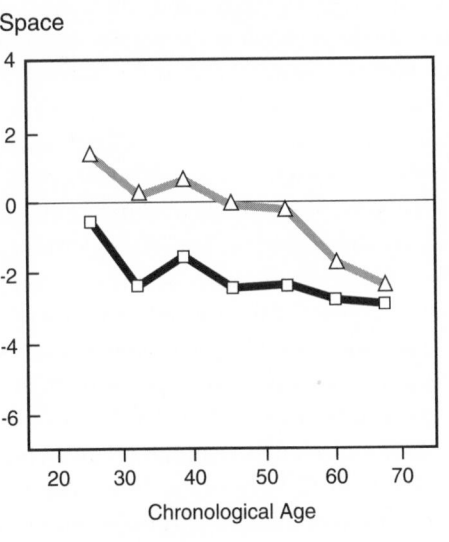

△ Longitudinal   ■□■ Cross-sectional

Figure 2.1 Differences in T-score units for three PMA subtests across seven years from longitudinal and cross-sectional comparisons. Adapted from T. A. Salthouse, *Theoretical Perspectives on Cognitive Aging* (Hillsdale, N.J.: Erlbaum, 1991), p. 111.

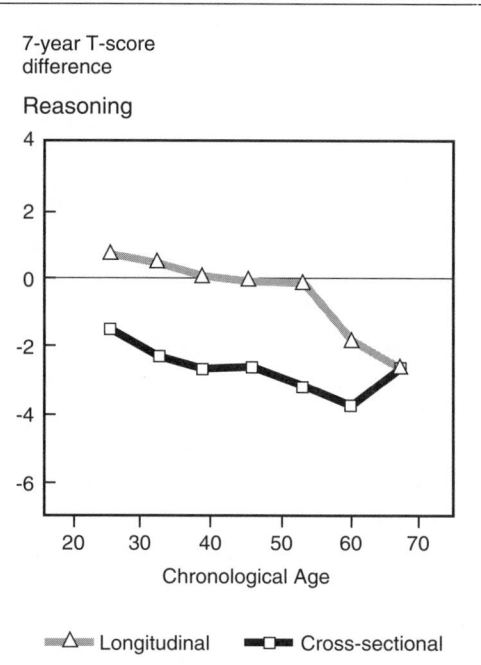

7-year T-score difference

Reasoning

Chronological Age

━△━ Longitudinal   ■□■ Cross-sectional

Figure 2.1 *(continued)*

It has been argued that cross-sectional data overestimate both the magnitude of age-related decline and how early it occurs. This has been found in measures of physiological and psychological characteristics as well as mental skills.[20] Examination of large numbers of studies, however, has found that the overall patterns of review by cross-sectional investigations generally correspond to the findings of longitudinal research. Evidence in support of this conclusion comes from a reexamination of the Seattle Longitudinal Study.[21] This study has examined over 5,000 subjects; some were first tested in 1956 and then again at approximately seven-year intervals thereafter. Since the data were initially cross-sectional, and new subjects were added cross-sectionally as the study progressed, both longitudinal and cross-sectional data were available. This is one of the few large sample investigations in which both types of comparisons could be made. Salthouse calculated the differences in the amount of change in several cognitive functions in both longitudinal and cross-sectional samples.[22] His results for three subtests of the Primary Mental Abilities Test are shown in Figure 2.1. Two clear patterns emerge from this figure. First, declines occur in all cognitive functions, whether the subjects were studied longitudinally or cross-sectionally. Second, cross-sectional studies found earlier and larger differences in verbal, spatial, and reasoning functions than did the results from the longitudinal design.

All in all, then, it seems likely that cross-sectionally derived data are adequate to answer the questions we wish to investigate. While we need to keep in mind the possibility that the data derived from different individuals in different age groups may overestimate both how soon the decline occurs and the magnitude of the loss, it seems reasonable to assume that if age-related changes in cognitive functions are discovered cross-sectionally, they are likely to generalize to the same subjects studied over time.

When we speak of the relationship between age and cognition in cross-sectional data, it is proper to refer to age-related *differences* in abilities, not age-related *changes,* because we are comparing the average test scores of groups of individuals with one another, not scores of the same people tested over time. However, in writing about this topic of differences in mean scores by age group, it is often easier to use a word such as "decline," "deterioration," "downturn," or "decay" to refer to this concept. The reader should assume that we have these age-related differences in mind when we use these terms.

3

Psychometric Properties of MicroCog

The psychometric properties are the vital signs of any test, telling us how well the instrument does what it is intended to do. Are the obtained scores reliable? How much might a second score differ from the first after retesting a day later, a week later, and a month later? How do subtests correlate with one another, and which ones contribute most to the overall score? When subtests are clustered into a few larger factors, do they fit our a priori notion of what is "in" MicroCog? Can the existence of such factors be confirmed by other neuropsychological tests known to measure memory, attention, reasoning, and visuospatial ability? And, perhaps most important, can Micro-Cog scores distinguish between cognitive impairment and normal cognitive aging?

Dahlstrom defined a psychological test as one that has standardized materials and procedures, creates a situation where subjects are optimally motivated, provides for immediate recording and objective scoring of the responses, and has appropriate norms and established validity: "Any device failing to meet all the criteria was not considered a test."[1] Much of this chapter will be devoted to judging how well MicroCog meets Dahlstrom's several criteria.

We have already described several of the essential psychometric properties of MicroCog in Chapter 2: the nature of the test, how it was administered, and the composition of the volunteer panels of subjects. Here we will present data on the statistical features of MicroCog, including means and standard deviations, reliability, and intercorrelations among the subtests. In addition, we will review our reasons for retaining the raw scores for this study and show why it was necessary to eliminate two of the subtests; we

Table 3.1 Samples of subjects and substudies mentioned in this book

---

Primary Subject Samples

MD Sample: 1,002 volunteer physicians ages 25–92, largely tested in Florida.

Normal Sample: 581 subjects who volunteered to take MicroCog and/or participate in one of the substudies.

Primary Substudies Involving Subgroups of MD and Normal Subjects

Test-Retest Reliability Study: 370 MD and Normal subjects were given MicroCog twice in intervals of time ranging from less than 3 days to 90–180 days.

WAIS-R/MicroCog Study: 184 MDs were given the WAIS-R and MicroCog to examine the correlations between the two tests.

Emotional State/MicroCog Study: To understand the extent to which emotions affected cognition, 188 MDs and 268 Normals were given two types of emotional state surveys along with MicroCog.

Pilot Validation Study: 16 normal and 27 mildly impaired subjects, largely from the Atlanta area, were given MicroCog to examine its sensitivity and specificity.

Florida Geriatric Research Group (FGRP) Construct Validation Study: 268 women and men ages 65–74, enrolled in the FGRP in Dunedin, Florida, took a battery of neuropsychological tests and MicroCog to study their comparability in classifying individuals as normal or impaired.

Atlanta Predictive Validation Study: 50 documented normals and 52 mildly impaired older volunteers were studied at the Emory Wesley Woods Center in Atlanta to determine how accurately MicroCog could predict both conditions.

---

will present factor analytic studies which show how the subtests group together in both the MD and Normal samples; we will define three cluster scores in MicroCog and attempt to confirm their presence by several statistical approaches; and finally, we will include studies on the validity of MicroCog.

Before turning to the statistical data, we present in Table 3.1 a summary of the subject samples and the several substudies that were carried out using smaller numbers of both MD and Normal subjects. This table should provide a useful guide for readers as they proceed through the book.

Descriptive Statistics for the MD and Normal Samples

The raw score means and standard deviations for both the MD and Normal samples are shown in Tables 3.2 and 3.3. The sequence and grouping of the subtests in Tables 3.2 and 3.3 reflect the cluster analyses shown in Tables 3.8 and 3.9. An analysis of variance (ANOVA) established that the differences among the total scores were statistically significant for both groups. Also significant is the fact that the variance of the total scores increases mono-tonically by age group among the MDs and Normals. The standard devia-tion of the total scores for MDs under the age of 35 was 10.49 points, as contrasted with 22.23 points for those 75 and older.

Among the specific subtests the same overall pattern held, though numer-ous exceptions occurred. In the larger and more homogenous MD sample, fewer irregularities appeared. In this group only six mean scores deviated from the lawful downward trend; all were within the smaller under-35 age group. There were seventeen exceptions to the trend toward increasing standard deviations, of which eight were in the youngest group.

A similar trend appeared in the Normal population. Eight subtest means were lower than those of the next older age group, half of them with the youngest subjects. Among the standard deviations, there were sixteen occa-sions in which the variance of the next older decade was less; this time the largest number of exceptions (seven) were in the oldest two groups.

Use of Raw Scores

Why did we not convert the raw test scores to standard scores? The short answer to this question is that converted scores provide no particular ad-vantage at this stage of test development. The initial system of essentially weighting subtests by the number of items they contained to obtain a total score was retained because the results worked well for research purposes, and standardizing the score distribution did not add to the usefulness of the data. However, the published version of MicroCog provides converted scores.

Initially, two approaches to weighting subtest scores seemed promising. The first approach was to weight each subtest by the first factor loadings; the second was to put the subtests on an equal footing by weighting the subtest scores in such a way that each had the same variance (that is, divid-ing each subtest score by the square of the standard deviation for that sub-test in the MD sample).

We examined the impact of these approaches to weighting the scores. For the first approach, we noted that the correlations between the first factor loadings and MicroCog raw scores were high ($r = .98$). This is not surpris-ing, because all of the values of the loadings fell within a narrow range. This means that this particular system of weighting would leave the relative con-tributions of subtest scores to the total largely unchanged.

The second approach in weighting the subtests, equalizing the variance, was accomplished by weighting each of the subtests inversely by the square

Table 3.2 Raw score means and standard deviations of MicroCog subtests by decade for 1,002 MDs

Age Group	Alphabet (15)	Wordlist 1 (16)	Wordlist 2 (16)	Numbers Forward (9)	Numbers Reversed (9)	Stories: Immediate (12)	Stories: Delayed (24)
MEANS							
<35	14.15	15.68	14.28	7.40	7.10	11.25	21.28
35–44	14.23	15.53	15.00	7.14	6.96	11.31	20.98
45–54	13.68	15.37	14.80	7.07	6.58	11.15	20.01
55–64	12.93	14.77	14.62	6.92	6.56	10.83	19.41
65–74	12.70	13.97	13.78	6.50	6.00	10.25	18.17
75+	8.89	11.23	12.16	5.79	5.07	9.44	16.42
STANDARD DEVIATIONS							
<35	2.87	0.76	3.23	1.53	1.60	1.08	1.68
35–44	2.80	0.96	2.00	1.24	1.46	0.82	2.16
45–54	3.67	1.19	1.73	1.37	1.50	1.05	2.72
55–64	4.63	2.03	2.16	1.35	1.39	1.17	2.51
65–74	4.65	2.91	2.45	1.43	1.49	1.41	2.68
75+	6.56	3.98	3.83	1.70	1.80	1.96	3.62

Notes: (1) Number of items are shown in parentheses below column headings. (2) Data for Alikes and Cubes not shown because these subtests were eliminated from battery.

of its standard deviation, which is the equivalent of computing a T-score. Doing so produces little more deviation from a linear relationship with the simple MicroCog total than was found using the first factor loadings. Here the correlation between the two forms of the scores was .97.

By converting MicroCog scores to T-scores, it puts the results on a standard scale familiar to many clinicians. However, since we were not using these score patterns clinically but only for research, the conversion did not appear to add enough to our understanding to justify their use.

Reliability

Reliability measures the degree to which a test is consistent in its measurements. Table 3.4 gives the reliabilities of the subtests in two different ways, internal consistency and test/retest. Cronbach's alpha, a method of calculating internal consistency, compares the magnitude of the error score to

Table 3.2 (continued)

Address (4)	Tictac (18)	Clocks (16)	Analogies (15)	Object Match (24)	Math (10)	Total (188)	Age Group	N
			MEANS					
3.58	15.68	15.13	11.95	22.78	9.27	169.51	<35	40
3.50	13.87	15.39	11.71	22.89	9.28	167.79	35–44	199
3.35	12.24	15.09	11.02	22.64	8.98	161.97	45–54	188
3.15	11.00	14.93	10.21	22.48	8.61	156.41	55–64	219
2.66	8.84	14.27	8.72	21.57	8.60	146.04	65–74	210
2.43	5.43	12.81	6.95	20.73	7.90	125.24	75+	146
							Total	1,002
			STANDARD DEVIATIONS					
0.68	2.94	1.62	2.14	1.29	0.82	10.49	<35	40
0.71	4.21	1.08	2.10	1.25	1.12	10.58	35–44	199
0.84	4.88	1.24	2.32	1.43	1.19	13.62	45–54	188
0.90	4.91	1.46	2.62	1.45	1.46	15.31	55–64	219
1.02	4.95	2.14	2.77	2.20	1.37	16.63	65–74	210
1.00	4.32	2.76	2.38	1.92	1.89	22.23	75+	146
							Total	1,002

that of the true score for each subtest. Test/retest measures reliability by comparing test and retest scores of subjects over time intervals ranging from a few days to six months. The subjects for the Cronbach's alpha reliability study were the 1,002 MDs. Volunteers for the test/retest investigation were drawn from both the MD and Normal samples. The most important reliability measure is that of the total MicroCog score, where the reliability coefficient of .95 is high. It is similar to the well-standardized WAIS-R intelligence test, where the full scale reliability is .97.

Reliability coefficients from the Cronbach's alpha and test/retest comparisons[2] indicate a high degree of stability for the total score, giving us confidence that if a person were to take the test again, and there were no intervening events, the score would be not significantly different. The strong reliability coefficients for total scores may have been attained because the computer effectively standardizes test administration.

The test/retest intervals were selected to be clinically useful. Some individuals might be retested right away because important decisions may hinge on the outcome. For instance, an initial finding that someone might be cognitively impaired could lead to retesting as soon as possible before

Table 3.3   Raw score means and standard deviations of MicroCog subtests
           by decade for 581 Normals

Age Group	Alphabet (15)	Wordlist 1 (16)	Wordlist 2 (16)	Numbers Forward (9)	Numbers Reversed (9)	Stories: Immediate (12)	Stories: Delayed (24)
			MEANS				
<35	14.42	15.66	15.15	7.04	6.68	10.87	20.40
35–44	13.91	15.71	14.49	6.89	6.23	11.14	19.77
45–54	13.14	15.17	14.00	7.17	6.50	10.78	19.50
55–64	12.31	14.57	14.12	5.86	5.26	10.22	17.96
65–74	10.97	13.05	13.29	5.60	5.11	9.59	17.00
75+	9.00	10.78	11.53	5.34	4.46	8.36	15.22
			STANDARD DEVIATIONS				
<35	2.12	0.73	2.31	1.36	1.27	1.06	2.35
35–44	3.28	0.96	2.95	1.41	1.68	1.00	2.91
45–54	4.33	1.91	3.75	1.70	1.34	1.07	2.68
55–64	5.02	1.79	2.77	1.93	1.50	1.40	3.81
65–74	6.02	3.22	3.19	1.98	1.67	1.81	3.18
75+	6.49	3.85	4.48	1.96	1.57	1.83	3.45

Notes: (1) Number of items are shown in parentheses below column headings. (2) Data for Alikes and Cubes not shown because these subtests were eliminated from battery.

commencing lengthy and expensive diagnostic procedures. The middle intervals, from one week to one month, are typically those found in clinics where retests need to be carried out but no emergency exists. The three- to six-month intervals were chosen because this time period is often employed in studies of test/retest reliability.

The correlations for the test/retest time intervals differ from .92 for the 8- to 30-day period to .83 for those tested three to six months apart. The recency of the retest appears to govern how much the total score improves on the second administration. The average test/retest gains on MicroCog for the shorter time intervals were 6 to 7 raw score points, about a 3% increase. The average gain in the three- to six-month interval was smaller, averaging just under 4 points, approximately a 2% increase.

Reliabilities of the subtests were much more variable than the total score. Looking at the Cronbach alpha reliabilities, we see that the high end is dominated by Alphabet (.98), Tictac (.92), Wordlist 1 (.92) and 2 (.84) and

Table 3.3 (continued)

				MEANS					
Age Group	Address (4)	Tictac (18)	Clocks (16)	Analogies (15)	Object Match (24)	Math (10)	Total (188)	Age Group	N
<35	3.64	15.00	14.96	10.89	22.32	8.90	165.93	<35	53
35–44	3.43	13.40	15.11	10.74	22.26	8.91	162.00	35–44	35
45–54	3.19	12.59	14.47	10.39	22.36	8.69	157.72	45–54	36
55–64	3.04	9.22	14.16	8.69	21.82	8.67	145.88	55–64	51
65–74	2.66	7.42	13.11	7.11	20.78	8.25	133.94	65–74	347
75+	2.05	6.10	12.31	6.32	20.14	7.43	119.03	75+	59
								Total	581
				STANDARD DEVIATIONS					
<35	0.56	3.87	1.27	2.03	1.57	1.18	11.66	<35	53
35–44	0.74	4.33	1.13	2.32	1.54	1.27	13.53	35–44	35
45–54	0.98	5.14	1.16	2.69	1.61	1.39	16.00	45–54	36
55–64	1.04	5.71	1.95	2.72	1.58	1.48	18.83	55–64	51
65–74	1.08	4.87	2.95	2.41	1.86	1.76	20.42	65–74	347
75+	1.29	4.65	2.71	2.22	1.90	2.20	20.80	75+	59
								Total	581

Analogies (.74). The lower boundary was established by Alikes (.46) and Address (.45). Those subtests which had a larger number of items and exhibited the greatest dispersion showed the highest reliabilities.

Because of the "eye-chart" method of giving numbers forward and reversed, the test/retest method for calculating reliability was more appropriate than the alpha. Here the coefficients were higher, though still moderate.

The test/retest reliabilities are in the same range as several reported by Matarazzo on an ancestor of the WAIS-R, the Wechsler-Bellevue-I.[3] The Full Scale I.Q. correlations ranged from .82 to .90. Subtest reliabilities varied greatly in seven separate studies. They are in the same range for comparable MicroCog subtests. Examples are Similarities scores ranging from .41 to .93, averaging .73. The reliability of MicroCog Analogies is .79. The reliability of Digit Span averaged .68 compared to MicroCog Numbers Forward (.57) and Numbers Reversed (.64). The remaining MicroCog subtests which are not similar to the Wechsler components have substantially lower test/retest reliabilities. It should be noted, however, that the published version of MicroCog reports higher reliabilities for both internal

Table 3.4 Reliabilities for MicroCog subtests

MicroCog Subtests	Internal Consistency	Test-Retest
ATTENTION		
Alphabet	.98	.42
Wordlist 1	.92	.57
Wordlist 2	.84	.50
Alikes	.46	.16
NUMERIC RECALL		
Numbers Forward	.52	.57
Numbers Reversed	.55	.64
VERBAL MEMORY		
Stories: Immediate Recall	.61	.45
Stories: Delayed Recall	.65	.51
Address	.45	.46
VISUOSPATIAL FACILITY		
Tictac	.92	.58
Clocks	.69	.49
Cubes	.60	.36
REASONING		
Analogies	.74	.79
Object Match	.50	.44
CALCULATION		
Math	.57	.46
Total Score	.95	.86

consistency and test/retest than this preliminary study. In the manual for MicroCog published by the Psychological Corporation, the overall test reliability (.95) is nearly the same as that found in our analysis. The reliabilities for the subtests, with one exception, are equal to or higher than those found in Table 3.4.[4]

Intercorrelation among the Subtests

Intercorrelations among MicroCog subtests and total score for the MD sample are shown in Table 3.5. Many of the subtests do contribute substantially to the MicroCog total score. Those with the highest correlations are Tictac (.75), Stories: Delayed Recall (.71), Analogies (.71), Wordlist 1 (.68),

Table 3.5 Pearson intercorrelation matrix for MicroCog subtests

MicroCog Subtests	Alphabet	Wordlist 1	Wordlist 2	Numbers Forward	Numbers Reversed	Address	Stories IR	Stories DR	Tictac	Clocks	Analogies	Object Match	Math	TOTAL
Alphabet	1.00													
Wordlist 1	0.41	1.00												
Wordlist 2	0.26	0.48	1.00											
Numbers Forward	0.24	0.28	0.18	1.00										
Numbers Reversed	0.28	0.30	0.18	0.64	1.00									
Address	0.29	0.32	0.27	0.24	0.28	1.00								
Stories IR	0.29	0.35	0.26	0.31	0.34	0.39	1.00							
Stories DR	0.34	0.38	0.26	0.31	0.39	0.47	0.68	1.00						
Tictac	0.31	0.37	0.23	0.36	0.37	0.36	0.42	0.46	1.00					
Clocks	0.27	0.41	0.20	0.23	0.33	0.31	0.35	0.37	0.40	1.00				
Analogies	0.34	0.45	0.28	0.34	0.34	0.42	0.41	0.49	0.47	0.43	1.00			
Object Match	0.30	0.37	0.28	0.23	0.27	0.31	0.32	0.37	0.39	0.30	0.41	1.00		
Math	0.22	0.27	0.17	0.26	0.28	0.24	0.26	0.30	0.35	0.29	0.31	0.22	1.00	
TOTAL	0.64	0.68	0.50	0.52	0.57	0.56	0.64	0.71	0.75	0.59	0.71	0.58	0.48	1.00

Stories: Immediate Recall (.64), and Alphabet (.64). Again, those subtests with more items and more challenging questions provided greater dispersion among the subjects, which resulted in higher correlations.

Correlations among the MicroCog subtests themselves were, on the whole, modest. Those which were of the same type exhibited the strongest associations: Stories: Immediate and Delayed Recall (.68), and Numbers Forward and Reversed (.64). The Analogies subtest had the highest correlations with the other subtests. Though these intercorrelations are lower than in the traditional I.Q. tests, they are not greatly different from traditional neuropsychological test batteries when these data have been reported.[5]

On the basis of low intercorrelations with MicroCog total score, low correlations with other subtests, and low reliabilities, we decided to eliminate the Cubes and Alikes subtests from the battery. They will not be included in further discussions of MicroCog or of cognitive aging.

Factor Analysis

Factor analysis is a widely used mathematical model that extracts fundamental dimensions which are inherent in quantitative data. It provides a way to examine the empirical results to determine if they correspond to the original a priori conceptions on which the test was conceived. Also, when examined by age group, factor analysis enables us to see if the factor structure is consistent across the age groups. In our search for such dimensions, we factor-analyzed the two data samples using principal components analysis (PCA). A PCA was carried out on the 1,002 physicians and 581 Normals and then separately with each of the six separate age groups. The factor analysis of the test scores of the entire MD and Normal groups provides the most stable estimate of the structure of the test. Comparing the results of the factor analyses by age group made it possible to determine how much age and years of education influenced the composition of the factor structures.

The resulting factors were rotated using a varimax solution. Only factors with significant eigenvalues of 1.0 or higher were included.

The PCA for the MDs defined two factors which accounted for 47.7% of the variance. All of the subtests loaded above .45 on the first, or general, factor. Varimax rotation produced one complex and one simple factor. The complex factor, listed in order of their contribution, consisted of four components, all loading .50 or higher, representing attention (Wordlist 1, Wordlist 2, and Alphabet), reasoning (Analogies and Object Match), verbal memory (Stories: Immediate and Delayed Recall and Address), and visuospatial functions (Tictac and Clocks). The second was a more sharply defined number recall factor. The resulting factor structure was rather over-simplified because of age heterogeneity. To gain further clarification, the MD sample was analyzed by age group.

A PCA was conducted with each of the six age groups (under 35 to 75 and over). These factor solutions were rotated using varimax criteria and the resulting loadings analyzed for content. The factor loadings by age group are shown in Table 3.6. As can be seen, verbal memory, attention, and numeric recall stand alone as a separate factor in each age group. Visuospatial recall (Tictac) defined a specific factor in the under-35 doctors and those aged 45–54, but made a far less distinct contribution to the three oldest groups. Reasoning, except at 75+, seldom stood alone. It appeared in the company of attention in the three youngest groups and with Clocks in the three oldest. Math, too, was always associated with other dimensions—for example, with visuospatial skills at 35–44, with number memory at 75+, or as part of one of the complex factors. This is reminiscent of the factor structure of the WAIS, where the math dimension (Arithmetic) was found to be associated with memory and attention.[6]

Our analysis was then extended to include the Normal sample composed of 581 subjects. For the entire group, three significant factors accounted for 55.8% of the variance. As with the MD sample, the first factor was most weighted by all subtests. Attention, as measured by Alphabet and Wordlist 1 and 2, was the major component of factor 2, while number memory largely defined factor 3. Rotation produced a first factor weighted by verbal memory—Stories: Immediate Recall (.77), Delayed Recall (.79), and Address (.47); visuospatial functions—Clocks (.68) and Tictac (.55); and reasoning—Object Match (.63) and Analogies (.60). Attention, as defined by Wordlist 1 (.70), Wordlist 2 (.80), and Alphabet (.61), loaded heaviest on factor 2. Numbers Forward (.87) and Reversed (.76) defined the third factor.

As before, these data were analyzed using a PCA for each age group. When the rotated factor solution, shown in Table 3.7, was run for each age group in the Normal sample, verbal memory, attention, and number recall again appeared as separate factors in each group. Neither visuospatial facility nor reasoning defined a specific factor in any group, though they often appeared in the company of other abilities. The highest Tictac loadings occurred most often when attentional or numeric recall weights were also heaviest. When Analogies contributed most, verbal memory often also loaded on that factor. This was clearest at ages 35–44, 45–54, 65–74, and

Table 3.6 Rotated factor structure of MicroCog by age group of 1,002 MDs

MicroCog Subtests	Age Group <35 Factors					Age Group 35–44 Factors					Age Group 45–54 Factors			
	1	2	3	4	5	1	2	3	4	5	1	2	3	4
Alphabet	.34		.39		.36	.63					.49		-.35	
Wordlist 1			.89					.75			.54		.36	
Wordlist 2	-.32				.54	-.41		.36				.89	.80	
Numbers F	.82							.36	.86			.89		
Numbers R	.83								.84			.86		
Address	.80							.60	.86		.75			
Stories: IR		-.30		.78			.81				.66			
Stories: DR		.33		.80			.86				.69			.30
Tictac		.86				.53			.38					.67
Clocks	.61		.63		.53					.89				.67
Analogies			.40	.44			.70	.69			.40		.48	
Object Match		-.69	.42		.81		.54			.31	.64		.30	
Math														.68
Percentage of Variance	29.5	12.5	11.7	9.8	8.8	21.2	11.2	10.6	10.1	7.8	26.5	11.2	9.8	8.8

Table 3.6 (continued)

MicroCog Subtests	Age Group 55–64 Factors				Age Group 65–74 Factors				Age Group 75+ Factors			
	1	2	3	4	1	2	3	4	1	2	3	4
Alphabet				.55		.36	.37			.59		.39
Wordlist 1	.39			.66			.80	.31		.75		
Wordlist 2				.77			.84			.81		
Numbers F		.89				.81			.77			
Numbers R		.87				.86			.73			
Address	.38		.47		.31			.51		.40		.41
Stories: IR			.81		.87							.83
Stories: DR			.85		.85						.61	.35
Tictac	.61							.49			.80	
Clocks	.77							.61	.42		.79	
Analogies	.63		.34					.53	.36		.52	
Object Match	.49			.49		.31	.35	.51		.52	.41	
Math	.41							.66	.75			
Percentage of Variance	27.1	11.6	10.0	8.4	26.5	10.7	9.8	8.0	31.0	11.7	8.7	8.3

Note: Only factor loadings of .30 or higher are shown.

Table 3.7   Rotated factor structure of MicroCog by age group of 581 Normals

MicroCog Subtests	Age Group < 35 Factors					Age Group 35–44 Factors				Age Group 45–54 Factors			
	1	2	3	4	5	1	2	3	4	1	2	3	4
Alphabet	.71				.38			.31	−.71	.49	.89		
Wordlist 1		.81					.76				.81		
Wordlist 2		.83					.68		.63		.80		
Numbers F			.76				.57		−.46	.77		.79	
Numbers R			.82					.51	−.41	.41	.37	.54	.46
Address			.60		.43	.82				.43	.69	.61	
Stories: IR				.87		.83				.71			
Stories: DR				.89		.82				.70			
Tictac	.46	.62				.50		.69		.48			
Clocks	.74					.73	.75			.42			
Analogies					.72			.78				.56	
Object Match					.68				−.31				.54
Math	.80					.66							.79
Percentage of Variance	27.3	14.1	12.0	10.0	7.9	33.1	14.1	11.6	8.8	30.0	16.9	11.1	8.3

Table 3.7 (continued)

MicroCog Subtests	Age Group 55–64 Factors				Age Group 65–74 Factors			Age Group 75+ Factors		
	1	2	3	4	1	2	3	1	2	3
Alphabet		.84			.67	.67				.53
Wordlist 1	.74				.67	.77				.79
Wordlist 2		.53		.42			.36			.79
Numbers F			.88		.80		.84	.80	.78	
Numbers R	.47		.62		.73		.80	.73	.81	
Address	.70			.41	.70	.34	.30			
Stories: IR				.73	.74					.46
Stories: DR			.32	.87	.57					
Tictac	.59			.32	.65			.53		
Clocks	.80				.52				.67	
Analogies	.42		.50	.30	.63				.51	.30
Object Match	.47			.33	.57			.34	.30	.42
Math	.39	.61							.32	.41
Percentage of Variance	35.5	10.6	9.5	8.3	32.8	10.0	8.0	28.2	11.3	9.9

Note: Only factor loadings of .30 or higher are shown.

75+. The highest Math weights accompanied strong loadings by at least one attentional subtest at every age.

In both groups the factor structure became more sharply defined in the decades beyond 55. This is most apparent in the more numerous and homogeneous MD sample. In the three youngest groups, the first factors were often loaded by more than one ability. For instance, factor 1 among the under-35 subjects was defined by a mix of number recall, verbal memory, and Clocks. In the next decade, the first factors were loaded by measures of attention, verbal memory, Object Match, and Clocks. At 55–64, the first factor was weighted by only two dimensions, visuospatial ability and reasoning. Factor 1 in the two oldest decades was verbal memory (65–74) and number facility (75+).

The Normals showed a similar pattern, with the number of significant factors shrinking from five for the under-35 subjects to only three among the two oldest decades. The first factor structure among the two oldest groups also was less complex than in the next youngest three decades, but not the under-35 subjects.

The PCAs carried out with each age group for both samples found a moderately strong linear and a lesser quadratic trend in the percentage of total variance explained by the first factor. Tables 3.6 and 3.7 show that the first factors are highest in the oldest and youngest MDs, and lowest among the Normals under 35 and 75+, revealing not much of a pattern. But if we take the ratio of the variance accounted for by the first and second factors, dividing the former by the latter, a clearer trend emerges. While still slightly curvilinear, a stronger linear pattern is shown by the ratios among the MDs: under 35 (2.36); 35–44 (1.89); 45–54 (2.63); 55–64 (2.34); 65–74 (2.48); 75+ (2.66). For the Normals the ratios for the six groups are 1.93, 2.35, 1.78, 3.35, 3.28, and 2.51.

Abilities, as measured by MicroCog, may become dedifferentiated with age. The number of factors decreased by decade. Moreover, the percentage of the variance explained by the first factor in the unrotated solutions, relative to the second factor, was largest in the oldest groups, suggesting that a general factor may become more prominent with advancing years. This observation finds support in the work of Cunningham and Owens[7] as well as earlier studies. The simplified factor structure among older subjects is consistent with Cohen's finding of four factors for his 60+ group from the WAIS standardization sample compared to five factors with the three youngest age groups.[8] Also consistent with our data is the fact that the percentage of variance accounted for by the first factor was highest among the oldest group.[9]

Cluster Analysis and LISREL

We decided to explore these relationships further using cluster analysis, another methodology that is useful for exploring intra-subtest relationships. Using the LISREL cluster model, we analyzed the data again. LISREL permits one to specify the components of each cluster and then determine the quality of the fit. For the 45–64 double decade in the MD sample, three clusters were found. Since these clusters were largely consistent with the theoretical assumptions about MicroCog's structure and the factor analyses, they were used as the basis for establishing clusters. The goodness of fit measures were obtained for the entire MD sample. The three LISREL clusters are shown in Table 3.8 for the MD subjects; they are verbal memory, visuospatial/numeric, and attention/reasoning.

In order to confirm the results of the MD data, the same LISREL analyses were applied to 268 Normal subjects from the Florida Geriatric Research

Table 3.8 Test results using the LISREL with the 407 MDs aged 45–64

MicroCog Subtests	Own Cluster	Next Closest
Cluster 1: Verbal Memory		
Address	.63	.30
Stories: Immediate Recall	.83	.50
Stories: Delayed Recall	.95	.53
Cluster 2: Visuospatial/Numeric		
Tictac	.89	.51
Numbers Reversed	.64	.36
Numbers Forward	.60	.36
Clocks	.62	.46
Math	.54	.34
Cluster 3: Attention/Reasoning		
Alphabet	.77	.39
Wordlist 1	.75	.49
Wordlist 2	.62	.30
Analogies	.70	.57
Object Match	.61	.44

Table 3.9 Cluster analysis results using the LISREL procedures
with 268 FGRP volunteers aged 65–74

	Cluster 1: Verbal Memory	
MicroCog Subtests	Own Cluster	Next Closest
Stories: Delayed Recall	.95	.58
Stories: Immediate Recall	.85	.51
Address	.61	.46
	Cluster 2: Visuospatial/ Numeric	
MicroCog Subtests	Own Cluster	Next Closest
Tictac	.88	.52
Numbers Reversed	.68	.47
Clocks	.67	.47
Numbers Forward	.62	.37
Math	.56	.39
	Cluster 3: Attention/Reasoning	
MicroCog Subtests	Own Cluster	Next Closest
Alphabet	.75	.32
Wordlist 1	.72	.47
Wordlist 2	.65	.35
Analogy	.59	.56
Object Match	.59	.50

Program (FGRP), ages 65–74. Table 3.9 shows that the three clusters discovered earlier were supported by this independent sample. On the basis of both the factor analyses and the LISREL procedures, it appears that the individual subtests of MicroCog could be condensed into three major components: verbal memory, visuospatial/numeric, and attention/reasoning.

Confirmation of the Content of MicroCog

To be more certain that these aptitude clusters in fact comprise MicroCog, we set out to confirm the existence of these elements by correlating them with other tests that are thought to measure these particular skills. Three separate approaches were used. The first was a factor analysis of MicroCog along with three well-established neuropsychological tests that share some of the same dimensions as MicroCog. The second was a regression analysis that evaluated how much these neuropsychological tests had in common with the MicroCog results. The third approach correlated the LISREL clusters with the neuropsychological test results.

The study that factor-analyzed MicroCog along with three neuropsychological tests was carried out with 268 volunteers of the Florida Geriatric Research Project (FGRP) in Dunedin, Florida.[10] The participants were recruited from the general ranks of those enrolled in the FGRP program between the ages of 65 and 74 who represented themselves as having normal cognitive functioning. FGRP participants were sent letters in which the purpose of the research and its design were presented, and in which they were asked to volunteer for the study. The remaining subjects were people in the same age cohort who read announcements about the study in the Dunedin area and chose to volunteer. Of the volunteers, 196 were females and 72 were males. The mean ages of women and men were similar. The males averaged 13.9 years of education, while the mean for females was about a year less. The subjects ranged from individuals with five years of education to those with doctoral degrees. Greater variability occurred among the males, as shown by their differences in standard deviation ($p = .004$).

Subjects were given MicroCog as part of an individually administered neuropsychological battery. The battery consisted of the Wechsler Memory Scale-Revised, the Wisconsin Card Sorting Test, and the Boston Naming Test.[11] Each of these tests assesses distinct mental activities. The Wechsler Memory Scale-Revised (WMS-R) is especially sensitive to memory and attention, while the Wisconsin Card Sorting Test (WCST) taps abstract reasoning. The Boston Naming Test (BNT) assesses the capacity to recall the proper names for pictorial objects.

Testing was divided into two sessions: the subjects were first given Micro-Cog and then were invited back at a later date for the neuropsychological tests. The latter set was designed to take about two hours, so that it would not be too taxing for older persons. The neuropsychological testing took place under the direction of Dr. Cynthia R. Cimino at the University of South Florida, who trained the test administrators and then supervised both the administration and scoring of the instruments.

Factor Analysis of MicroCog and Neuropsychological Tests

In an effort to gain a clearer picture of the MicroCog structure, the test was factor-analyzed along with several subtests of the WMS-R. These subtests were selected as marker variables to assist in understanding the components of MicroCog. The initial analysis with the WMS-R produced three

Table 3.10 Rotated factor loadings of MicroCog and WMS-R subtests

Subtests	Factor 1	Factor 2	Factor 3
Alphabet		.52	
Wordlist 1			.75
Wordlist 2			.60
Numbers Forward		.40	.47
Numbers Reversed		.43	.41
Address			
Stories: Immediate Recall	.35	.68	
Stories: Delayed Recall	.38	.68	
Tictac			.31
Clocks		.52	
Analogies			
Object Match			
Math		.55	
WMS-R Verbal Memory	.83		
WMS-R Visual Memory	.70		
WMS-R General Memory	.93		
WMS-R Attention/Concentration			.67
WMS-R Delayed Recall	.86		

Note: Only factor loadings of .30 or higher are shown.

primary factors. Rotation produced the factor structure shown in Table 3.10. The verbal memory subtests of the WMS-R and the immediate and delayed recall story subtests of MicroCog contributed to the first factor, suggesting that MicroCog and the WMS-R share a common recall component for verbal content. The second factor also was loaded by memory-related MicroCog subtests, but heavy loadings came from Math and Numbers Forward and Reversed. The third factor was more clearly attention-based, due to the loadings from Wordlist 1 and 2 and Alphabet from MicroCog, and the WMS-R Attention/Concentration.

The MicroCog subtests were also analyzed with subtests of the WCST to assess the degree to which there might be other common factors upon which both might load. We were especially interested in whether a reasoning factor common to both subtests might emerge. The unrotated solution produced the now-familiar trio: general learning, memory, and attention. Rotation produced memory and attention factors along with the third factor, which might be labeled visuospatial, but no clear reasoning component.

Table 3.11 Multiple regression values with MicroCog as dependent variable and summary indices as independent variables

Independent Variables	Beta Value	(*f*) Value	Probability Value
WMS-R Verbal Memory	−.203	1.18	.236
WMS-R Visual Memory	−.000	0.00	.999
WMS-R General Memory	.445	1.93	.054
WMS-R Attention/Concentration	.252	5.61	.000
WMS Delayed Recall	.094	1.24	.214
BNT Total Score	.161	3.45	.000
WCST Errors	.328	4.16	.000
WCST Perseverative Errors	.057	0.73	.465

Regression Analysis

The second attempt to examine the relationship between MicroCog and eight summary indices from the neuropsychological tests used regression analysis, the results of which are depicted in Table 3.11. Using MicroCog total score as the dependent variable and the eight summary indices as independent variables, it was found that total scores are quite predictable with a multiple correlation of .68. The findings revealed that four independent variables contributed significantly to the regression equation (WMS-R General Memory and Attention/Concentration, BNT word finding, and WCST Errors), suggesting that MicroCog is associated with these useful neuropsychological factors.

Correlation of LISREL Clusters

The third effort to confirm the content of MicroCog correlated the three LISREL-derived clusters of verbal memory, visuospatial/numeric, and attention/reasoning to eight of the neuropsychological indices. The results are shown in Table 3.12. (It should be noted that some of the correlations are negative: this is because several scales such as the WCST Perseverative Errors are scored on a reverse scale.) The results in Table 3.12 show that the correlations among the variable constructs were significant, but there was also evidence that the differential predictive power was relatively small. For example, the Wechsler Verbal Memory score is substantially correlated (.43) with MicroCog's Verbal Memory factor. WMS-R General Memory also correlated significantly with MicroCog Verbal Memory (.51) and with

Table 3.12　Correlations among MicroCog clusters and eight neuropsychological
　　　　　　subtest scores with 268 volunteers, aged 65–74, from the FGRP

Neuropsychological Subtests	Cluster I Verbal Memory	Cluster II Visuospatial/ Numeric	Cluster III Attention/ Reasoning	MicroCog Total Scores
WMS-R Verbal Memory	.43	.24	.20	.22
WMS-R Visual Memory	.39	.33	.39	.96
WMS-R General Memory	.51	.34	.34	.46
WMS-R Attention/Con- centration	.17	.47	.37	.43
WMS-R Delayed Recall	.47	.30	.33	.43
Boston Naming Test Total Score	.31	.25	.26	.34
WCST No. of Errors	.20	−.38	−.29	−.38
WCST Perseverative Errors	.28	−.43	.33	−.45
Cluster I	.55	.45	—	.70
Cluster II	.38	—	.45	.83
Cluster III	—	.38	.55	.84
MicroCog Total	.70	.83	.83	—

the other clusters (.34). The WCST scores correlated significantly with MicroCog Attention/Reasoning as expected. But because they also were associated with the two other cluster scores, MicroCog's discriminate power in this case is modest.

These explorations provided insight into the general structure of MicroCog using factor analysis, regression, and cluster analysis. From these studies it appears that MicroCog might be said to have three well-defined dimensions: verbal memory, visuospatial/numeric, and attention/reasoning.

Validity Studies

Validity studies of MicroCog addressed the question, "How accurately does the test differentiate between normal and impaired individuals?" Three studies of validity were completed. The first was a pilot study of 43 normal and mildly impaired subjects; the second was a concurrent construct validation study with the 268 volunteers from the Florida Geriatric Research Program; the third was a predictive validation study with 102 carefully documented normal and mildly impaired subjects at Emory University's Wesley Woods Geriatric Center in Atlanta.

Table 3.13 Pilot validation study: Accuracy of classification of normal and impaired subjects using MicroCog total cutoff score of 68% correct

MicroCog Total Score	Normal	Mildly Impaired*
≥68%	11	3
≤67%	5	13
Totals	16	16

*11 additional subjects diagnosed as cognitively impaired could not complete the test.

Pilot Validation Study

Twenty-seven women and men who had been diagnosed independently by neurologists as mildly cognitively impaired were tested with MicroCog. Their results were compared with those of 16 self-assessed "normal" volunteers from the same geographic areas—Boston, Atlanta, and Fort Lauderdale—who matched the impaired group in terms of age and education. Initially, we guessed that a MicroCog total of at least 68% correct would predict normal cognition. This hunch was based on clinical observation of those individuals scoring above and below 68%. The number of correct classifications is shown in Table 3.13. Using this simple prediction model, we found that of the 32 subjects who completed the test, 24 were correctly classified for an accuracy rating of 75%. Eleven additional subjects failed to complete the test, largely because of inability to understand or recall the instructions. All subjects self-assessed as normal finished MicroCog. If those 11 subjects originally diagnosed as mildly impaired were included, the total "hit rate" would be 81%, with a sensitivity of 89% and a 69% specificity rate. The sensitivity rate refers to those impaired subjects accurately classified, while the specificity rate is the percentage of normal individuals who are correctly identified.

FGRP Concurrent Construct Validation Study

A concurrent construct validation study was carried out with 268 subjects aged 65–74 from the FGRP.[12] The 268 subjects were divided into three groups on the basis of MicroCog total score: 68% and above correct (Probably Normal), 60–68% correct (Possibly Normal), and below 60% correct (Probably Impaired). Then the neuropsychological (NP) test scores for each individual were similarly grouped. Those whose subtest scores were

Table 3.14   Rate of agreement in classification between MicroCog total score
and eight neuropsychological test scores

Neuropsychological Test Scores	% Agreement with MicroCog Cutoff Score	χ^2	*p* Value
WMS-R General Memory	73.1	21.17	<0.001
WMS-R Verbal Memory	69.4	4.39	0.336
WMS-R Visual Memory	78.0	60.61	<0.001
WMS-R Attention/Concentration	75.7	30.08	<0.001
WMS-R Delayed Recall	71.6	30.08	<0.001
Boston Naming Test	76.9	28.04	<0.001
WCST Number of Errors	76.5	39.89	<0.001
WCST Perseverative Errors	76.1	37.85	<0.001

less than −1.0 standard deviation (S.D.) from the mean were identified as Probably Normal; those from −1.0 to −1.5 S.D. were classified as Possibly Normal; and those greater than −1.5 S.D. were categorized as Possibly Impaired.

The degree of concurrence among the eight separate NP subtest scores and the MicroCog results can be seen in Table 3.14: the range is from 69% to 78%. The percentage of similar classification between the total score on the BNT and the MicroCog total was one of the highest—76.9%. It is possible that many of the relationships with the WMS-R and the WCST would have been even stronger if either of these instruments had had a total score for comparison purposes. Nonetheless, with the exception of the comparison of MicroCog total and WMS-R Verbal Memory, all of the relationships were significant.

In an effort to simulate clinical judgment as a criterion, the investigators devised a Clinical Composite Score based on eight individual NP subtests. Subjects with a Clinical Composite Score less than −1.0 S.D. from the mean were called Probably Normal; those from −1.0 to −1.5 S.D. were labeled Possibly Normal; and those beyond −1.5 S.D. were classified as Possibly Impaired. The subjects were then divided into three groups on the basis of MicroCog total score. This enabled the investigators to compare the cutoff score thresholds of 68% and 60% with NP test classification sensitivity and specificity. As can be seen in Table 3.15, the overall agreement of the MicroCog total score with the NP tests is highly significant. There is more

Table 3.15 Concurrent construct validation study: MicroCog cutoff scores and agreement with clinical composite scores from neuropsychological tests

MicroCog Total Score	Probably Normal	Possibly Normal	Possibly Impaired	Totals
≥68%	119	58	19	196
67%–60%	11	17	10	38
≤59%	2	10	22	34

Threshold Score	Agreement	Sensitivity	Specificity
<68%	78%	63%	82%
<60%	85%	43%	94%

$\chi^2 = 71.07; p < .001.$

concordance at the lower threshold of 60% than at the level of 68% correct. The two cutoff scores offer interesting trade-offs: the lower threshold correctly identifies a large proportion of the normals (96%) but has less sensitivity to impairment; the higher cutoff score works in the opposite direction.

Discriminant analysis is a method of determining the effectiveness of a series of independent variables in predicting group membership. If subjects are classified as normal or mildly impaired using a MicroCog score of 68% as the cutoff, it can be determined with what frequency the WMS-R, the BNT, and the WCST will predict membership. The most effective discriminant analysis uses all of these independent variables including the subtest scores. The accuracy of classification was 81.3%.

The reasonably high rates of correspondence between the total MicroCog score and the individual NP test indices, and the significant agreement with the clinical composite scoring, provide evidence of construct validity. We were pleased with the agreements from 85% to 81% depending on the criterion. We were not pleased, however, with the low degree of sensitivity. We suspect that part of the problem is that the criteria for probable impairment may have produced a high number of false positives. This can be judged by the large proportion of individuals labeled as Possibly Impaired by the clinical composite score from the NP tests. Fifty-one of those volunteers, or 19%, were viewed as Possibly Impaired by this index, which is considerably out of line for this age group. As we shall see in Chapter 7, 2% to 3% would be a more accurate estimation among community-dwelling subjects. We felt that a more accurate evaluation of the normal and impaired subjects would produce a more accurate estimate of the validity of MicroCog. This step was carried out in the Atlanta Predictive Validation study.

Atlanta Predictive Validation Study

To explore more completely the validity of the test, colleagues from Emory University's Wesley Woods Geriatric Center in Atlanta, Georgia, conducted an independent evaluation of MicroCog's predictive accuracy with 52 mildly impaired and 50 normal subjects.[13] Both groups were documented to be either normal or mildly impaired by extensive medical and neuropsychological diagnostic procedures. The mildly impaired subjects were drawn from a group seen clinically by Emory University Medical School's neurobehavioral program. For the purposes of this study, "impaired" subjects conformed to the following criteria: reported decline in functional level; below-average Verbal or Performance IQ on the WAIS-R or memory impairment as demonstrated by below-average scores on the California Verbal Learning Test, the Logical Memory subtest from the WMS-R, or the Visual Reproduction subtest from the WMS-R; poor neurological test scores (including MR imaging); and diagnosis of a neurological disorder confirmed by a neurologist who had excluded depression. Normal subjects had to meet the following criteria to be considered normal: Verbal and Performance IQ within the average range on the WAIS-R; scores on selected neuropsychological tests within the average range (for subjects above age 74, average performance is considered to be within 1.5 standard deviations

Table 3.16   Characteristics of subjects in the Atlanta Predictive Validation Study

Characteristic	Normal		Mildly Impaired	
	Mean	S.D	Mean	S.D.
Age	68.7	5.0	71.2	10.1
Education	15.4	2.3	14.7	2.3
Gender (% female)	70%		54%	
N	50		52	

Source: R. C. Green et al., "Screening for Cognitive Impairment in Older Individuals: Validation Study of a Computer-based Test," *Archives of Neurology,* in press.

of the mean); no evidence of CNS dysfunction; normal EEG and MRI; absence of psychiatric or neurological medication; and no neurological disorder confirmed by a neurologist.

The characteristics of the subjects are shown in Table 3.16. We can see that the normal group was significantly younger and slightly better educated. More females were included in this group as well. The authors of the Atlanta study did not believe that the slightly older and more heavily male mildly impaired group significantly biased the data, since each individual was independently documented to be either normal or mildly impaired.

Instead of setting arbitrary cutoff scores to determine how well MicroCog performed at separating normals from those with cognitive impairment, the percentage of those correctly identified in each group was calculated for different MicroCog scores. The distribution of accurate predictions is shown in Table 3.17. As discussed earlier, sensitivity refers to individuals correctly identified as impaired, while specificity refers to those correctly classified as normal. The "hit rate" is the percentage of both normal and impaired subjects who were classified correctly on the basis of a particular cutoff threshold.

Setting a higher percentage correct (82%) as the cutoff score enables the test to identify correctly all of the individuals with cognitive impairment. This threshold, however, misclassifies about two-thirds of the normals, calling them impaired. This is called a "false positive" error. The other side of the coin is to set too low a cutoff threshold. For example, a total of 58% correct enables MicroCog to identify all of the normals correctly, but then

Table 3.17 Sensitivities, specificities, and "hit rates" of MicroCog with various cutoff scores

Total MicroCog Percent Correct	Sensitivity Percent	Specificity Percent	"Hit Rate" Percent
58	69	100	84
60	83	96	89
63	83	96	89
68	92	88	90
73	96	74	85
77	98	52	74
82	100	32	67

Source: R. C. Green et al., "Screening for Cognitive Impairment in Older Individuals: Validation Study of a Computer-Based Test," *Archives of Neurology,* in press.

it yields 31% false negatives, individuals incorrectly labeled as normal when they are in fact impaired. Examining the number of miscalculations, we see that a cutoff score between 68% and 60% correct yields roughly the same number of misclassifications. We will have more to say on this subject in Chapter 8.

Validity of MicroCog as a Screening Test

The validity of the best-established, individually given neuropsychological tests in correctly classifying normal and cognitively impaired subjects varies considerably from report to report. It depends upon many factors, including the magnitude of the difference in the degree to which intellectual functions are compromised in the impaired and control groups.[14]

As discussed earlier, the validity of neuropsychological tests for diagnostic purposes is measured by their hit rate, the degree to which they can successfully classify individuals into their diagnostic categories as determined by other criteria. As Lezak aptly points out, the hit rate may have little to do with the intrinsic properties of the tests, but rather can be influenced by a number of factors.[15] One factor that can affect the hit rate is the base rate of the condition which the test was intended to evaluate. Less frequent conditions are harder to detect and lead to more misclassifications. Another related factor is severity of impairment. The hit rate of any test can be increased by including a large number of severely impaired individuals to be compared with normals.

The Halstead-Reitan Neuropsychological Test Battery is one of the most commonly used instruments for evaluating neurobehavioral syndromes.[16] It consists of seven basic subtests and can require more than a day to administer. Hit rates as high as 90% (correct classification of brain-damaged patients) have been reported for this battery.[17] The Trail Making Test,[18] a more recent addition to the battery, was found to classify 81% of non-brain-damaged subjects and 88.5% of brain-damaged patients correctly.

Another, briefer psychometric measure for detecting brain damage is the Luria-Nebraska Neuropsychological Battery.[19] In an early study, the test with 14 scales was administered to 50 brain-damaged patients (all etiologies) and 50 control subjects. The average age of subjects was about 45. The hit rate of the various subtest scales ranged from 74% to 96% in the control group, and 64% to 86% in the brain-damaged group. A subsequent discriminant analysis was performed which successfully classified all 50 brain-damaged patients and 43 of the 50 control subjects. For three other test batteries that have been used in the past to detect cognitive impairment, sensitivity rates have been reported from 68% to 95%, while specificity percentages have varied from 84% to 100%.[20]

On the basis of this literature, it seems reasonable to assume that a 75% hit rate is an acceptable standard for neuropsychological tests that attempt to differentiate normals from mildly impaired subjects. Our three validity studies show that cutoff scores between 60% and 68% correct differentiate normal from mildly impaired subjects 81%, 85%, and 90% of the time. Moreover, the most rigorous of the validation studies yielded the highest percentage of correct classifications. These validation data await confirmation from other researchers. So far, however, it appears that MicroCog has the potential to join the company of the most accurate of the tests for detecting mild to moderate cognitive impairment.

4

Cognitive Changes over the Life Span

In this chapter we present data on the cognitive changes that occur in the adult years. First, we will consider the question of whether the decline of intellectual functioning is global or specific. That is, does aging bring with it a deterioration of particular abilities while everything else remains stable, as when an otherwise healthy person becomes hard of hearing, or is the downward trend in specific skills nested within a global decline? We will also investigate how early we can detect subtle changes in global and specific cognition and will identify those abilities that diminish earliest and those that are retained longest. Particular attention will be paid to the growing variability among individuals in older age groups in both overall mental ability and particular aptitudes. These empirical findings will be illustrated by anecdotal reports from more than 400 physicians.

We will use a number of different terms to denote mental or intellectual functioning that have slightly different meanings. When we use the terms "cognition," "intellectual functioning," or "mental operations," we have in mind global intelligence or a capacity that is composed of several specific abilities. An IQ test such as the WAIS-R is an example. When we refer to "abilities," "aptitudes," or "skills," we are referring to specific mental faculties such as attention, memory, or reasoning.

Age-Related Physiological Changes

Before looking at what happens to cognitive functions over the life span, it is instructive to consider the extent to which certain physical indices change over the adult years. Figure 4.1 traces the decline of five physical functions

% function remaining

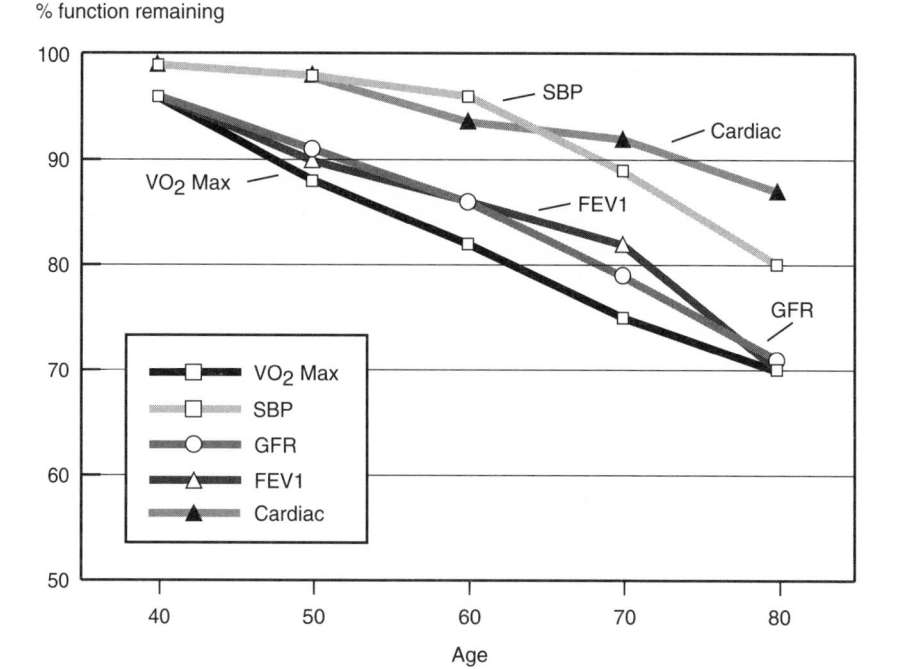

Figure 4.1 Age-related decline in five physiological functions. VO_2 Max = maximum oxygen consumption; SBP = percentage with normal systolic blood pressure; GFR = glomerular filtration rate; FEV_1 = forced expiratory volume in one second; Cardiac = heart rate per minute during maximal exercise.

by decade from age 40 to age 80.[1] The lines graph the percentage of function relative to age 30. The first is a cardiovascular index, VO_2 max, which is a measurement of maximum oxygen consumption per kilogram of body weight as a function of age. The second is the percentage of men and women with normal systolic blood pressure. The third curve is a measure of kidney function, the GFR or glomerular filtration rate. The fourth line follows the trajectory of one measure of the pulmonary system, the FEV_1 or forced expiratory volume of air in one second. The fifth is a cardiac index, the heart rate per minute during maximal exercise. It is striking to see how well so many of the physical measures hold up through age 60. The percentage of function remaining varies from a high of 96% (systolic BP) to 82% (VO_2 max). At age 70, VO_2 max diminishes to 75% along with GFR (79%), while cardiac function remains relatively high at 92%. By age 80, all of the physical indices are notably lower.

It should be recognized that although these curves are representative, other studies of these vital signs or other physiological variables could have been selected that show more or less loss of function. This is because the plots are based on subjects who may differ greatly among themselves in characteristics such as dietary habits, drinking and smoking, physical activities, personal characteristics, and stress levels. In addition, these curves do not show the variability around each of the age-related means because they are not provided in many cases by the authors of this study. An exception is the VO_2 max score, where there is an increase in the variability with age. For instance, among the 40-year-old subjects the range of scores on VO_2 max was about 40% of the mean, while among 80-year-olds the difference between the highest and lowest scores was 56% of the average score. Other evidence on the dispersion of scores by age groups suggests that the variance grows by age group with physiological as well as psychological and cognitive measures.[2]

These percentages of biological properties remaining provide a useful context in which to understand the changes that occur by decade in the intellectual functioning of our subjects.

Age-Related Cognitive Changes

What happens to our intellectual functions over the life span? Do they parallel the decline in the physiological domain? What areas are most dramatically affected? How soon can we detect these losses? In this section we present the results of our investigation with both the MD and Normal subjects. We will begin with the "big picture," tracking global cognitive function over the life span, and then will turn to the "smaller picture," a more fine-grained analysis of the effect of growing older on particular cognitive operations.

Figure 4.2 shows the percentage of correct answers for MicroCog total score among both the 1,002 MDs and the 581 Normals from the 25–34 age group to the 75+ group. The overall profile of cognitive functioning for both groups is similar until age 50. We see a relatively gentle downward slope for the first three decades among the MDs, and then a more rapid decline after 60. The average 60-year-old MD scored only 8% lower than a young doctor, while the same-decade Normal subject was 12 percentile points lower than someone of age 30. After age 60 the mean scores decline far more rapidly, the differences compared to the younger groups nearly doubling with each advancing decade. For instance, the total MicroCog score of MDs at age 70 was 14% lower than the youngest doctors; at age 75+ the total scores were 26% lower.

% correct

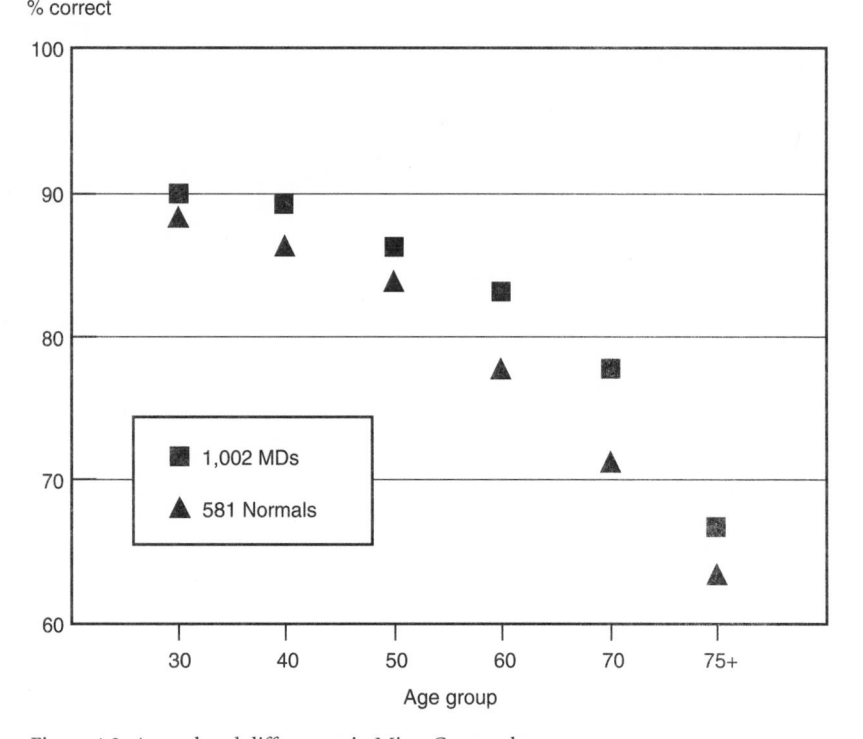

Figure 4.2 Age-related differences in MicroCog total score.

The age-grouped means dropped off slightly more rapidly after age 50 among the Normal subjects. Indeed, in the two decades after 60, the Normal women and men scored in about the same range as physicians ten years older. After age 75, the gap between the two groups narrowed. At all measurement points the Normal subjects scored below the doctors. This likely is due to the lower educational level of the women and men in the Normal pool, who averaged 14.13 years of education compared with the 20+ years of the medical group. We will see in Chapter 6 that number of years of education is strongly correlated with higher test results.

The curves shown in Figure 4.2 follow a pattern familiar to clinicians and gerontological researchers alike. For instance, changes in the age group scores on the Wechsler Intelligence Test resemble the MicroCog pattern. Figure 4.3 shows Full Scale IQ scores by age group from 25–34 to 75+.[3] These WAIS Full Scale IQ data were obtained by entering the mean score of the scaled scores into the WAIS IQ table for age group 25–34. The mean scores for groups 35–44 through 55–64 were drawn from Wechsler, and the

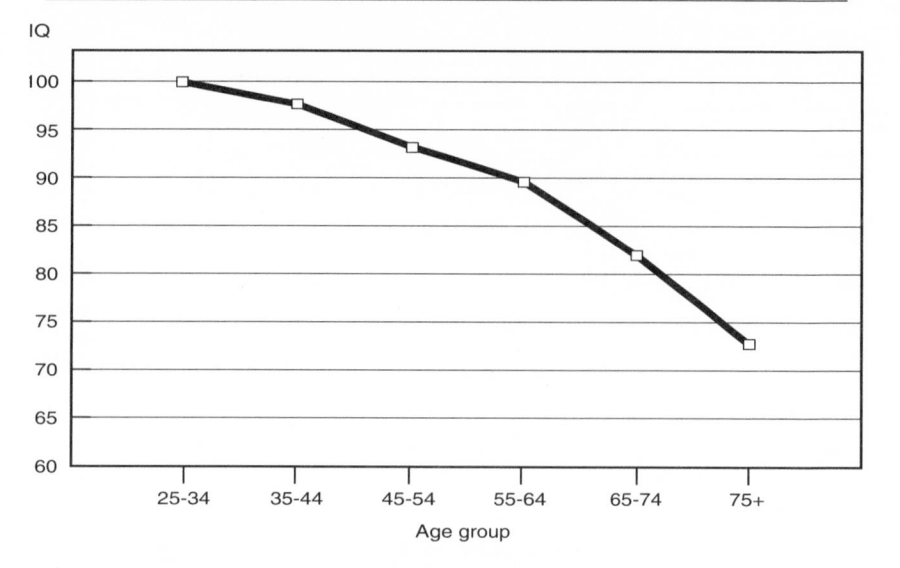

Figure 4.3 Average WAIS Full Scale IQ scores for age groups 25–34 to 75+. *Source:* A. S. Kaufman, *Assessing Adolescent and Adult Intelligence* (Boston: Allyn-Bacon, 1990), table 7.1, p. 185.

mean scores for age groups 65–69 through 75+ were computed from an older age sample reported by Doppelt and Wallace.

We can see the relatively slight decline in Full Scale IQ through ages 55–64. These individuals in the 55–64 group scored on average about 10% less than the 30-year-olds. In the next ten years overall IQ dips another 9%, and at 75+ the total score drops 11% more. This profile of scores looks remarkably similar to the pattern of MicroCog average total scores by decade. Comparable patterns of age-related scores were found on both older (W- B I) and newer (WAIS-R) forms of the Wechsler intelligence tests.

Not all aptitudes follow the same trajectory as the WAIS Full Scale IQ. The differences in the rate of change for the two halves of the Revised Wechsler Adult Intelligence Scale are portrayed in Figure 4.4.[4] We notice right away that the verbal component of the WAIS-R (made up of subtests such as vocabulary, general information, and reasoning tasks as well as mental arithmetic and digit span) shows a gradual downward movement by advancing decade. On the other hand, the performance tests, which place a premium on visuoperceptual and visuoconstructional tasks, nose down rapidly after ages 25–34. The Verbal IQ at ages 70–74 is less than 10% lower than for those at age 30, while Performance IQ declines roughly 25% during the same interval.

Verbal IQ

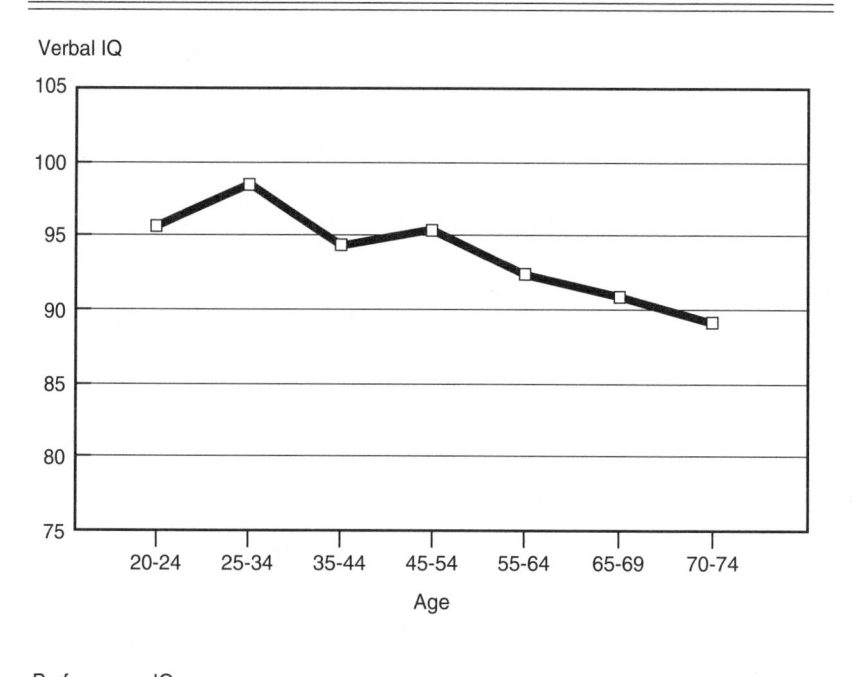

Performance IQ

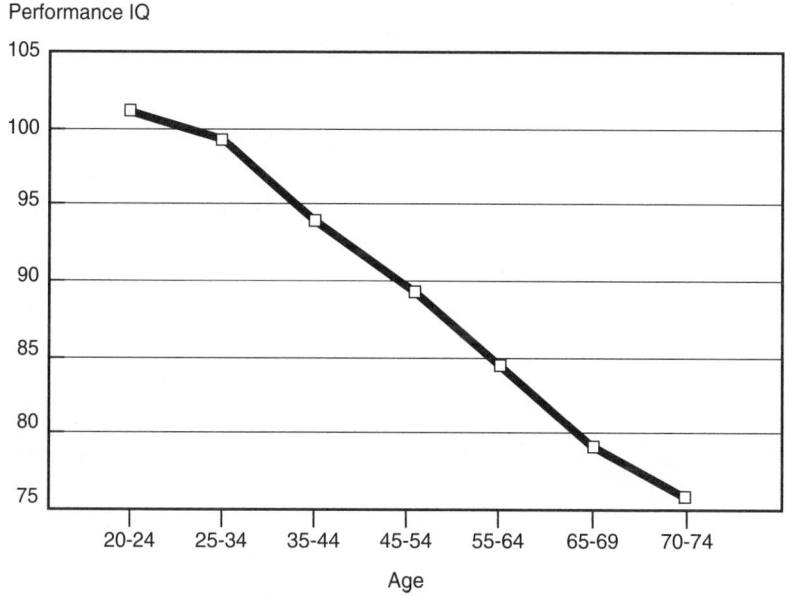

Figure 4.4 Change in WAIS-R Verbal and Performance IQs across the 20- to 74-year range (IQs were based on norms for ages 25–34). *Source:* Data from A. S. Kaufman, *Assessing Adolescent and Adult Intelligence* (Boston, Allyn-Bacon, 1990), fig. 7.1, p. 193.

Not all aptitudes fall at the same rate. Table 4.1 shows the extent to which different abilities are adversely influenced by age. It presents the negative correlations of the top and bottom four subtests as well as the total Micro-Cog score with age. Among the four highest correlations, three are thought to decline most rapidly over a normal lifetime: reasoning skills (Analogies), visuospatial facility (Tictac), and verbal memory (Stories: Delayed Recall). The "outlier" among these higher correlations is Wordlist 1, which is an attentional task. The bottom four subtests in the hierarchy are those which are often thought to be more resistant to aging—attention (Alphabet, Wordlist 2, and Numbers Forward) and calculation skills (Math). We also note that the total MicroCog score is more strongly correlated with aging than any particular subtest score. This suggests that the decline of specific skills is nested in a global downward trend.

The downward progression of aptitude scores varies greatly: some fall off sooner and more steeply, while others hold up until later life. Figure 4.5 shows the declining curves for scores on visuospatial memory, reasoning, and verbal memory after delay compared with overall performance across the age group for both MDs and Normals. In both the MD and Normal data sets, we see that the same patterns occur. Mean scores on visuospatial memory as defined by Tictac fall off the most steeply. Reasoning (Analogies) runs second, while verbal memory after delay is in third place. All are well below the slant of the total MicroCog score. The rate at which these skills trend downward after ages 45–54 is dramatic for those aptitudes most negatively correlated with age: the 50-year-old MD gives 24% fewer correct responses than does the 30-year-old in the visuospatial domain. From 50 to

Table 4.1 Negative correlation with age: Highest and lowest four MicroCog
             subtests (1,002 MDs)

Subtests	Correlation
Analogies	−.284
Tictac	−.267
Wordlist 1	−.263
Stories: Delayed Recall	−.216
Alphabet	−.168
Wordlist 2	−.165
Numbers Forward	−.146
Math	−.140
Total Score	−.376

1,002 MD subjects

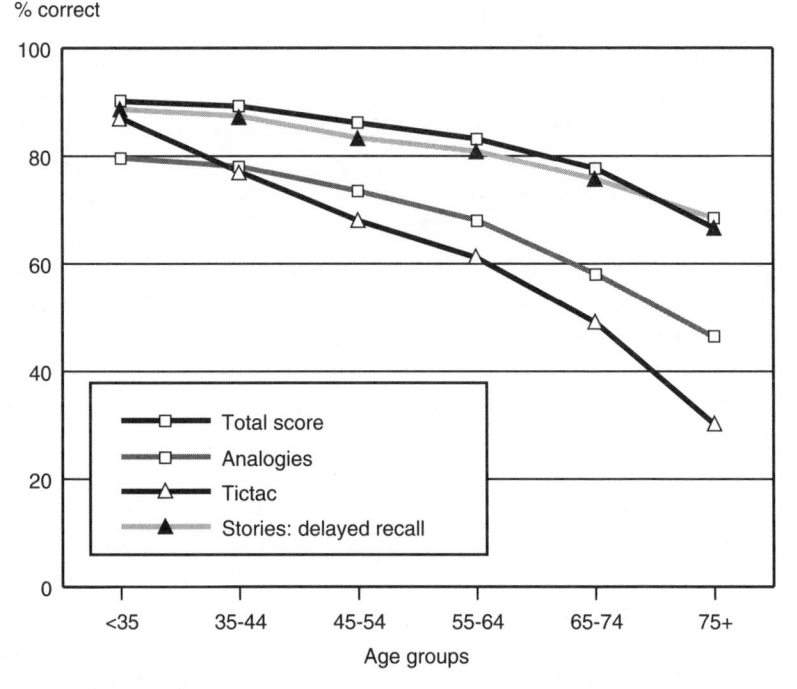

% correct

Figure 4.5   MicroCog aptitude scores that decline significantly by decade compared with total.

60 the drop-off is 10%, and the percentage of correct responses on the Tic-tac subtest for physicians aged 75+ was 39% lower than for doctors aged 65–74. The rate of decline is slower for Normal subjects, perhaps because they start off with lower scores to begin with. This is not surprising since the MD sample had to demonstrate visuospatial ability in both science and math courses as part of their academic preparation.

Reasoning skills also declined, though less steeply. In fact, these data suggest that reasoning is negatively influenced by age about a decade later than visuospatial functions. Evidence comes from both data sets in the similarity of correct responses for Tictac and Analogies. For instance, the 60-year-old MDs averaged 68.1% correct responses on Analogies compared with 68.0% on Tictac for 50-year-old physicians. The age-75+ doctors answered 46.3% of the Analogies correctly, a figure close to the 49.1% for visuospatial memory among the MDs in the 65–74 decade. The same pattern did not occur among the Normal subjects. This is because reasoning scores started lower than visuospatial

581 Normal subjects

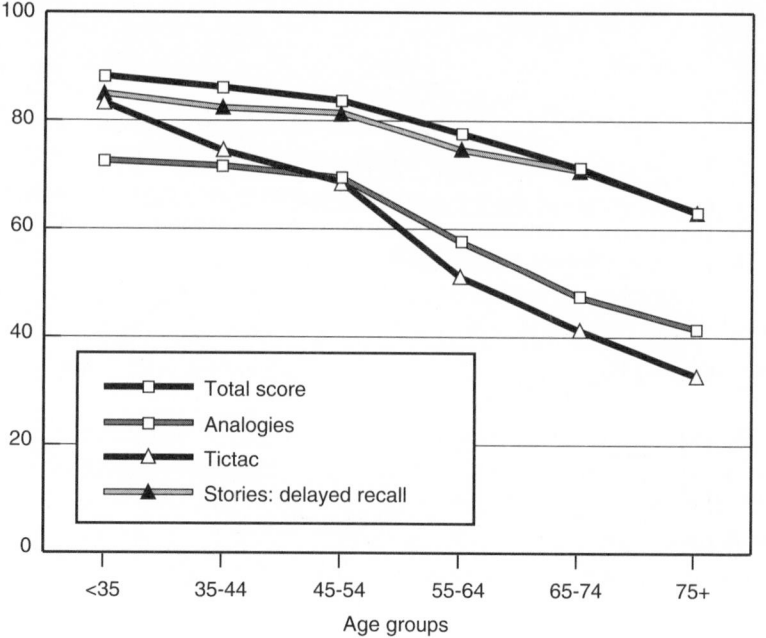

Figure 4.5 *(continued)*

facility, and this trend continued until the 55–64 decade. After this point the Tictac scores nosed downward more rapidly than Analogies.

Some aptitudes are far more resistant to aging. Figure 4.6 displays the mean scores of three of the subtests with the lowest correlations to age. One is attention-related (Wordlist 2), while Clocks requires visuospatial skill. Math speaks for itself. For comparison purposes, these subtests are plotted against the slope of the total MicroCog score. Attention appears to be sustained at a high level relative to total score in all age groups. If we use Wordlist 1 as a criterion, we see that scores on this subtest hold up well through the 65–74 decade, declining only about 11% from the mean of the youngest age group. Beyond age 75, however, this score drops another 21%. Clocks and Math scores follow a similar pathway: these skills decline relatively gently through ages 65–74 and then more rapidly thereafter.

Attentiveness does not seem to be much influenced by educational level. At nearly every checkpoint, the Wordlist 1 scores are nearly identical for the

MD and Normal samples. The mean scores for Clocks follow suit. The Math facility of the MDs is just slightly above the Normals in the two older age groups, but not earlier.

How Early Do Differences Emerge?

A systematic way to gain a global view of what happens to all aptitudes over the decades is to carry out an analysis of variance (ANOVA) for each of the subtests as well as the MicroCog total score. The ANOVA is useful because it enables us to tell whether the differences among average scores in the age groups are reliably greater than the variability within each decade.

The ANOVA compared the MicroCog scores of the subjects across the six age groups. There was a consistent and statistically significant decrease in the MicroCog scores for both the MDs and Normals for total and each subtest score ($p < .001$) with advancing census decade.

Although an ANOVA and correlations are useful in that they tell us that age affects particular cognitive functions over a lifetime, these statistics do not pinpoint where the decrease in average aptitude scores is significantly lower than for the previous decade. To understand the extent to which certain cognitive skills decline or remain stable over a lifetime, the subjects were divided into age groups. *t*-tests were calculated between each pair of adjacent average scores for both the total and subtest data. For example, the 35–44-year-old MDs were compared with those aged 45–54, and the 45–54 group against those aged 55–64. Pairwise comparisons are presented for the MDs only because of their greater educational and occupational homogeneity.

We employed two types of statistical indices to assess the relationship between age and cognition: the significance test and the effect size estimate. An excellent summary of these procedures is presented by Hall.[5] The first, the test of statistical significance, is familiar to most. Stated in terms of a *p* value, the significance test tells us how confident we can be that the observed difference between the means of 50- and 60-year-olds in, say, verbal memory, would occur again in a replication of this investigation with the same age groups. Thus we use the designation $p = .03$ when we expect the observed difference three times in a hundred, or $p < .001$ when the result is likely to happen less than one time in a thousand.

Valuable as the significance test is in informing us as to how certain we can be that the differences between the scores are reproducible, it tells us little about the magnitude of the relationship. This is why we use the effect size (ES) estimate, which is usually stated in the form of a correlation. The ES

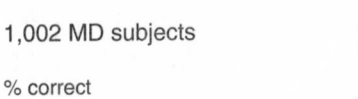

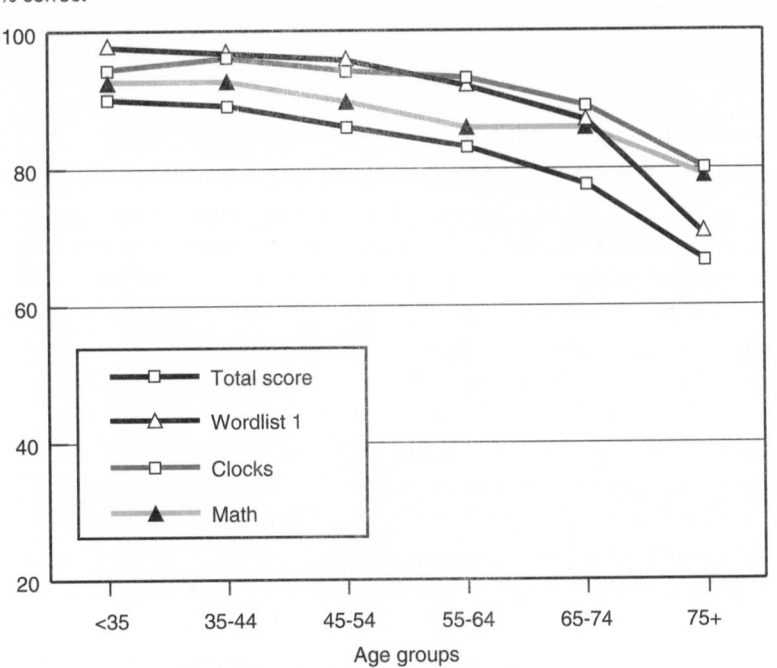

Figure 4.6 MicroCog aptitude scores that remain stable by decade compared with total.

correlation is composed of two elements: the significance test and the size of the study.[6] ES correlations have three virtues that make them useful in studies such as this. First, they enable us to make clearer statements about statistically significant findings in the data. For example, one problem that researchers often have is that it is possible to have statistically significant findings where the relative difference in raw scores is relatively slight. With large numbers of subjects as we have in this study, investigators often find p values less than .05 between many variables when the absolute differences in scores are tiny. For example, we may discover that 40-year-olds outscore 50-year-olds on a test of math skills by about 3 percent. Because we have several hundred subjects in each group, the significance test shows a p value of less than .02. Here we have statistical significance without much practical importance. Such findings tend to undermine the value placed in significance testing by health care professionals, other clinicians, and applied scientists as

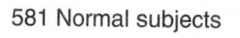

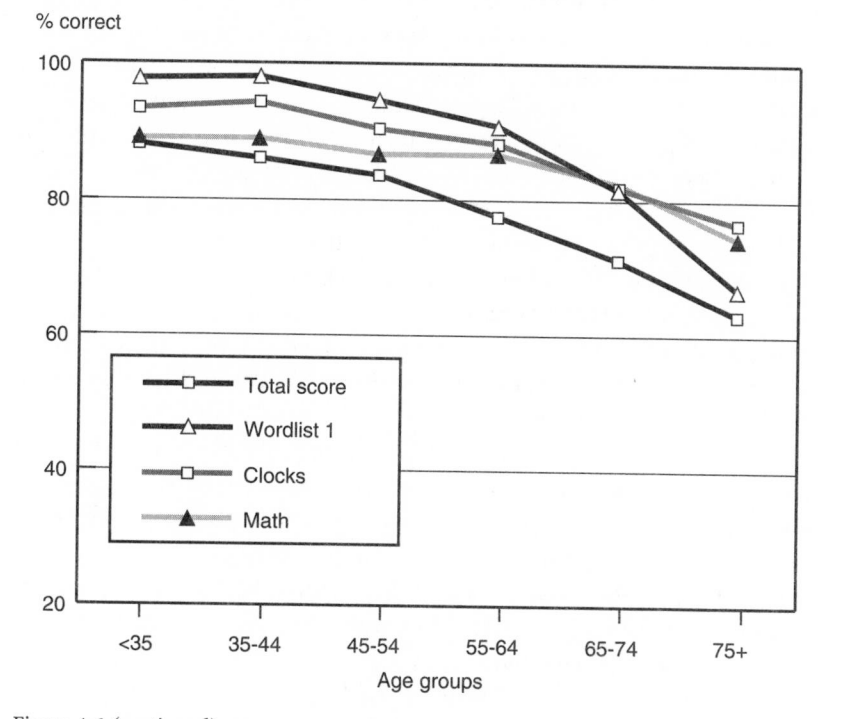

Figure 4.6 *(continued)*

well as others who try to use these data in real life. If we calculate the ES estimate using both the significance test and the size of the study we obtain a correlation of .13, confirming what our intuition had already told us when we looked at the raw data: namely, the association between age and reasoning is quite small though detectable. By the same token, we might find statistically significant findings of $p < .001$ when comparing the Tictac of MDs aged 65–74 with those aged 75+. If we look at the raw score averages for these two groups, they appear to be quite large, a matter of 39%. The significance test of $p < .001$ gives us a hint that the differences between these two older groups may be considerable, but it doesn't tell us by how much. Here the ES correlation is quite useful because it shows a correlation of .34, a substantially greater effect than the math score differences in the two younger groups which also had reached statistical significance.

The second virtue of the ES correlation for this research is that it provides a scale for quantifying what we observe to be dramatic changes in the trajectory of certain intellectual skills with age. Consider the mean scores of 65, 70, 75, and 80-year-olds on Alphabet, a test of attention. Inspecting the average scores for these half-decades in the MD sample, we found that there is a greater decline in mean scores between the 75–79 and 80+-year-olds than between the 65–69 and 70–74-year-old MDs. The ES correlation between the two younger groups revealed a correlation of .14, while between the two older groups it was .29. Thus the ES correlations provide us with a means of quantifying these changes so that we can more clearly grasp what appears to be the growing power of age to disrupt attention.

The third virtue of the ES correlation is that it provides a metric to make comparisons with other investigations on cognitive aging much easier. One problem with comparing research studies is that different scientists employ different methods for analyzing their findings. When trying to assess whether our results are comparable to those of others, we face the problem that we have used *t*-tests for significance testing while others may have used F tests or chi square or something else. The ES correlations can be easily calculated from these other statistical results, allowing us to put all of the studies on the same footing for comparison purposes.

Four comparisons were made for the MD sample: the scores of those aged 35–44 with those 25–34; those 45–54 against those 35–44; and so on. ES correlations were computed for the statistically significant findings to determine the magnitude of the influence of aging. Table 4.2 excerpts these data to provide an overall pattern of decline in specific cognitive functions for the MD subjects. It contrasts each decade with the next lowest age group. Since no significant findings emerged when the 35–44 group was compared with those under 35, the contrasts for those groups are not reported here.

One finding that immediately stands out in this table is the growing negative association between advancing age and declining intellectual powers. That all ES estimates favor the younger age groups is no surprise. What is interesting is that the magnitude of the age effect grows dramatically with each decade. This is illustrated by the ES correlations for Total score. At Comparisons I and II, where the 10-year groups under 65 were set against one another, the downward trends were relatively shallow. But afterward the magnitude of the ES correlations increased to medium effects (.312) when the mean scores of the 65–74 interval were contrasted with those a decade their junior, and to large effects (.479) when the 70-year-olds were compared with those aged 75+.

The negative influence of growing older broadens by decade. At Comparisons I and II, seven subtests, in addition to the total score, differentiated

Table 4.2   Differences in MicroCog subtest scores by decade among MD subjects: Effect size correlations

MicroCog Subtests	Decade Comparisons			
	I	II	III	IV
	35–44 vs. 45–54	45–54 vs. 55–64	55–64 vs. 65–74	65–74 vs. 75+
ATTENTION				
Alphabet				.323[a]
Wordlist 1		.176[a]	.157[a]	.370[a]
Wordlist 2			.180[a]	.250[a]
NUMERIC RECALL				
Numbers Forward			.150[b]	.222[a]
Numbers Reversed	.128[b]		.192[a]	.271[a]
VERBAL MEMORY				
Stories: Immediate Recall		.143[b]	.220[a]	.234[a]
Stories: Delayed Recall	.195[a]	.114[c]	.239[a]	.269[a]
Address	.101[c]	.114[c]	.248[a]	.110[c]
VISUOSPATIAL FACILITY				
Tictac	.177[a]	.126[b]	.214[a]	.337[a]
Clocks	.132[b]		.178[a]	.286[a]
REASONING				
Analogies	.155[b]	.161[a]	.266[a]	.317[a]
Object Match			.238[a]	.196[a]
CALCULATION				
Math	.128[b]	.139[b]		.209[a]
Total	.238[a]	.189[a]	.312[a]	.479[a]
N	387	407	419	356

Note: All comparisons favor younger age groups.
a = $p \leq .001$; b = $p \leq .01 > .001$; c = $p \leq .05 > .01$.

the oldest group from physicians 10 years their junior. At Comparison III, 11 of 13 subtest means were lower for the doctors aged 65–74, while the 75+ age group scored lower on every measured skill than the previous decade.

We can also see the rising association between age and diminished cognition in specific aptitudes early on. Those that are more greatly affected are visuospatial facility, reasoning, and verbal memory after delay. For instance, the ES correlations for Tictac and Analogies just about double from Comparison I to Comparison IV. The ES estimates for Stories: Delayed Recall move from .195 at Comparison I to .269 when MDs in the 75+ group are compared with those aged 70.

It should be noted in Table 4.2 that there is a distinct "flattening" in the magnitude of the decline in MicroCog scores from ages 50–60 compared with the decades on either side of this age span. This is shown by the slightly lower ES correlations for Total score and many of the specific subtests at Comparison II. For example, the Total score ES correlation when the 35–44 group was contrasted with those 45–54 was .238 compared with .189 when the scores of 50-year-old doctors were stacked up against those of 60-year-olds. This flattening of the overall cognitive decline curve in the fifties can be seen with the naked eye in the MD curve in Figure 4.2. It can also be seen that the Normal data set does not parallel this line; rather, the shallowing of the decline occurs about ten years later.

Data provided by Schaie[7] offer partial support for the thesis that the falling off of global intellectual functions flattens in the fifties compared with the adjacent decades. Among independent samples drawn from the Seattle Longitudinal Study, Schaie and his colleagues found that the composite score for intellectual ability dropped 2.45 T-score points from 46 to 53 and 3.95 T-score points from 60 to 67. In the 53–60 interval, the decline was only 1.53 points. This same pattern held true for each of the five PMA subtests. As with our two samples, not every one of the Seattle groups followed this pattern. For example, of the four longitudinal cohorts only the 1963 and 1970 samples traced the flattening in the fifties curve of cognitive decline. The 1977 cohort resembled this profile except that there was less decline from ages 46 to 53 than in the next seven years. In the 1956 sample the flattening occurred as with our Normal group in the decade of the sixties.

At this point it appears that the slowing of the decline in overall, and possibly many specific, cognitive functions does occur in late mid-life. Some cross-sectional as well as longitudinal evidence indicates that it happens in the 50–60 decade. But there are also data indicating that the flattening of the curve can occur in the first five to seven years of the sixties.

We have already noted that the decline in mean score steepens dramatically after age 65. In order to understand more fully the timing of this decay in cognition, finer-grained analyses of the differences among older MDs were carried out by breaking the sample into five-year age groups from age 60 onward and then computing the comparisons. The significant ES correlations are reported in Table 4.3. The ES correlations are somewhat smaller in this table because the absolute differences in mean scores were less, and

Table 4.3 Differences in MicroCog subtest scores by 5-year age groups among MD
subjects: Effect size correlations

| | Age Group Comparisons | | | |
| | A | B | C | D |
MicroCog Subtests	60–64 vs. 65–69	65–69 vs. 70–74	70–74 vs. 75–79	75–80 vs. 80+
ATTENTION				
Alphabet			.243[a]	
Wordlist 1		.155[c]	.219[b]	.237[b]
Wordlist 2		.139[c]		.223[b]
NUMERIC RECALL				
Numbers Forward	.169[b]		.187[b]	
Numbers Reversed		.164[c]	.187[b]	
VERBAL MEMORY				
Stories: Immediate Recall	.169[b]			.198[c]
Stories: Delayed Recall	.153[c]	.149[c]		.189[c]
Address				
VISUOSPATIAL FACILITY				
Tictac			.283[a]	
Clocks		.152[c]	.230[a]	
REASONING				
Analogies	.189[a]		.234[a]	
Object Match	.211[a]		.232[a]	
CALCULATION				
Math			.173[c]	
Total	.189[a]	.211[b]	.351[a]	.193[c]
N	234	210	198	146

Note: All effect size correlations favor younger groups.
a = $p \leq .001$; b = $p \leq .01 > .001$; c = $p \leq .05 > .01$.

because of the lower number of subjects in both groups. Though the overall
decline in intellectual capacity was less at each of these five-year comparisons than with the decade contrasts, we still see small to medium age-related
correlations on each occasion. From age 65 onward, the doctors in each
half-decade scored on average notably lower than the next youngest group.

It would appear from Table 4.3 that the downward sloping of specific
abilities as well as in global cognitive functioning is relatively mild until 70–

74, with all but one of the ES estimates less than .20. At Comparison C, when the subjects aged 75–79 are measured against those five years younger, both the number of significant findings and the size of the correlations increased remarkably. The ES estimates for the total score move from .211 at Comparison B to .351 at Comparison C. Nine of thirteen subtests among subjects aged 75–79 were substantially lower. Those most greatly affected were the now familiar faces of visuospatial functioning and reasoning, as well as facility with numbers and attention. At Comparison D, lower verbal memory, both immediate and delayed, along with attention as measured by Wordlist 1 and 2 distinguished the 80+ MDs from those five years their junior.

Reaction times are not reported in Tables 4.2 and 4.3 because none of the ANOVAs produced significant findings. Pairwise *t*-testing yielded only one statistically significant comparison (Image 2, age groups 45–54 versus 55–64), which could well have occurred by chance. All groups responded more quickly to sound than image, and the mean scores were faster when the reaction time subtest was repeated in the second half of the test. Overall, the amount of improvement in response time to sound and image achieved by the oldest two groups matched that of the younger subjects.

This finding—the insignificant change in reaction time to sound, image, or both over the decades—is at odds with much of the literature.[8] It could be that the relatively simple demand of the task on computer administration may have been responsible for the lack of decline by age group. Or it is possible that the older volunteers were unusually capable and not representative of their age cohort. A more likely hypothesis is that older subjects can respond about as rapidly on a simple reaction time test as younger ones, but far more slowly when the task requires accuracy as well as quick response.

A confirming piece of evidence comes from the research of Sharps and Golin.[9] They compared the response times of younger (17–22) and older (66–83) subjects on a test requiring a decision as to whether a pair of perspective line drawings were the same or different. They found that when the subjects were instructed to respond as quickly as possible, there was no difference in the reaction time of the two groups. When the instructions were modified so that the subjects were told to answer "as accurately, but also as quickly as you possibly can," the younger ones were nearly twice as fast as the older group. These results parallel our findings. Our subjects were told to respond as rapidly as possible on the reaction time test. On the more complex tests, the subjects were instructed to stress accuracy first, then speed. These data show a pattern similar to the findings of Sharps and Golin under these two different conditions. When subjects aged 35–44 were compared on reaction times with those aged 65–74, no differences were found. But when the average reaction times on Analogies and Math were compared for the younger and older subjects, the differences for both subtests were statistically significant ($p = .037$ for Analogies; $p < .001$ for Math).

Protecting against Chance Findings

In the process of seeking differences among scores on 14 separate MicroCog subtests over four or five age groups, we have calculated a large number of significance tests. If there were no true differences between the scores, how many might be expected by chance? In order for us to be reasonably certain that the p values exceeding .05 in our t-tests represent real differences between mean scores, we need to consider ways of protecting against the possibility of capitalizing on chance.

Statisticians have been writing about this problem for several decades. Excellent summaries of the variety of procedures that can be employed to avoid what are called Type I errors (errors of "gullibility," concluding that differences occurring by chance are true differences) are readily available.[10] They provide a useful comparison of the numerous approaches that might be used for data such as ours where the number of subjects in each group is unequal and the variances are heterogeneous. The primary method we used to control for chance findings was to compute ANOVA for each of the MicroCog scores across the age groups. If that F was significant, we then calculated t-tests because we could conclude that these comparisons would therefore likely be significant. In most cases this is an adequate solution to the Type I error problem. There is another more conservative approach that might also be employed, which is to divide the alpha level of .05 by the number of t-tests for each subtest across the comparisons. For instance, if we make five age comparisons with, for example, the Analogies subtest, the p value we would accept to be significant is $.05/5 = .01$. Using this more conservative technique, the difference between the means would have to reach a confidence level of $p \leq .01$ before we could say with confidence that reliable differences exist.

Because it is our intention to share with the reader all of our findings, we will report p values of various magnitudes throughout the book. Doubtless those who are sophisticated in this area will have their own opinions based on their experiences as to what constitutes a significant p value.

The Order of Decline in Aptitudes

These data cause us to believe that certain cognitive skills decline before others. Visuospatial facility, reasoning, and verbal memory were early casualties of the aging process. Attention and number facility remain intact for a much longer period. Specifically, MDs with a mean age of 50 had detectably lower scores on Address and Stories: Delayed Recall as well as Tictac and Analogies at Comparison I. For the most part these early relative declines signal continued deterioration in later decades. For example, scores on Tictac and Analogies were significantly lower at each comparison.

A small amount of early loss may foreshadow greater loss later on in groups of individuals. As with weak eyesight, the younger the age at which lower performance for a particular ability is detected, the more likely it is that this aptitude will deteriorate more rapidly with advancing years. At Comparison III, the highest ES correlations were in the area of reasoning, delayed verbal memory, and visuospatial abilities. While it is true that 70-year-olds as a group show other losses as well, as shown in Table 4.2, it does seem that early detectable losses are correlated with later, greater cognitive decline in those particular skills.

For the most part, these differential patterns of age-related performance declines are consistent with the reports of others. A comprehensive review of the literature is provided by Salthouse.[11] Figure 4.7 presents his analysis of the patterns of decline for verbal memory, inductive reasoning, and visuospatial memory. The tests on which the aptitude scores are based do not measure ability in these spheres in precisely the same way as the MicroCog subtests, but they show several similarities. First, all data were collected under untimed or slightly timed conditions. Second, most of the subjects tested were more highly educated. Third, all of the studies had representative numbers of older subjects. Fourth, all data are derived from cross-sectional studies.

The curves presented in Figure 4.7 generally follow the same slope of other tests of verbal memory, reasoning, and visuospatial ability reported by Salthouse. With respect to verbal memory, data are based on recognition tests involving previously presented material. The inductive reasoning material comes from a series completion test. A study of the Analogies subtest found that the World War I Army Alphas confirmed these findings. Of the eight subtests in the Alphas, verbal analogies had the greatest negative correlation with age. A limitation of this research is that no data are reported for subjects beyond age 60. The visuospatial ability curves are derived from the performances of college men on the geometric design subtest of the Benton Retention Test.

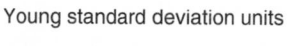

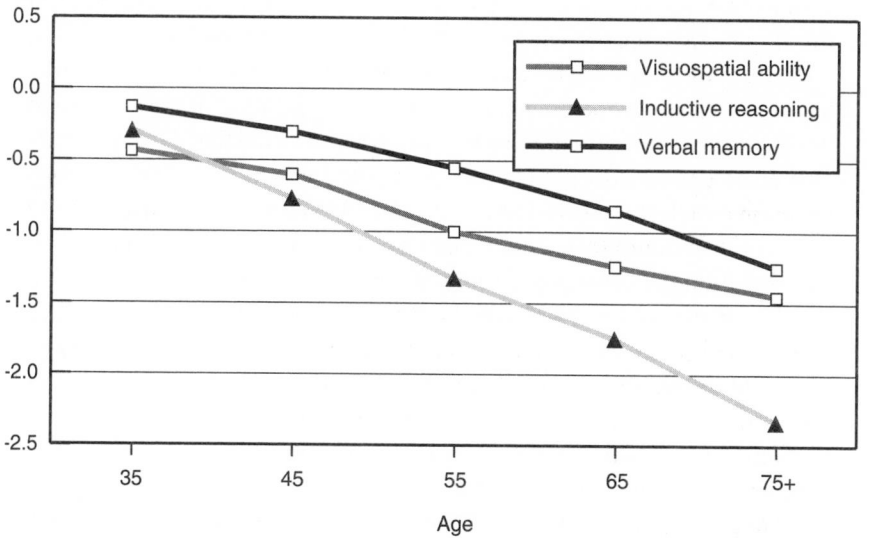

Figure 4.7 Age-related differences in memory, reasoning, and visuospatial ability of subjects aged 35–75; decline expressed in young adult (22–28) standard deviations. *Source:* Adapted from T. A. Salthouse, *Theoretical Perspectives on Cognitive Aging* (Hillsdale, N.J.: Erlbaum, 1991), fig. 2.5, p. 48; fig. 6.5, p. 239; and fig. 7.4, p. 279.

Others have pointed to losses with advancing age in the visuospatial area. Farver and Farver found age-related changes in visual organization and visual discrimination on the Hooper Visual Organization Test, as well as on three other tests—the Poppelreuter Superimposed Figures Test, and the Finger Identification and Clock Setting subtests of the Boston Diagnostic Aphasia Examination.[12] Performance subtest scores on the Wechsler Adult Intelligence Scale—Digit Symbol, Picture Completion, Block Design, Picture Arrangement, and Object Assembly—are particularly vulnerable to aging.[13] Benton and colleagues noted a significant decline by age cohort on visual memory.[14] In their 65–69-year-old group, 7% of their subjects had difficulty on a test measuring visual retention. Memory deficiencies in the older group (80- to 84-year-olds) increased: 38% failed on visual retention.

Evidence has been accumulating that increasing chronological age is correlated with lower scores on several types of reasoning problems. Heaton and colleagues found a significant age-related decline on the Similarities subtests of the WAIS in cross-sectional studies.[15] In a study of concept learning requiring serial hypothesis testing, a sample of adults aged 65 to 81 scored significantly lower than a sample of college students in selecting correct hypotheses.[16] Other investigators reported that a group of subjects with a mean age of 71.2 years had significantly lower "abstraction ages" on the Shipley Institute of Living Scale than did younger subjects.[17]

Declines in both primary and secondary memory associated with aging have been carefully documented. In particular, verbal recall after delay and interference is diminished. Inman and Parkinson found that 64- to 80-year-olds when compared with a 17- to 28-year-old group scored substantially lower on a Brown-Peterson delayed recall task. When subjects had to recall letters after an interpolated digit reading or digit summing tasks, the difference between the older group and the younger group was significant and directly related to the length of the retention interval.[18] Lezak compiled mean scores for young and aging normal adults on the Wechsler Memory Scale and documented progressive declines with age in these areas: the capacity to learn paired word associates, the immediate recall of a brief narrative, and the immediate reproduction of geometric designs.[19] Haaland and colleagues, using the Russell variant of the Wechsler Memory Scale, demonstrated a progressive decline by 5-year age cohort in well-educated normal subjects 65 and older.[20]

Earlier, Rey introduced the variable of educational level into the question of how cognition is affected by aging. He measured average recall of words from a word list on five successive trials and found that there was progressive decline for both learning and recall of verbal material.[21]

Tables 4.2 and 4.3 do not contain entirely bad news for seniors. Performance on attentional tasks and facility with numbers are spared until quite late in life. Numerous studies have found that attention and calculation skills are maintained in the face of aging. For instance, studies of normal subjects aged 20–75 found attention to decline from 3 to 15%.[22] Recall of number strings has been found to be among those tests which are spared during much of the life span. Data show that with auditory presentation, forward digit span remains relatively intact in normal older men and women.[23] Benton and colleagues reported that decrements in digit span in normal subjects aged 80–84 were only 8% lower than in a sample under age 65.[24] The capacity to carry out mental calculations has been found to remain relatively stable with age. An investigation of the Arithmetic subtest of the WAIS-R, controlling for education, found that scores declined less than 10% between ages 25–34 and 70–74 in cross-sectional data.[25]

Not everyone has found monotonic decline in these cognitive areas. Schaie and his colleagues followed 97 women and men for nearly 30 years. They were the survivors of an original sample of 500 of the Seattle Longitudinal Study.[26] Tested with the Thurstone Primary Mental Abilities (PMA) test at seven-year intervals on four occasions, these subjects averaged slightly higher scores on subtests of vocabulary and spatial orientation from age 40 to age 50. Although the PMA items and format differ from similar subtests of MicroCog, and the heavy attrition of the subjects from the study makes us wonder if these remaining women and men might be very special, this investigation suggests caution in assuming that all grouped aptitude scores decline with age.

Our data are consistent with the findings of others that average scores for specific skills decline by age group in the context of a falling-off in global functions. These findings confirm the research of Reed and Reitan thirty years ago and the more recent reports of Moehle and Long.[27] However, this evidence runs counter to some of the prevailing theory in neuropsychology that normal cognitive aging is specific and focused rather than entailing a general mental decline.

It is important to understand that we can have statistically significant findings without a great deal of practical importance.[28] Because of the large number of MD subjects in our sample, we were able to detect reliable differences in scores among the various decades, when the actual disparity in raw subtest scores was often tiny. This was especially true in the younger age groups where the variances were small. For instance, the difference between the mean scores of the 45–54 and 35–44 age groups for Analogies was about 5%; for Math it was only 3%. The differences were larger for Tictac 1 and 2 (11% and 7% respectively.) This contrasts with considerably larger subtest differences between older age group pairs. For instance, the raw score difference at Comparison IV for Analogies was 11%, and 7% for Math. Even among the 5 year older age group pairs, the raw score differences were often quite large. On Tictac, the raw score of the 75–79 group was 12% less than for those in the 70–74 group.

It is also true that the growing variability among individuals 65 and older means that a substantial portion will continue to function at a level comparable to that of younger people. We will see in Chapter 8 on normal cognitive aging that four out of five MDs aged 70–74 function as well as doctors in the prime double decade 45–64. Over half of those 75 and older measure up to the same criteria. In Chapter 9, on optimal cognitive aging, we find that a surprisingly high proportion of individuals over 70 function at or above the mean for individuals in their prime.

5

Other Influences on Cognitive Aging

Chronological age is not the only influence on cognitive changes over a lifetime. Several other factors affect how well older adults retain their intellectual vigor, including physical and mental health, intellectual ability, and continuing employment. Are seniors in the best physical health also cognitively the most vigorous? Do certain types of physical problems have a higher probability of reducing overall or specific mental operations? Are older people who may be depressed or anxious more likely to score lower on cognitive tasks? Are those who have higher IQ scores to begin with more likely to retain their abilities for a longer period, or does getting older bring everyone down to about the same level? Do older people who remain employed after 65 score higher on intellectual measures because they continue to use their minds, while those who are retired stagnate mentally? In this chapter we will examine the influence of each of these factors on the intellectual functioning of our subjects.

Physical Health

Since our mental state ultimately depends on our physical state and since we know that many illnesses and serious medical events increase with advancing age, it is not surprising to find considerable professional opinion, as well as common sense, predicting that health negatively affects the cognitive abilities of the elderly.[1] Researchers carrying out normative studies of older individuals routinely rule out most healthy subjects who in the past have had strokes, lost consciousness, had brain tumors, or suffered head injuries. Also excluded have been those with high blood pressure, diabetes, seizures, thyroid conditions, and learning disabilities. Additional subjects left out of the "normal" aging groups are those who have been alcoholic or drug-dependent, have smoked, or have been exposed to toxic materials.

Investigators who have not excluded the less healthy subjects in their studies of cognitive aging, however, have failed to confirm the common wisdom of physical and intellectual vigor being highly correlated among the elderly. For example, the association between health and intellectual functioning was examined with 57 members of the Berkeley Older Generation Study who had been interviewed and tested in both 1969 and 1983.[2] At these two periods the subjects averaged 69 and 82.7 years of age. The health index was constructed on the basis of four variables: present health, health today compared with 20 years ago, effect of health on activity level, and energy. The researchers compared the health ratings with WAIS Verbal and Performance IQ scores and discovered no connection between health and Verbal IQ at either the 1969 or 1983 testings. A significant correlation was found with Performance IQ in the later testing but not at the earlier period.

A potential problem with this study is that it relied entirely on self-reports of health. This question was largely answered by the work of neuropsychologists at the Mayo Clinic.[3] As part of their ongoing studies of aging and intellectual functioning, they abstracted the complete Mayo Clinic medical records of 540 subjects aged 55–97. They then looked at the relationship between scores on intellectual measures and physical status. Specifically, they divided their subjects into three groups with respect to their physical status: "worst," "common," and "best" health. The subjects' medical condition was determined by the number of diagnoses, the number of physical symptoms involved, and the number of medications being taken. The investigators then calculated the mean scores of the three groups on the WAIS-R and WMS-R and found little relationship between the number of symptoms involved or the number of medications taken and cognitive scores. They were able to detect a small association between the number of diagnoses and WAIS-R Performance IQ and with the WMS-R Visual Memory Index. The correlations, however, were small, accounting for no more than 2% of the test variance.

These findings confirm earlier reports by Salthouse, whose extensive review of the literature concluded that "the age trends in a variety of measures of cognitive functioning appear to be independent of either the self-rated or objectively assessed health status of the participants."[4] A portion of the evidence he cites comes from research in his own laboratory. Figure 5.1 traces the decline from age 30 to age 70 in three abilities—memory, spatial, and

Standard deviation
for all subjects

Memory (N=362)

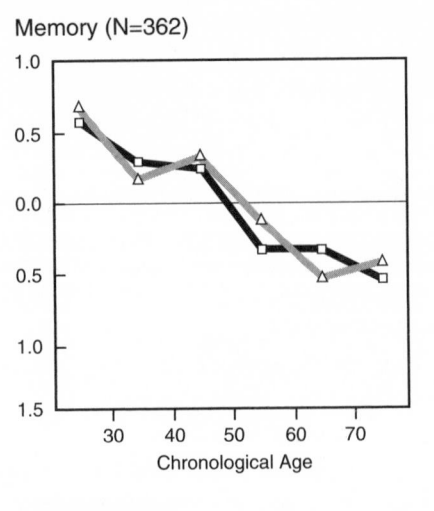

Spatial (N=383)

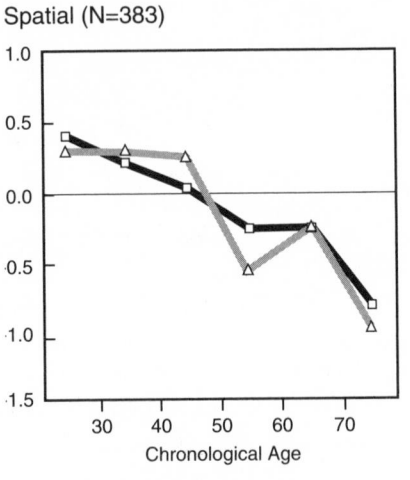

■□■ All subjects

▲ Only participants reporting
excellent health

Figure 5.1 Composite measure of cognitive performance in three areas in the adult years: all subjects and only those reporting excellent health. *Source:* Adapted from T. A. Salthouse, *Theoretical Perspectives on Cognitive Aging* (Hillsdale, N.J.: Erlbaum, 1991), fig. 2.9, p. 63.

Standard deviation
for all subjects

Reasoning (N=383)

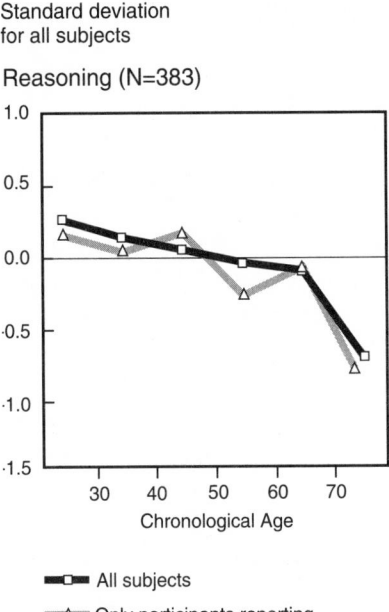

Chronological Age

■□■ All subjects

▲ Only participants reporting

Figure 5.1 *(continued)*

reasoning—by two different groups of subjects.[5] The first are those who re-port themselves to be in excellent health; the second are all subjects. We immediately notice how closely the curves of the two groups match. Those who say they are in the best health do not differ in any important ways from all subjects over the decades. It is possible that other factors (for example, educational level) may have confounded these results. On the whole, how-ever, it seems reasonable to conclude that, among volunteers for studies such as this, health status is largely independent of age effects on cognition.

In order to examine the influence of medical history and medication in our subjects, we selected the MD panel because of their larger numbers, their sensitivity to their own health, the greater likelihood of their reporting accurately, and the homogeneity of occupation and socioeconomic status. The last factor provides a limited degree of control for job-related stress and health care behaviors.

All of the subjects were living independently in the community and rep-resented themselves as normal for their age. On the day the physicians took MicroCog, they also completed a medical history form. Their answers were then coded for health behaviors, major medical symptoms, medications, and hospitalizations. The medical history questionnaire asked whether the respondent had a history of 20 different health behaviors, illnesses, and medical events. A problematic health behavior cited by almost half of the doctors was smoking. Other frequently cited health issues included a history of high blood pressure, heart conditions, neurological problems, and head injury.

Table 5.1 shows the percentage correct for MicroCog total scores for subjects with a variety of medical conditions. Little evidence for direct association between medical history and the MicroCog total score is apparent.

There were some subjects with substantially lower cognitive scores than others at the same age; for example, those who had motor problems, cataracts, or heart conditions had MicroCog totals significantly lower than those of their age-mates. It is not surprising that those whose hands shook or who had eye problems had some difficulty with MicroCog because of the necessity of operating a keyboard and the visual acuity required. Neither is it surprising that those with a cardiac history scored lower: studies of pa-

Table 5.1　Total MicroCog score and medical history, medication, and hospitalization of 1,002 physicians

Medical History	N	MicroCog Percent Correct	Hospitalization/ Medication	N	MicroCog Percent Correct
Alcohol-dependent	15	79.2	Hospitalized	842	82.6
Arthritis	175	77.7	Hospitalization:		
Cancer	94	77.5	Cortical Only	55	84.5
Cataracts	85	74.2	Motor Only	5	79.6
Depression	63	84.3	Cortical and Motor	5	73.8
Diabetes	44	77.9	Take Medication	489	80.0
Electroshock	3	87.9	Medications:		
Epilepsy	10	88.6	Cortical Only	88	79.9
Head Injury	121	85.9	Motor Only	3	70.1
Heart Condition	165	76.0	Cortical and Motor	1	83.6
High Blood Pressure	212	79.4			
Learning Problem	68	84.0	All Subjects Mean	1,002	83.0
Neurological	116	83.1	All Subjects S.D.	1,002	10.2
Smoke: Now	73	83.4			
Smoke: Ever	498	81.5			
Thyroid	42	81.2			
Toxic Material	26	84.7			

tients with severe heart conditions have found that these individuals have cognitive deficits in numerous areas. Furthermore, among patients awaiting coronary bypass or valvular replacement surgery, neuropsychological testing has revealed compromised attention, organization skills, verbal learning, reasoning, and motor speed.[6] Patients who have had open heart surgery typically did not show substantial improvement, and what improvement there was resulted from enhanced motor speed due to better physical condition. In fact, some researchers have found that abstract reasoning deteriorates following open heart surgery.[7]

Several findings were surprising. Individuals with a history of head injury from which they had recovered scored about three points higher than their age-mates ($p = .02$). Other findings that run counter to prevailing thinking were that subjects who presently smoke scored above the mean, as did those with a history of depression, though at the time of testing they were functioning within normal limits.

Because we did not ask specific questions concerning what kinds of heart conditions the subjects experienced, we have no way of knowing how severe their problems were. Doubtless most had not had a cardiac transplant and were well short of the criteria for open heart surgery. Still, the fact that individuals with heart problems showed measurable impairment suggests that we should not be surprised to find that subjects who list themselves as having heart conditions would perform at a lower level on a cognitive test than subjects in their cohort without a cardiac history.

Almost half of the respondents (489) reported that they were taking medications at the time of testing, and 842 reported that they had been hospitalized at some time. A senior psychiatrist colleague, Dr. Randolph Catlin, coded the medications to identify those that might have had an adverse effect on intellectual functioning, such as tranquilizers and sedatives. Eighty-eight respondents were taking medications that could affect cognitive functioning. There was, however, no demonstrable medication effect, with the exception of those subjects who were on high enough doses of tranquilizers that their capacity to perform complex motor tasks was compromised.

With the exceptions noted, our data analyses found little evidence to confirm the direct effects of physical condition or drug-rendered regimes on cognitive functioning among these volunteers. Though these findings may seem counterintuitive, they do follow a general trend emerging in the literature cited earlier. Following a comprehensive analysis of the relation between health status and cognitive aging, Salthouse concluded that "contrary to intuition and popular opinion, there's little evidence that declines in cognitive performance associated with increased age are mediated by declines in health status."[8] This does not mean that medical status has no influence on intellectual functions or that certain physical disabilities may not interact with advancing age to accelerate mental decline. Rather, the evidence available from this and other investigations indicates that overall health status, among those who volunteer to participate in this type of research, does not greatly change the effect of age on cognitive functioning.

Emotional States

Emotions can have an adverse impact on cognition. Evidence exists that depression, anxiety, and anger are correlated with lower levels of intellectual functioning. Since it is not difficult to imagine those emotions increasing in magnitude among the aged, it seems crucial to examine these affects with respect to their potential detrimental influence on intellectual functioning. In particular, it has been argued that depression may worsen with the inevitable losses and stresses associated with aging. Some have maintained that we may misdiagnose an older person as having Alzheimer's disease when in fact that individual is depressed. Depression and dementia share many common features, primary among them being memory loss, difficulty in concentrating, impaired problem-solving ability, and psychomotor retardation.[9] It is possible that depression could cause cognitive deficits in the absence of actual neurological impairment. The term "depressive pseudodementia" has been suggested to describe cognitive impairment caused by depression rather than a dementing illness.[10] However, research that has attempted to sort out depression effects on cognition from those related to dementia has been equivocal.

Anxiety is a less obvious confound of cognition. It is well established that high levels of stress impair new learning, especially on more difficult tasks. Pioneering experiments by Spielberger and his colleagues demonstrated that highly anxious subjects had greater problems with complex design recall, initial concept formation, and academic performance than did low-anxiety individuals.[11] Summarizing two decades of research on the effect of state and trait anxiety on cognition, Hertzog and Blanchard-Fields presented evidence that high levels of anxiety are associated with problems in concentrating, shorter working memory, difficulty in processing information, and slower performance.[12] Some believe that anxiety is greater in older people and that as a result they may often score poorly on mental performance tasks.[13] It seems equally plausible, however, that older people would have less need to prove themselves in test-taking situations than younger adults and thus would be less anxious.

Considerably less is known about the impact of anger on cognitive functions. Clinically, one sees individuals whose angry feelings adversely affect intellectual performance. But research has been scanty. It has been found that angry interactions with parents are associated with lower grade point averages among adolescent males.[14] Among college students and older adults, higher scores on the hostility scale of the Multiple Affect Adjective Checklist[15] were inversely correlated with simple and complex verbal recall.[16]

We took two approaches to the problem of assessing the extent to which emotional state adversely affects cognitive functioning. Both involved self-reports. The first approach used subjects from the MD sample, and the second drew selected members from the Normal panel. To measure the emotions of depression, anxiety, and anger, 188 physicians were given the Cambridge Research Mood Survey (CRMS)[17] and the State-Trait Personality Inventory (STPI).[18] The CRMS is a self-administered device consisting of 23 scales designed to be sensitive to variations on the manic as well as the depressed side of the affective continuum, and is designed for use with non-clinical populations. CRMS total score correlates with the Beck Depression Inventory (1983) at .779.[19] The STPI measures state-trait anxiety and anger as well as curiosity. The anxiety and anger items were drawn from the most powerful questions from Spielberger's other well-known state-trait tests.[20]

The total scores from these instruments were correlated with MicroCog results, as shown in Table 5.2. Looking at the relationship among these variables, we note that only state anxiety correlates significantly with lower

Table 5.2 MicroCog total score correlations with mood and state-trait anxiety and anger (N = 188 MDs)

Emotion	Correlation with MicroCog Total Score	*p*
Mood	.05	.25
State Anxiety	.13	.04
Trait Anxiety	.09	.11
State Anger	−.04	.29
Trait Anger	−.04	.29

Note: All *p* values are 1-tailed.

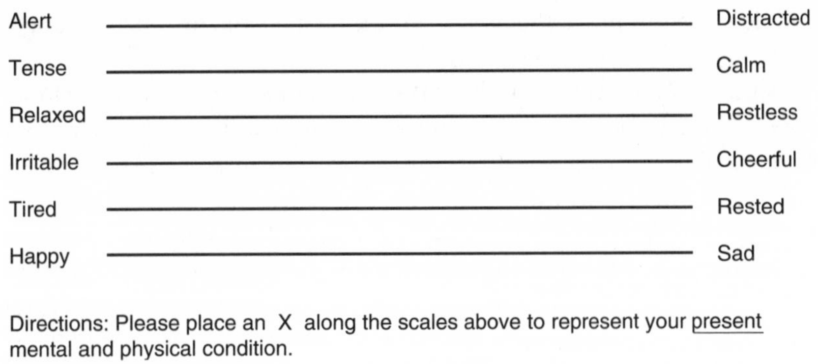

Alert	——————————————————————————	Distracted
Tense	——————————————————————————	Calm
Relaxed	——————————————————————————	Restless
Irritable	——————————————————————————	Cheerful
Tired	——————————————————————————	Rested
Happy	——————————————————————————	Sad

Directions: Please place an X along the scales above to represent your <u>present</u> mental and physical condition.

Figure 5.2 Emotional state scales for self-rating.

scores on MicroCog. Otherwise the MicroCog total score is not notably impacted by mood or anger at the time of taking the test.

The impact of emotional state on MicroCog score was examined in two related studies. In the first, 154 physicians who participated in a sleep deprivation study were asked to rate their moods. The scales are shown in Figure 5.2. In a second study, 268 women and men aged 65 to 74 who participated in the validation research in Florida were asked to rate their moods on the same scale. The correlations are presented in Table 5.3. These data are consistent with the first study. All of the correlations are low, and are insignificant with only one exception: that higher levels of tension are associated with slightly lower MicroCog scores in older subjects.

Because these data were not consistent with the views of so many others that depression should retard intellectual functioning, we wondered

Table 5.3 Correlations between self-ratings of emotional states
              and MicroCog total score

Emotional State	154 Physicians		268 Normal Subjects, 65–74	
	Correlation	*p*	Correlation	*p*
Alert/Distracted	.09	.14	.04	.28
Calm/Tense	.02	.39	.13	.01
Relaxed/Restless	.01	.44	.02	.35
Cheerful/Irritable	.09	.15	.05	.23
Rested/Tired	.09	.13	.05	.22
Happy/Sad	.04	.32	.05	.22

Note: All *p* values are 1-tailed.

Table 5.1 Total MicroCog percentage correct and affects by quartiles

	First Quartile of Affect Score (1% to 24%)	Second Quartile of Affect Score (25% to 49%)	Third Quartile of Affect Score (50% to 74%)	Fourth Quartile of Affect Score (75% to 100%)	r	p
Mood						
Overall Mood Question						
MicroCog Mean	83.1	85.0	86.5	83.1		
S.D.	—	6.3	6.8	9.2	.031	.35
N	1	13	22	147		
Total CRMS Survey Score						
MicroCog Mean	80.2	80.7	84.1	83.1		
S.D.	5.8	8.2	10.0	6.3	.082	.16
N	2	11	136	32		
Anxiety						
State						
MicroCog Mean	84.1	84.1	84.1	82.1		
S.D.	7.3	10.6	7.7	10.6	.006	.23
N	60	45	39	40		
Trait						
MicroCog Mean	83.1	85.0	82.6	84.1		
S.D.	7.7	10.0	10.6	7.7	.013	.43
N	37	30	50	67		
Anger						
State						
MicroCog Mean	n/a	83.6	83.1	85.5		
S.D.	n/a	9.2	9.2	6.3	.004	.50
N	n/a	150	31	3		
Trait						
MicroCog Mean	82.6	83.6	82.6	85.5		
S.D.	8.7	8.7	10.0	7.3	.074	.46
N	36	39	63	46		

whether we might have had a population that was insufficiently dysphoric to depress the MicroCog scores. Therefore, we decided to separate the groups into quartiles on the basis of their scores on emotional status. The results are shown in Table 5.4, where we can see that no significant differences emerged among these groups. There is little or no difference between the first and fourth quartiles on mood, anxiety, or anger. From these data, it does not appear that those scoring in the highest quartiles of mood showed cognitive impairment.

Useful as statistics are, it is always helpful when you can see with your own eyes the phenomenon being described. A clinical vignette may help illustrate the surprisingly low association between MicroCog score and depression. During the period when this potential confound was being examined, a 29-year-old depressed patient (DR.MTM59) was referred to one of our research teams for evaluation and treatment. He complained of memory loss as well as depression. He was given MicroCog, the CRMS, and the Beck Depression Inventory (BDI) twice during this period. The first time he was depressed; the next time he was feeling better. The results are shown in Figure 5.3. As the figure shows, when DR.MTM59 was first interviewed in December, he was notably depressed on the basis of the CRMS and the BDI. By the following May, his mood had clearly improved. His MicroCog total scores at these times, however, were nearly the same (93% correct in December and 94% the following May).

The absence of significant correlations between mood and cognitive functioning intrigued us. We had expected to find more depression attending lower MicroCog scores among the individuals participating in this study. A closer look at the data on aging and depression as well as the notion of depressive pseudodementia suggests that our findings may not be so different from what others have actually found. A recurring theme in gerontological literature is that aging brings with it an increased risk of depression. The inevitable physical limitations, decimated social networks, and other losses associated with growing older have been thought to produce higher rates of depression among older adults.[21] We are aware, however, that others have argued the opposite position, namely that this assumption is lacking empirical evidence.[22] A careful review by Newmann of 21 major research studies carried out in the United States since 1970 on aging and depressive symptomatology stated that it is "difficult to draw any definite conclusions regarding the age-depression relation at this time."[23]

The fact that some investigators have found a high correlation between aging and depression while others have not may be related to the presence

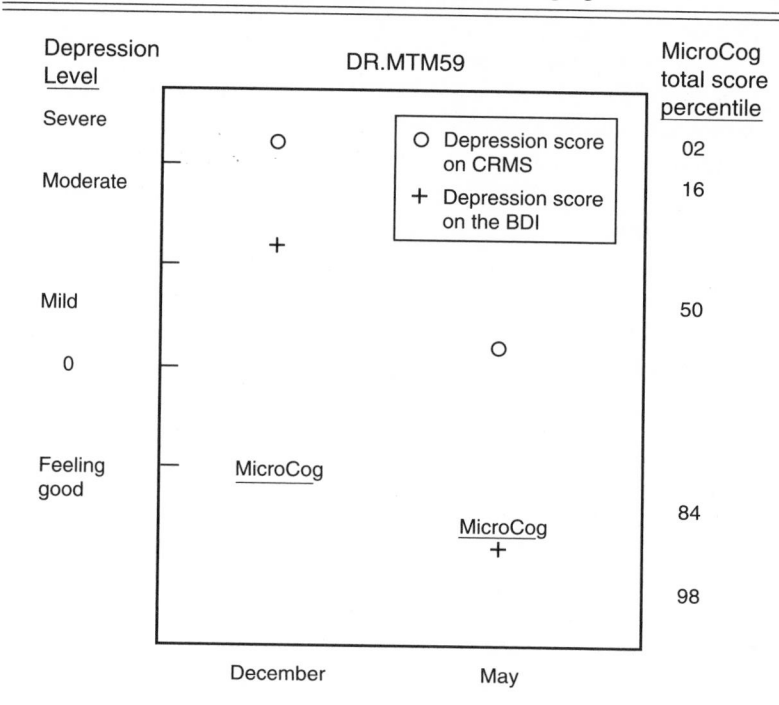

Figure 5.3 MicroCog total score and overall severity of depression.

or absence of stressful factors that may also be correlated with depression. For instance, Duke University researchers studied 3,998 community-dwelling volunteers aged 65 and older and found that depression was indeed correlated with advancing age. But they also discovered that when stressors such as lower income, physical disability, and lack of social support were controlled, the association between age and depression reversed in both the young-old and old-old populations.[24]

Another problem with many of the studies of depression and cognitive decline is that they correlate scores on depression ratings with intellectual performance at a given moment in time. It is possible that depression may precede a cognitive decline that does not become obvious until later. Older individuals may become despondent at minor lapses in word finding, orientation, or memory because they believe these are precursors of a future mental downward turn. Depression may develop in response to these assumptions, resulting in less effort to remain mentally vigorous and leading in turn to intellectual deterioration.

A study of 201 elderly women and men over a two-year period by Parmalee, Kleban, and Lawton addressed these questions as well as the cross-sectional relationship between depression and cognitive functioning.[25] These analyses found a small statistically significant correlation between scores on a depression scale and a short measure of cognitive impairment.[26] A small, but again significant, association was found between depression and subsequent cognitive status over one-year intervals. Although the relationship was not strong, it appeared that for some individuals greater depression produced greater later intellectual impairment. Turning to the question of whether the strength of depression influences mental operations, here again a careful look at the data suggests caution in inferring a strong relationship. For instance, the correlations we found between mood and MicroCog totals are slightly lower but in the same range as the data from Parmalee and colleagues.[27] At nine intervals their correlations between mood and cognition were .01, .04, .11, .13, .14, .18, .19, .21, and .22.

With respect to the depressive pseudodementia, a number of carefully crafted studies have compared the degree of depression with scores on cognitive tests of memory. They discovered that those depressed elders who complain about "having Alzheimer's" perform normally.[28] An extensive survey of those investigations which attempted to find a link between depression and impaired test performance concluded that this relationship could not be consistently demonstrated.[29]

It may be that the term "depressive pseudodementia" is no longer a particularly useful concept for clinicians and researchers who are attempting to disentangle the effects on cognition of dementia versus depression. On the basis of more than a decade of research, Emery[30] has concluded that instead of the usual dichotomy between depressive dementia (which may be reversible) and AD with depression (which is not), a continuum viewpoint should be adopted ranging from depression without dementia to dementia with depression. This concept would be more useful for both clinical practice and research. We have seen many depressed seniors who complain of diminished intellectual functions but score normally on cognitive tests. We have also seen numerous cases of older individuals with documented cognitive impairment who seem depressed in the clinical interview but who score normally on mood scales. It is possible that another group of older individuals who were more severely depressed and whose intellectual skills were assessed more comprehensively over a longer period would evidence signs of diminished cognition associated with their mood. It may also be possible that the depressive symptoms must include psychomotor retardation before cognition is severely affected.[31] But this remains to be clearly demonstrated.

In thinking about our findings that anxiety was associated with lower scores on our cognitive test while mood was not, and that some other studies have found a correlation between depression and intellectual functioning but others did not, we wondered whether a possible explanation for these disparities might have to do with the relationship between anxiety and depression. We know that these two affects coexist in populations of any age. It is not unusual to find patients who are depressed also reporting higher levels of anxiety, and many individuals seeking treatment for anxiety also manifesting symptoms of depression. We wonder whether studies that have successfully isolated the elusive "depressive pseudodementia" may have inadvertently overlooked anxiety concealed in the shadow of the depression. It may be the anxiety that was responsible for the lower cognitive scores, not the melancholy state. Since most studies did not exclude anxiety, they may have been blind to its impact on intellectual functioning.

To summarize our findings on the relationship of emotional states and intellectual performance, we were able to discover one significant association with MicroCog total score. In one of the MD samples and among the Normal 65- to 74-year-olds, we found that individuals who scored high on state anxiety and rated themselves as more tense obtained slightly lower cognitive scores. Otherwise, little effect of emotional state on intellectual functioning was found, whether the subjects were young or older, whether highly educated or not, or whether the measures were a formal test or self-ratings on a scale.

Intellectual Ability

To what extent does overall intelligence in one's prime shape the course of the inevitable decline in the later years? Specifically, do people who have scored higher on aptitude tests as young adults retain their abilities longer than those who begin the post-65 years with lower scores?

For some time, experts have surmised that those who start with greater intellectual endowment have higher levels of cognition in later years. For the most part, however, the evidence is based on clinical observation and indirect evidence from investigations on the effect of education. Clinical data come from two sources. First, the medical reports of individuals with brain trauma have shown that those with higher measured ability prior to the trauma exhibited higher levels of intellectual functioning afterward.[32] Second, some neurologists and neuropsychologists have found that cognitively impaired patients with higher IQ levels are difficult to detect on traditional tests because their higher pre-morbid ability masks the effect of the impairment.[33]

In no longitudinal studies that we are aware of have the researchers given their subjects IQ tests, stratified them into higher and lower scoring subgroups, and then compared the slope of the decline on intellectual aptitudes across the decades. The indirect evidence comes from studies showing a positive correlation between years of education and less decline in abilities in the later decades.[34] We might then infer that because IQ is known to correlate strongly with years of education, and the amount of education is associated with less decline in cognition among the aging, then how well abilities are maintained in the later years may be influenced by young adult IQ.

There are two problems with this line of reasoning. First, studies showing this relationship are largely cross-sectional in nature. This means that we don't know whether the differences discovered among groups of one hundred 35, 55, and 75 year olds on a cognitive test would be the same if we followed one hundred women and men over time, testing them at twenty-year intervals. Second, we have no way of knowing whether the number of years of education had the same influence for those educated in the 1930s, the 1950s, and the 1970s. There are far more opportunities for a college education today than half a century ago, especially for females, and college curricula have changed greatly.

The best way to investigate this phenomenon would be to carry out a longitudinal study with a group of subjects with different amounts of education. So far no one has been able to accomplish this because survivors in longitudinal studies tend to have higher levels of education than the cohort who began the study. The problem of comparing cross-sectional age groups with one another can be overcome to some degree if we can compare younger, middle-aged, and older adults who have had the same type of education and training. Therefore, it would seem that our MD sample might be useful in helping us understand the impact of intellectual ability on patterns of cognitive aging.

Our first approach was to compare individual IQ test scores with cognitive functioning as measured by MicroCog across age groups. If those with higher IQs had substantially higher scores on MicroCog, then we would

Table 5.5 WAIS-R IQ scores on 184 physicians by age group

Age Group	N	Full Scale Mean IQ	S.D.
35–44	27	123.1	11.58
45–54	37	124.2	8.70
55–64	43	129.9	10.64
65–74	51	126.9	10.74
75+	26	120.3	9.29
TOTAL	184	125.6	10.75

Notes: (1) 55–64 subjects' total scores were significantly higher than 75+ ($p = .0002$), 35–44 ($p = .007$), and 65–74 ($p = .0056$) age groups. (2) 65–74 subjects' total scores were significantly higher than 75+ ($p = .0064$). (3) 45–54 subjects' total scores were significantly higher than 75+ ($p = .0468$). (4) p values are 2-tailed.

have indirect evidence that young adult IQ can result in higher-quality intellectual functioning in later life.

The Revised Wechsler Adult Intelligence Scale (WAIS-R) was given to 184 physicians on the day they took MicroCog. The IQs for each group are shown in Table 5.5. This table indicates that the MDs are relatively tightly bunched in terms of relative IQ—ranging from an average of 129.9 among the 55–64 group to the 120.3 of the 75+ subjects, with all of the means above the 90th percentile or in the superior range. The variability, as indicated by the standard deviation, remained relatively constant. The significantly higher Full Score IQ of the 55–64 group is somewhat deceptive because on an age-graded test such as the WAIS-R, fewer correct answers are required to obtain a specific IQ when the subject is 60 as compared to 40. To achieve an IQ of 100, a 40-year-old must generate about 108 correct answers on the WAIS-R, while a 60-year-old needs only 95 correct answers.

Table 5.6 provides a view of the relationship between measured IQ and MicroCog total percentage correct. It shows that average MicroCog scores and WAIS-R IQ follow the same pattern: the highest MicroCog means are obtained by those with IQs greater than 130, while the lowest occur with WAIS-R totals in the 90–109 range. The table further shows that among doctors over 65 compared with those in the two youngest groups, a more lawful, stepwise association occurs between measured IQ and cognitive functioning as assessed by MicroCog.

It is possible that the WAIS-R and MicroCog measure essentially the same

Table 5.6 Mean MicroCog raw total percentage correct and WAIS-R Full Scale IQs by
age group (184 MDs)

WAIS-R Full Scale IQ	Mean MicroCog Total Percentage Correct					
	75+	65–74	55–64	45–54	35–44	Total
130+	81.8	84.3	89.9	93.4	93.5	88.5
	(N = 7)	(N = 19)	(N = 23)	(N = 11)	(N = 8)	(N = 68)
120–129	77.2	80.1	84.8	86.4	88.6	83.9
	(N = 4)	(N = 20)	(N = 15)	(N = 16)	(N = 10)	(N = 65)
110–119	68.2	76.0	81.5	87.3	89.0	77.8
	(N = 13)	(N = 10)	(N = 3)	(N = 8)	(N = 5)	(N = 39)
90–109	73.2	63.0	72.7	80.0	86.1	76.9
	(N = 2)	(N = 2)	(N = 2)	(N = 2)	(N = 4)	(N = 12)
Totals	73.6	80.2	86.7	88.3	89.7	83.8
	(N = 26)	(N = 51)	(N = 43)	(N = 37)	(N = 27)	(N = 184)

abilities, so we should not be surprised that the scores follow the same curve. It is well established that standard intelligence and aptitude batteries are highly related; for example, the total IQs of the recent versions of the Stanford-Binet and the Revised Wechsler Adult Intelligence Scale correlate in the range of .85.[35]

We compared the scores on MicroCog with individual IQ test data. The correlation between MicroCog total score and WAIS-R Full Scale IQ was .47 (± .15). The correlations with Verbal IQ and Performance IQ were .46 and .36, respectively. These correlations indicate that the Full Scale IQs explain about 20% of the variance of MicroCog total scores in this sample.

These lower than expected correlations could be attributable to the relatively narrow range of IQs in this population and the smaller standard deviations. The correlation between pairs of variables is reduced by selection of subjects from a narrow range of one of the variables. Prigatano studied the relation between the Wechsler Memory Scale and WAIS IQ and found correlations in the range of .40 among those with superior IQs.[36] Correlations in a sample more representative of the general population, however, were much higher, about .80.

Because the obtained standard deviation of the WAIS-R Full Scale score among the MDs was only about two-thirds of that of the standardization group, a correlation for restricted range was calculated to estimate what the coefficient might be between the two tests if the standard deviation of the WAIS-R had been based on a normally distributed population. The formula predicts an *r* of .67, slightly outside the higher confidence interval limit of .62, for the correlation between MicroCog and WAIS-R total scores if the population were normally distributed.

It appears that IQ in the prime of life has a modest effect, but nonetheless a demonstrable one, on the extent to which overall abilities are maintained or diminished with advancing age. Specifically, having greater intelligence to start with may slow the detectable onset of impairment because of the higher starting point. But we must be cautious in assuming too large an effect. We have seen a very rapid decline among extraordinarily talented individuals because of the ravages of Alzheimer's disease. It is also possible that the importance of higher intellectual ability lies in its interaction with other factors known to benefit cognitive aging, such as providing the possibility of higher education and achieving the socioeconomic status that would lead to better nutrition and access to medical care, or the opportunities to engage in other health-enhancing activities.

Continued Employment

Nowhere is the "use it or lose it" thesis more alive and well than in the notion that regularly exercising our intellectual skills enhances the probability of remaining intellectually vigorous. The other side of the coin, we suppose, is that not vigorously exercising one's mental capacities may cause them to atrophy like other physical capacities. The "use it or lose it" theory has numerous backers, among them some of the most influential and thoughtful experts in gerontological research.[37]

Efforts to demonstrate this common wisdom, however, have largely failed to produce the expected results. Salthouse and his colleagues at the Georgia Institute of Technology have subjected the "use it or lose it" theory to rigorous scrutiny and have found little empirical support. First, they looked at studies of older and younger people employed in the same occupations. They found that the patterns of cognitive functioning between older and younger individuals followed the expected declining curves whether they were teachers or truck drivers, nuns or executives, pilots or nurses.[38] The intellectual tasks on which the younger members of the occupation outperformed their older colleagues included verbal memory, reasoning, visuospatial facility, and reaction time.

Two criticisms of these investigations might be raised: first, we don't know whether the activities performed by the subjects in the younger and older groups were the same—older faculty, for example, might be functioning as administrators rather than teachers; second, the tests given might not have been sufficiently specific to the job tasks whose continuing use preserves specific cognitive functions—for example, the work of a business executive may not reinforce the maintenance of the ability to substitute symbols for digits under time pressure.

Several investigations addressed these criticisms. In one project, older and younger working architects were tested using visuospatial tasks. The differences again favored the younger architects.[39] In another study, the research team looked carefully at the relation between scores on the visuospatial tasks and how many hours subjects spent on particular daily activities presumed to correspond to visuospatial functions. They examined women and men from ages 20 to 70.[40] Their results showed that visuospatial scores were negatively (−.37) correlated with age. They also found that experience contributed only a small amount (about 15%) to their relationship. Moreover, the impact of experience was relatively small whether the subjects spent 50 hours a week on visuospatial activities or 5. The conclusion drawn from these studies about the "use it or lose it" theory is that the age-related decline in basic skills is largely independent of experience.

We believe that we have an opportunity to put the "use it or lose it" theory to a test with the physician sample because of their educational and vocational homogeneity. Among the older doctors are a large number who have continued to work and others who have retired, providing a useful sample by which to test whether continuing to utilize one's skills would result in a higher level of intellectual functioning than if one gave up the practice of medicine.

We divided the MD sample into five-year age groups from 55 onward and separated them into working and retired categories. The differences in the total score on MicroCog by five-year age groups among the working and retired MDs are shown in Figure 5.4. We immediately see that the difference in MicroCog scores between working and retired physicians is not noticeable until after age 70. The gap in total scores between working and retired MDs is only significant among the 75–79 age group and is in the predicted direction with the 80+ group. Larger numbers in the oldest group might have yielded a more robust result.

The differences in overall MicroCog scores caused us to examine individual subtest scores to determine whether patterns emerged among these subjects. We found that in all cases where the subtest differences in scores occurred, they favored the working physicians in the age groups beyond 65.

% correct

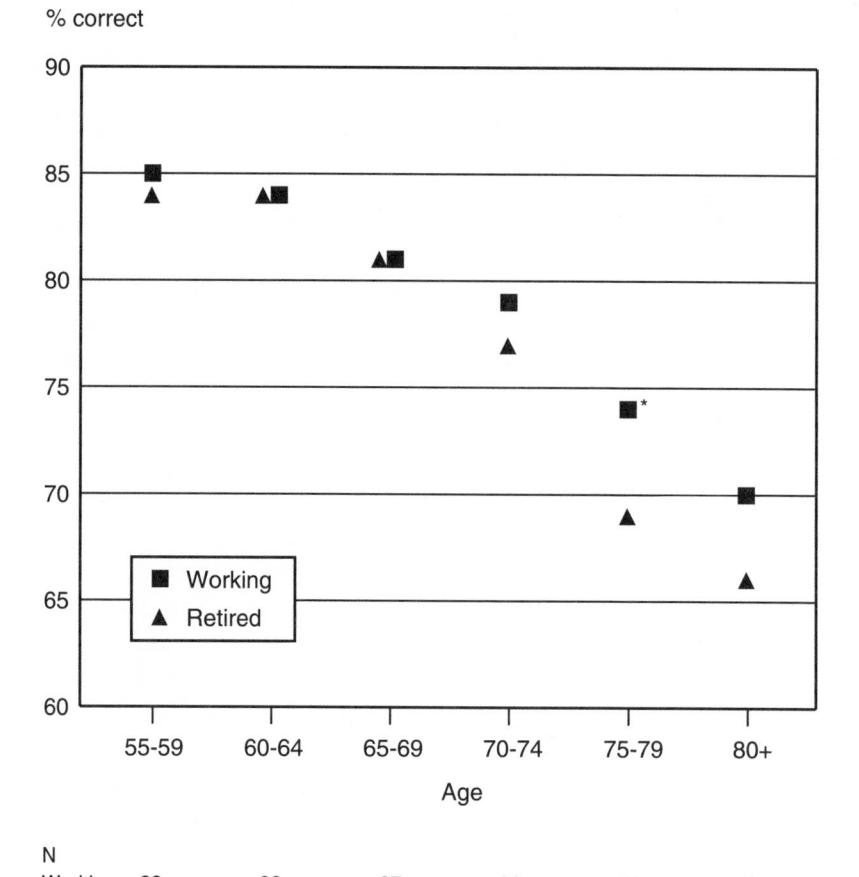

N
Working 89   93   67   36   26   10
Retired   7   21   39   56   70   35
* *p* = .017 (effect size *r* = .216). Other pair-wise *t*-tests are not significant.

Figure 5.4 MicroCog scores of working and retired MDs.

We wondered whether those abilities which were known to be the most dramatically affected by age, such as visuospatial function, memory after delay, and reasoning, would differentiate the working and retired MDs. Alternatively, was it possible that the attention-based cognitive skills which we earlier found to vary most among individuals beyond the age of 70, and which also differentiate normals from the cognitively impaired, would separate the employed from the retirees? Table 5.7 shows that verbal memory

Table 5.7 Significant differences in MicroCog subtest scores among working and retired MDs after age 70: Effect size correlations

MicroCog Subtests	Age Groups		
	70–74	75–79	80+
Wordlist 1	.219^c		
Alphabet			.30^c
Numbers Reversed		.223^c	
Address	.176^c	.227^c	.326^c
Tictac		.221^c	
N	92	96	45
Working	36	26	10
Retired	56	70	35

a = $p \le .001$; b = $p \le .01 > .001$; c = $p \le .05 > .01$.

and attention are primary abilities that distinguish MDs who continue to work from those who are retired after the age of 70. Prior to the age of 70, the only significant findings favoring the employed physicians involved an attention subtest, Wordlist 1. The Address subtest significantly separated the working from the nonworking doctors in all three groups. Two of the attention-related subtests (Wordlist 1 and Alphabet) were also higher for the employed physicians.

A potential explanation for the broad differences in the aptitude scores of MDs in the middle seventies and beyond is that those who retired may have done so because they were aware that they were losing ground intellectually. Their sense of having diminished capability relative to what they believed was needed to continue a competent medical practice may have been the reason for leaving the field.

One needs to be cautious about making too much of these findings. The significant effect size correlations are in the small to medium range. It is also true that the largest number of computations among the working and retired physicians found no between–age group differences sufficiently strong to overcome the variability within the age group. Moreover, on many of the subtests measuring attention and memory, the employed and retired physicians performed at the same level. For instance, there was no difference in Alphabet at any age except 70+; Wordlist 2 had no significant findings after age 65. Most of the memory subtests, including Stories: Immediate and Delayed Recall, found the two groups scoring at the same level.

The unanswered question in this investigation is whether working or retired physicians were different to begin with, especially those beyond age 75. Our data cannot tell us whether the working doctors at 75 were the intellectual cream of the crop when they were 40. What we can say with some conviction, however, is that the differences are not big differences. Working or not working beyond 65 matters little with respect to maintaining cognitive proficiency. One possible explanation for the largely insignificant findings is that there are other ways to remain intellectually vigorous in the seventh decade and beyond besides working. We will look at this subject in more detail in Chapter 9, which deals with optimal cognitive aging.

6

The Effects of Gender and Education

Does gender matter with respect to how well certain cognitive abilities are preserved as we move through the life cycle? To what extent does the amount of education play a role in the retention of intellectual skills? Might there be an interaction between gender and education as we enter into the later decades? In this chapter we will investigate the relationship between gender and aptitude scores over the adult years. We will also look at how these differences are retained or diminished in later adulthood. Finally, we will see how years of education influences both gender differences and the maintenance of intellectual aptitude in the years beyond 65.

Gender Differences in Aptitude

Much of our understanding of cognitive as well as other changes over the life cycle is based on small samples of males, usually well-educated and middle-class males. Examples are the Harvard Study of Adult Development, begun in 1938, which initially followed male undergraduates.[1] Levinson's research reported on 40 males living in the New Haven, Connecticut, area.[2] Other research has followed a similar pattern.[3] Not all longitudinal studies are based on males of elite backgrounds, however. For example, Vaillant followed a group of inner-city youths.[4] The Oakland Growth and Guidance Study examined a group of children, mixed by gender and socioeconomic status, in the years 1928–1929 and has followed them since. The surviving parents of these subjects, now ages 74 to 93, have been formed into the Berkeley Older Generation Study.[5] The Seattle Longitudinal Study has enrolled representative numbers of males and females.[6]

Lowenthal and her colleagues originally studied subjects balanced for gender at four potential crisis points in their lives and have now followed them into middle and later adulthood.[7]

The educational level of subjects continuing in longitudinal studies considerably exceeds the national average. Even those projects which have selected a wide range of community-dwelling individuals to begin with find that the volunteers who stay in the study have spent considerably more years in school than the average from which their cohort was drawn. An example is the Berkeley Older Generation Study. Of those subjects, 59% had 13 years of education, whereas only 14% of women and men in those age groups nationally had one or more years of college.[8]

Overall, the common wisdom has been that women outperform men in the verbal domain, while men score higher in the math and science areas. A closer look at the data, however, reveals four problems with this generalization. First, most studies show no statistically significant differences. Second, most of the differences occur among adolescents and young adults. Many fewer studies have been done with older people. The third problem is that the age-group cohorts may have had very different educational experiences. For example, females entering school after 1960, with teachers more sensitized to developing quantitative skills in girls as well as boys, will have received far more encouragement to perform up to the level of their abilities in math and science. One result has been the dramatic increase in the number of women applying to and graduating from medical school. Finally, studies that are more representative of the population at large report fewer differences between males and females than those with more elite groups.

The first comprehensive review of the differences between males and females in specific aptitudes was compiled by Eleanor Maccoby and Carol Jacklin in 1974.[9] A summary of their findings, reframed to fit the intellectual functions tested by MicroCog, is shown in Table 6.1. Maccoby and Jacklin's review of nearly 300 studies on the relationship between gender and intellectual performance from infancy through adulthood found that males and females did not differ significantly throughout life. As the authors put it, "beginning in early infancy the two sexes show a remarkable degree of similarity in the basic process of perception, learning and memory."[10] In the verbal sphere, where females often are superior, Maccoby and Jacklin reported the outcomes of 98 studies. In 37 of them, females had higher scores, nearly three times the number of occasions in which males were superior. In the majority of reports (48), however, no differences were found. This caused Maccoby and Jacklin to conclude: "It is true that when-

Table 6.1 Possible gender differences among intellectual aptitudes

MicroCog Subtests	Possible Gender Differences
ATTENTION	None (p. 51)
Alphabet	
Wordlist 1	
Wordlist 2	Females stronger (p. 50)
NUMERIC RECALL	
Numbers Forward	None (pp. 58 and 59)
Numbers Reversed	
VERBAL MEMORY	
Stories: Immediate Recall	Females show better memory for verbal content (p. 59)
Stories: Delayed Recall	
Address	
VISUOSPATIAL FACILITY	Males stronger (p. 93)
Tictac	Males superior at recalling designs (p. 59)
Clocks	
REASONING	None (p. 110)
Analogies	
Object Match	Males better at breaking set (p. 105)
CALCULATION	
Math	Males better (p. 85)

Source: Adapted from E. E. Maccoby and C. N. Jacklin, *The Psychology of Sex Differences* (Stanford, Calif.: Stanford University Press, 1974).

ever a sex difference is found, it is usually the girls and women who obtain higher scores, but the two sexes perform very similarly on a number of verbal tasks in a number of sample populations."[11]

Gender-related contrasts in the quantitative domain could not be found until adolescence. From that stage onward, males generally outscored females in most reports, though a large number found that the sexes could not be distinguished. Since much of science requires facility with math, it is not surprising that males scored higher than females on aptitude tests in chemistry and physics. Maccoby and Jacklin raised the question of whether superiority in science is a result of greater math ability or whether a third factor, visuospatial ability, may be at work. They reviewed findings of the Harvard Project Physics in which the physics achievement test was given to a large sample of high school students.[12] On those physics questions that required visuospatial aptitude the boys were stronger, but when a task called for verbal ability the female students had higher scores.

Unlike verbal or mathematical skills, visuospatial aptitude encompasses a wide range of tasks. Four types of visuospatial tasks are shown in Figure 6.1. The first is a spatial perception task in which the subject must visualize how the line of water would appear if the bottle were tipped 45°. The second, an embedded figures item, requires the individual to locate a simple shape within a complex pattern of lines. The third visuospatial task is paper folding. Here the problem is to imagine where the holes would be when the paper is unfolded. The fourth is a mental rotation problem in which the subjects must identify which two of the four shapes match the standard by moving the possible responses around in their mind until they can tell whether they conform to the model or not.

The results of nearly 100 studies in the visuospatial domain reviewed by Maccoby and Jacklin found the mirror image of the studies of gender differences in verbal aptitudes. This time the differences were in the direction of higher scores for boys and men. These differences were greatest in early adolescence onward. Again, more than 60% of the research reports discovered no gender differences.[13]

A limitation of the work by Maccoby and Jacklin is that their review of hundreds of studies simply indicated the direction of the difference of whether the findings were statistically significant or not. Had their book been written a decade later, these studies might have been reported meta-analytically. Meta-analysis, or the "analysis of the analyses," is a family of relatively new statistical techniques that allow researchers to combine findings from many studies on the same topic.[14] Instead of merely counting the number of research reports favoring girls or boys or neither, significant and nonsignificant studies can be aggregated, putting together larger numbers of subjects, significance tests, and effect size (ES) estimates. This results in two benefits. First, the added power of more subjects can result in a clearer picture of whether or not substantial differences exist. Second, the accumulated significance tests and ES estimates tell how large these discrepancies in aptitude may be between the sexes.

Three meta-analyses covering verbal, mathematical, and visuospatial abilities have been carried out in the last 10 years. Hyde and her colleagues examined gender differences in verbal and mathematical skills. They located 165 reports on scores of males and females in the verbal domain.[15] Overall they found the weighted mean ES (Cohen's d) for all studies to be 0.11, or about a 4% statistical advantage for females. The authors

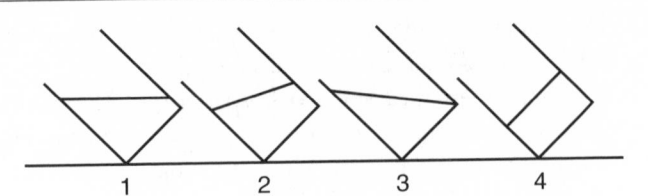

Spatial perception item. Respondents are asked to
indicate which tilted bottle has a horizontal water line.

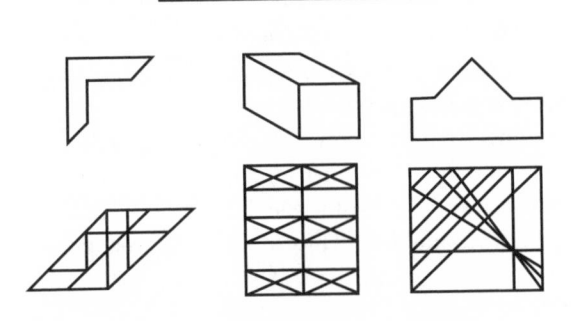

Spatial visualization item. Embedded figures:
respondents are asked to find the simple shape
shown on the top in the complex shape shown
on the bottom.

Figure 6.1 Examples of visuospatial test questions. *Source:* M. C. Linn and A. C. Peterson, "Emergence and Characterization of Sex Differences in Spatial Ability: A Meta-analysis," *Child Development,* 56 (1985): fig. 1, p. 1482; fig. 2, p. 1483; fig. 3, p. 1485.

concluded that the general differences are so small as to be negligible. Subdividing the verbal domain, they discovered some notable differences in component skills. For example, average scores of females were approximately 13% higher in speech production and 10% better in essay writing and anagrams. Interestingly, males were slightly stronger in analogies. They also outscored females on the verbal portion of the 1985 SAT.

In mathematics, these researchers found 100 statistical studies of gender differences.[16] Meta-analysis produced results that were the mirror image of the studies of verbal skills. Averaged over all studies (excluding the SAT data), the *d* favoring males was 0.15, or about a 6% difference. One of the most interesting aspects of this meta-analysis was the point where these researchers found the differences beginning to emerge. In the elementary and

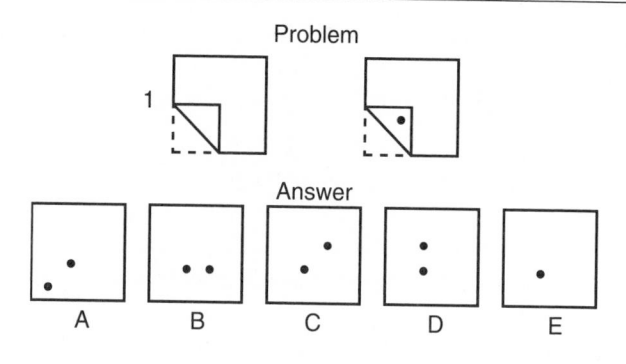

Spatial visualization item. Paper folding: respondents are asked to indicate how the paper would look when unfolded.

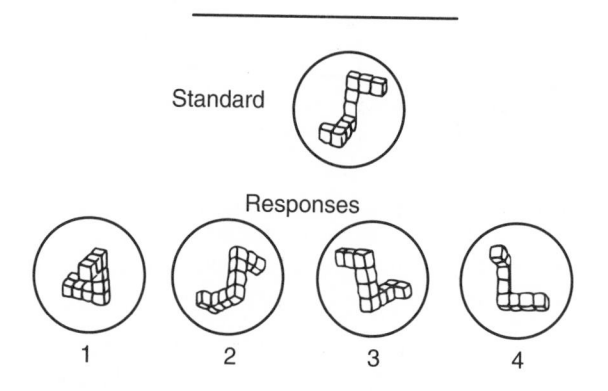

Mental rotation item. Respondents are asked to identify two responses that show the standard in a different orientation.

Figure 6.1 *(continued)*

middle school years, boys and girls tested just about the same on arithmetic tests. Actually, pre-adolescent girls were slightly superior to boys in computation. But from high school onward, male subjects began outperforming their female classmates noticeably. In high school, males scored approximately 12% higher; in college, the differences were closer to 15%; and among adults, the group differences in performance averaged 22%. The math skill in which males were consistently higher was problem solving.

Visuospatial ability has been described by Linn and Peterson as the ability to represent, transform, generate, and recall symbolic nonlinguistic information. They found 172 ES estimates on gender differences in this domain and then subdivided the kind of visuospatial ability into three of the sorts of problems shown in Figure 6.1: spatial perception, spatial visualization, and mental rotation.[17]

On the whole, Linn and Peterson found that males were superior to females on many but not all of the visuospatial problems. In mental rotation tests, men outperformed women on most studies, the average difference being approximately 27%. In the spatial perception studies, the genders did not differ significantly under the age of 18. After 18, males outscored females moderately. On the spatial visualization tasks, no sex differences were discovered.

While it can be said that the difference in ability scores between the sexes is small and the gap may be narrowing, it remains a fact that the differences are not trivial. For example, Rosenthal and Rubin make the point that even if the average score for female subjects on a verbal test is only 4% higher than that of their male counterparts, this means that 6 out of 10 women will score above average while only 4 out of 10 men will exceed the mean.[18] The mirror image of this ratio occurs in the math and visuospatial spheres.

A very interesting discovery about changes in the magnitude of gender differences emerged from the meta-analysis of Hyde and her co-workers. They found that the gap between the sexes in average scores on verbal and mathematics tasks has been narrowing. They compared the average difference between females and males in studies published prior to 1974 and the average differences in reports appearing afterward and found that the separation between females and males has narrowed by about one-half in the verbal area (9% before 1974 compared with 4% after). In math, the same trend is apparent. In research published prior to 1974, males on average were 12% higher than females. Since 1974, the differences have shrunk to approximately 6%.

It is not obvious why the gender differences in both verbal and mathematical skills have narrowed in the past two decades. One factor may be greater efforts to encourage women to take math courses, as well as to excel in vocations that have typically been male-dominated such as engineering, medicine, public accounting, and piloting of airliners. But this does not explain why boys are performing better relative to girls in the verbal sphere. It may be that other forces are at work. One potential explanation is that the pool of subjects being tested after 1974 compared to previous ones may be quite different. We know that more selective cohorts produce greater differences between the sexes than a pool of normally distributed subjects. The past two decades have brought greater encouragement and incentives to individuals from all walks of life to remain in school and to attend college, and this has broadened the representativeness of students in schools and colleges. Since most of the testing for gender differences has been carried out with students in high school and college, it may be that this more representative sample of males and females is yielding truer findings about the real "differences" between the sexes.

A final explanation is that since Maccoby and Jacklin's work there has been greater interest in studies showing no differences between the genders. If one adds to this the fact that the number of professional journals in the field of education and psychology has proliferated since the mid-1970s, it is possible to imagine a much larger number of studies with nonsignificant findings between the genders appearing in the literature. It will be necessary to continue to study gender differences in ability into the next decade before we can conclude with greater certainty that the gap between the scores for verbal and math skills is closing.

A limitation of the work on gender differences has been the relative absence of studies of adults. For example, in 98 of the 100 studies on verbal ability surveyed by Maccoby and Jacklin, the subjects were under 25 years of age.[19] Their survey of reports on mathematical aptitude included none with subjects in the adult years. With the growing interest in aging in the past two decades, we might expect that more articles would address gender differences in the adult years. But the more recent meta-analyses of gender differences in aptitude found that only 7 of the 84 investigations of verbal ability used subjects aged 25–60,[20] while of the 100 reports in the mathematics sphere, all but 9 studied subjects 24 and under.[21]

Because most of the data on gender differences comes from studies of young people, we do not know whether differences in aptitudes found among 14-year-olds or college sophomores extend to a geriatric population. For example, Schwartz and Karp reported that the male superiority exhibited on visuospatial tasks in a sample of younger subjects was not found among individuals 58–92 years of age.[22] More recent work at the Mayo Clinic supports the findings based on young subjects.[23] Examining the relationship between gender and scores on well-known cognitive tests (the WAIS-R and WMS-R) with subjects aged 55 to 85+, Mayo Clinic researchers confirmed the now familiar pattern of females being higher on the verbal portion of the testing and males being stronger on the visuospatial side.

The Interaction of Gender and Education

When substantial differences did occur, it was when the effect of education was weighed in. In their normative studies on older Americans, the Mayo Clinic team divided the subjects into six groups based on the subject's number of years in school. They found that the amount of education substantially correlated with all but one of the eleven WAIS-R subtests (the exception being Object Assembly). Especially impressive was the correlation of schooling to the verbal aptitudes—Information and Vocabulary as well as the reasoning-related Comprehension and Similarities subtests. As would be expected, the Performance subtests had a smaller relationship with years in school. In nearly every case the association between education and intellectual aptitude was stronger than the correlation between gender and ability. To a lesser degree, these same patterns were observed with the WMS-R.

The limitation of this excellent work is that the subjects covered a 30-year age span. This lumping together of older individuals of vastly different ages might obscure the influence of gender and education. It could be, for example, that education would be far more influential with older subjects than with younger ones.

Earlier, Heaton and his colleagues compared IQ subtest scores on a large number of older males and females.[24] Using a sample of 2,423 subjects, they found a significant correlation between all 11 subtests of the WAIS and WAIS-R intelligence tests and education. Those with more schooling had substantially higher scores, especially on Performance subtests in the 35–64 decades. Of particular interest, however, was what they called "regression to the mean." Adults at age 35 with more years in school scored substantially higher than those with less education. Beyond age 65 the average scores for those groups with more and less education narrowed dramatically. After age 65, the advantage of more education diminished with respect to scores on these IQ subtest comparisons.

Comparisons also were made using 1,108 men and women matched for age and education. In both batteries men outscored women on Information, Arithmetic, and Picture Completion. Women were better at Digit Symbol, a measure of visual memory. On the WAIS-R the average scores of men were higher than those of women on three performance subtests— Picture Arrangement, Block Design, and Object Assembly—as well as the three IQ scores. Though the mean scores were statistically significant, Heaton and his colleagues point out that "sex differences on the whole were modest in size."[25]

Of particular interest for our purposes was whether a significant interaction effect was discovered between education and gender with respect to I.Q. None was found.

A question that comes to mind when observing the powerful relationship of education to cognitive function is whether education is just a synonym for IQ. After all, we know that IQ is highly correlated with the number of years in school. This question has been addressed by Stephen Ceci.[26] In a lengthy review of the evidence bearing on the relationship between IQ and number of years of school, he concluded that it is education that affects IQ more than IQ influences education. Specifically, he discovered that (1) IQ is correlated with the number of years of school completed; (2) IQ diminishes during summer vacation from school or with intermittent attendance; and (3) IQ is adversely affected by starting school later or dropping out earlier. These data support the notion that years of education and IQ influence each other, perhaps even slightly favoring duration of school attendance.

Gender Differences across the Decades

In order to investigate the questions of gender differences in cognitive aging as they may be influenced by education, we carried out three increasingly focused studies. The first was an overall analysis of the male-female test scores in the Normal sample across the decades. The second was a more detailed examination of the differential effects of education for men and women among 268 Normal subjects aged 65–74. The third looked at the MD sample, which provided more control for education, in an attempt to discover if gender differences could be found within separate age groups.

Gender Differences in Cognitive Aging among Normal Subjects

MicroCog scores from the Normal panel were compared by gender for each decade from under 35 to 75+. Then we divided the subjects over 65 into five-year intervals for a finer-grained analysis. Table 6.2 shows those comparisons that were statistically significant (the effect size correlations are shown in parentheses). Because of the small number of subjects in all but the 65–74 group, *p* values trending toward significance are shown.

On the whole, our data look a good deal like the summary of the literature

Table 6.2   Significant gender differences in MicroCog subtest scores by decade: Effect size correlations for Normal sample

MicroCog Subtests	Age				
	35–44	45–54	55–64	65–74	75 +
ATTENTION					
Alphabet		F (.313^d)			
Wordlist 1	F (.309^d)				
Wordlist 2	F (.296^d)			F (.144^b)	F (.245^d)
NUMERIC RECALL					
Numbers Forward				M (.169^b)	M (.290^c)
Numbers Reversed				M (.132^c)	
VERBAL MEMORY					
Stories: Immediate Recall					
Stories: Delayed Recall					
Address	F (.320^d)				
VISUOSPATIAL FACILITY					
Tictac					
Clocks				M (.106^c)	
REASONING					
Analogies			F (.257^d)	M (.096^d)	
Object Match			F (.397^b)		
CALCULATION					
Math					
Total Score					
N: Female	23	21	40	251	40
N: Male	12	14	11	96	19

Note: Because of the small number of subjects in all but one of the comparisons, the differences trending toward significance ($p > .05 \leq .10$) are included in this table.

a $= p \leq .001$; b $= p \leq .01 > .001$; c $= p \leq .05 > .01$; d $= p > .05 \leq .10$.

on gender differences by Maccoby and Jacklin. In all, 70 comparisons (five age groups × 14 test scores) between males and females were made. Of these, 64 produced insignificant findings. Six of the differences between genders were statistically significant, a greater than chance number. Seven others trended in the direction of significance.

No global differences approached significance. The few places where the gender scores were significantly different follow the pattern of previous re-

Table 6.3　Significant gender differences in MicroCog subtest scores by 5-year intervals: Effect size correlations for Normal sample

MicroCog Subtests	Age		
	65–69	70–74	75+
ATTENTION			
Alphabet			
Wordlist 1			
Wordlist 2		F (.175^c)	
NUMERIC RECALL			
Numbers Forward	M (.163^c)	M (.182^c)	M (.290^c)
Numbers Reversed			
VERBAL MEMORY			
Stories: Immediate Recall	M (.175^c)		
Stories: Delayed Recall			
Address			
VISUOSPATIAL FACILITY			
Tictac			
Clocks			
REASONING			
Analogies			
Object Match	M (.153^c)		
CALCULATION			
Math			
Total Score			
N: Female	113	138	40
N: Male	42	54	19

a = $p \le .001$; b = $p \le .01 > .001$; c = $p \le .05 > .01$.

search. Males exhibited strength on one of the visuospatial tasks and numeric recall, while the attentional skills of females were higher. It is interesting to note that all the differences reported in Table 6.2 prior to age 65 favor women. Beyond age 65, most of the comparisons find the men with significantly higher scores.

By far the largest share of the $p < .05$ findings were in the 65–74 decade. It may be that the reason is relatively simple: that the larger number of subjects in this group allowed for more powerful statistical tests. It is also possible that the differences in certain skills between the sexes are more pronounced at this time.

As we looked at the sudden appearance of a large number of significant ES estimates in the 65–74 age group, two questions came to mind. First, we wondered whether we could improve our understanding of just when these gender differences emerged by dividing the group into five-year intervals. Second, we wondered whether there might be differences in the young-old subjects (say, 65–69) that would melt away with the older groups. With these questions in mind, we subdivided the Normal subjects over 65 into five-year intervals and carried out *t*-tests between females and males. The results, shown in Table 6.3, are not greatly different from the 10-year groupings. Males continue to outperform females in the ability to recall numbers, while women are in the ascendance in attentional abilities. The sole exception to this pattern is the strong showing of the men aged 65–69 on immediate story recall.

It is possible that other factors besides gender influenced the retention of intellectual aptitudes in the later years. For example, years of education might make a difference in how well certain abilities are preserved later in life.

Gender and Education Effects on Aptitude among Normal Subjects Aged 65–74

In order to examine the question of the influence of gender and education on aptitudes among older individuals, we used the cohort of women and men aged 65–74 (195 women, 73 men) from the Florida Geriatric Research Program in Dunedin, Florida. We picked this group because they were the only decade with a large enough number to examine educational effects by gender. The characteristics of this subgroup were described in Chapter 3. For the purpose of looking at gender differences in aptitudes, this cohort had several advantages. First, the subjects were close to the same age and thus were educated at about the same time and shared cultural experiences (for example, the Great Depression and World War II), both of which potentially influence intellectual growth. Second, this sample met criteria for "normal" closely approximating those reported by the Mayo Clinic team: they were living independently and viewed themselves as normal; they had no neurological or psychiatric disorders sufficient to impair cognitive status; and they were taking no medications that would compromise intellectual functioning.[27]

Table 6.4 gives the means and standard deviations for males and females

Table 6.4 MicroCog subtest scores by gender among Normal subjects aged 65–74:
Percentage correct

MicroCog Subtests	Females (N = 251)		Males (N = 96)	
	Mean	S.D.	Mean	S.D.
ATTENTION				
Alphabet	.747	.391	.692	.425
Wordlist 1	.820	.186	.803	.235
Wordlist 2	.848[c]	.171	.784	.254
NUMERIC RECALL				
Numbers Forward	.599	.226	.682[b]	.190
Numbers Reversed	.553	.183	.608[c]	.187
VERBAL MEMORY				
Stories: Immediate Recall	.793	.190	.816	.185
Stories: Delayed Recall	.704	.155	.719	.166
Address	.674	.258	.638	.294
VISUOSPATIAL FACILITY				
Tictac	.398	.303	.450	.330
Clocks	.808	.222	.851[c]	.182
REASONING				
Analogies	.464	.157	.499	.168
Object Match	.864	.077	.871	.079
CALCULATION				
Math	.829	.172	.816	.188
Total Score	.731	.094	.741	.116

$a = p \leq .001; b = p \leq .01 > .001; c = p \leq .05 > .01.$

separately on the MicroCog subtests. Visual inspection of the scores for men and women finds few gender differences existing in these data. Total scores were nearly identical (74% and 73% correct respectively). Most of the scores obtained by women and men were statistically indistinguishable. Four were significant at $p < .05$ or better. Again, females scored higher on a measure of attention, Wordlist 2. But none of the other attentional subtests were elevated. Males outperformed females on numeric recall and Clocks.

As a group, the men were far more widely scattered in their performance than the women. This can be seen in their much larger S.D. for MicroCog total score. The variability of the males was approximately 23% greater than that of the females ($p \leq .001$).

To sharpen our perspective on the effect of schooling on cognitive functioning, we divided the subjects into three educational groups and compared their MicroCog scores with one another. We then subdivided them by gender to see whether the amount of school impacted their aptitudes differently. This enabled us to investigate several questions about the relationships between education and gender. For instance, is the greatest educational effect among these subjects between those who are college graduates and those who did not go beyond high school? Or is some amount of college sufficient to make a difference? To address these questions, we carried out three sets of comparisons. Comparison I contrasted those subjects with the most schooling (≥ 16 years) with those with the least (≤ 12 years); Comparison II set the scores of individuals with some college (13–15 years) against those with none; Comparison III looked at whether the scores of subjects with some college differed from individuals with a bachelor's degree.

Table 6.5 shows the relationship of years of education to aptitude scores by gender. The magnitude of the influence is provided by ES correlations. Each is derived from pairwise t tests for each of the three comparisons. The significance of the p values is indicated by the letter superscripts.

Inspecting Table 6.5 across aptitude areas, we can see that most are powerfully enhanced by years spent in school. We are not surprised to find reasoning highly correlated. The capacity to solve analogies is the only subtest where all subjects with more education scored significantly higher on all three comparisons. Years of education also was associated with the ability to "break set" as measured by Object Match. College graduates substantially outscored those with ≤ 12 years of education on this task. Visuospatial functions as measured by Tictac also distinguished those with more schooling on two occasions.

Those with the most education also surpassed those with the least amount of school on the subtests assessing attention and verbal memory. Alphabet and Wordlist 1 had at least one significant contrast. Memory after delay as measured by Stories: Delayed Recall and Address exhibited the greatest differences, though only one of the p values exceeded .05. Numbers Forward decisively differentiated the 16+ group from those with a high school education or less.

The ES estimates in Table 6.5 show the extent to which several cognitive abilities are influenced by years of education. If years of education matter,

Table 6.5 Relationship of years of education to aptitude scores by gender among Normal subjects 65–74: Effect size correlations

MicroCog Subtests	I Years of Education ≤ 12 vs. 16+			II Years of Education ≤ 12 vs. 13–15			III Years of Education 13–15 vs. 16+		
	All	Females	Males	All	Females	Males	All	Females	Males
ATTENTION									
Alphabet	.158[c]	.189[c]							
Wordlist 1				.180[b]	.315[c]				
Wordlist 2									
NUMERIC RECALL									
Numbers Forward	.195[b]	.186[c]							
Numbers Reversed									
VERBAL MEMORY									
Stories: I R									
Stories: D R					.161[c]				
Address	.182[c]	.222[b]							
VISUOSPATIAL FACILITY									
Tictac	.207[b]	.230[b]		.119[c]					.279[b]
Clocks	.160[c]				.170[c]			.186[c]	
REASONING									
Analogies	.531[a]	.469[a]	.544[a]	.143[c]			.422[a]	.447[a]	.348[c]
Object Match	.244[a]	.296[a]						.250[c]	
CALCULATION									
Math									
Total Score	.284[a]	.343[a]		.211[b]	.218[b]			.243[c]	
N	189	138	51	215	165	50	132	89	43

Note: All differences are in the direction of higher scores associated with more years of education.
a = $p \leq .001$; b = $p \leq .01 > .001$; c = $p \leq .05 > .01$.

then the comparisons between aptitude scores of those subjects with the most schooling and those with the least should reveal significant differences. As can be seen in the table, that is exactly what occurred. The greatest differences were between those who graduated from college and those who did not venture beyond high school. Eight of the ES estimates for all subjects were significant at Comparison I. Subjects with some college also had an edge over those with none. Comparison II yielded four significant differences. When the scores of individuals with some college were contrasted with scores of subjects with college degrees, only Analogies differentiated the two groups.

The cognitive benefit of education appears to be strongest for women. Looking at the effect size correlations for females only, we find that 15 were significant. Among males, by comparison, only three of the differences in scores were statistically notable. Two were on Analogies.

The superiority of the best-educated women in reasoning can be seen at both Comparison I and Comparison III. When females with college degrees were compared with the women with ≤12 years of education, the scores of the former were higher on at least one subtest in every aptitude area. The greatest differences were in reasoning. Verbal memory also correlated with years in school. Memory after delay was notably stronger among the best-educated females. Attentiveness as measured by Alphabet was greater for women with college degrees when compared with those with high school or less. Women with college degrees surpassed those with less education on the Tictac subtests, indicating greater visuospatial ability.

Why does a college education make so much difference in the cognitive functioning of women in this sample while men with a bachelor's degree scarcely differ from males with no more than 12 years of school? A possible explanation is that there may have been something very special about the women who attended college in that generation. They would have begun their higher education in the decade of the 1930s. In those times slightly more females then males graduated from high school. In 1930, for instance, 55% of those completing twelfth grade were female; in 1940 the proportion was 53%. But despite the larger number of females graduating from high school, far fewer completed four years of college. In 1934 the number of females who were awarded college degrees was 15% of the total number of women graduating from high school four years earlier. In contrast, the percentage of males receiving a college diploma in 1934 was 27% of the 1930 number graduating from high school—nearly twice the female proportion.[28] These data stand in sharp distinction to the graduation rates of women a half-century later. The ratio of females completing the twelfth grade was nearly the same in the 1980s as in the 1930s, but 51% of all college graduates in 1988 were female.[29]

Since they were going against the trend of their times, these college women of the 1930s may have been not only brighter but more highly motivated, and they may have come from homes that strongly valued intellectual activities. The other side of the coin, of course, is that the males going on to higher education in the decade prior to World War II may have been less unique. In those years, a much larger percentage of men continued their schooling after high school. If males attending college were a more heterogeneous group in terms of ability, motivation, and the academic values of their homes, this could also explain why males differed so little as a function of education while college experience made so much difference among females.

Gender Effects on Aptitude among Physicians

So far, we have found that small gender-related differences occurred in the Normal data set. Specifically, men exhibited stronger abilities in visuospatial functions, such as Tictac and Clocks, and in the recall of numbers after age 65. Prior to 65, all of the reliable differences, and those trending toward significance, favored females. At every age women dominated the attentional skills (Wordlist 1 and 2). Controlling for education in the 65–74 age group from the Normal sample, we found that those with more years in school scored higher than those with less education. The differences were far more pronounced among women.

We are aware that a disadvantage of the Normal group is its restricted age range. We wondered whether the patterns we found would be reproduced across a broader span of years. In addition, we found ourselves questioning whether individuals more closely matched for education would show the same differences as the Normal sample. We turned to the MD sample to see if they might shed light on these questions. Though the numbers of women in this sample are decidedly skimpy (72 females versus 930 males), closely reflecting the percentages of women in these age groups in the AMA, the fact that educational experience as well as vocation is held constant for all subjects is an advantage. Not only are the women equivalent in terms of number of years of education, but they are also likely to have been similar in both high school and college course work and the academic achievement required to enter medical school.

An interesting question is whether age affects the aptitudes of women and men differently. The small numbers of females in the older age groups precluded comparisons among the doctors by decade. We combined the sample into three groups (≤44, 45–64, and 65+) to gain more statistical power. The results of the statistical analysis of the differences between scores of male and female doctors are shown in Table 6.6. Overall, we are more

Table 6.6 Gender differences in subtest scores among physicians in three age groups: Effect size correlations

MicroCog Subtests	All	≤44	45–64	65+
ATTENTION				
Alphabet			M (.103)[c]	
Wordlist 1			M (.118)[a]	
Wordlist 2				
NUMERIC RECALL				
Numbers Forward			M (.084)[c]	
Numbers Reversed				
VERBAL MEMORY				
Stories: Immediate Recall				
Stories: Delayed Recall				
Address			M (.103)[c]	
VISUOSPATIAL FACILITY				
Tictac				
Clocks			M (.147)[b]	
REASONING				
Analogies				
Object Match	M (.084)[c]		M (.101)[c]	M (.156)[b]
CALCULATION				
Math				
Total Score			M (.153)[b]	
	M = 930	M = 206	M = 387	M = 337
	F = 72	F = 33	F = 20	F = 19

a = $p \leq .001$; b = $p \leq .01 > .001$; c = $p \leq .05 > .01$.

impressed by the similarities of the abilities between the sexes than the differences. Of the 56 comparisons, 47 found no significant differences between men and women. In addition, the ES estimates for the significant findings, shown in parentheses, were on the small side.

For the total sample of 1,002 physicians, statistical analyses of the scores revealed only one significant difference; men were stronger in "breaking set" (Object Match), a finding that conforms to previous research. This area of male superiority was found among the doctors in the two oldest groups.

A striking finding is that no statistical differences were found among the younger doctors, and only one in the oldest age group. Only in the 45–64 age group did the male physicians score notably higher in several domains than their female counterparts. The stronger showing of men was in areas of traditional male competence—breaking set, number recall, and the visuospatial domain. In this age group the males were also stronger in aptitudes not usually thought to be the province of men, namely verbal recall and attention. Because of the relatively small proportion of females in this sample, it seems reasonable to consider the findings from the 45–64 subgroup as interesting results requiring further support from other research.

These data, however, are consistent with the observations from the meta-analyses reported earlier in this chapter in which the differences in aptitude scores between the sexes have been narrowing in more recent generations of students. The preponderance of doctors in the 45–64 group would have completed their educations prior to 1974, whereas all of the MDs 44 and under were in school after 1974.

These data lend themselves to one further analysis: a within-gender comparison of the degree to which particular aptitudes hold up or diminish through the decades. Are certain abilities retained or not retained differentially among men and women as they grow older? Because we have a sample of subjects controlled for education and occupation, we can be somewhat more certain that the differences we discover are likely to be a function of the aging process rather than of external factors. Table 6.7 shows the comparisons of the MicroCog scores of younger (≤44) with middle-aged (45–64) doctors and of middle-aged MDs with those 65+. To examine gender differences, the group is divided into males and females.

The short answer to the question posed in the previous paragraph is that older and younger men and women in medicine resemble one another closely as they age cognitively. Though the familiar age-related differences are seen, no substantive gender effects were discovered with respect to specific abilities. We note, for example, that the global difference among younger and middle-aged doctors for both sexes was larger than the decline in any specific ability. This can be seen at Comparison I in the ES estimates, which are larger for the total score than for any of the subtest findings (.304 for males and .527 for females). The total score ES estimate at Comparison II is also higher than any component score for men but not for women.

The longer answer to the question of whether males and females age

Table 6.7   Age group comparisons for MD males and females: Effect size correlations

MicroCog Subtests	I ≤44 vs. 45–64		II 45–64 vs. 65+	
	Males	Females	Males	Females
ATTENTION				
Alphabet	.108[b]	.309[b]	.219[a]	
Wordlist 1	.150[a]	.352[b]	.375[a]	
Wordlist 2			.296[a]	
NUMERIC RECALL				
Numbers Forward			.269[a]	
Numbers Reversed	.127[b]		.295[a]	.219[d]
VERBAL MEMORY				
Stories: Immediate Recall	.163[a]	.258[c]	.382[a]	
Stories: Delayed Recall	.257[a]	.402[a]	.374[a]	.446[a]
Address	.143[a]	.448[a]	.340[a]	.286[c]
VISUOSPATIAL FACILITY				
Tictac	.248[a]	.453[a]	.380[a]	
Clocks	.116[b]	.365[b]	.361[a]	
REASONING				
Analogies	.238[a]		.451[a]	.289[c]
Object Match	.112[b]	.310[c]	.373[a]	.252[d]
CALCULATION				
Math	.177[a]	.352[b]	.161[a]	
Total Score	.304[a]	.527[a]	.521[a]	.279[c]

Notes: (1) All effect size correlations favor younger doctors. (2) Because of the small number of female subjects, differences trending toward significance $p > .05 \leq .10$ are included. (3) Because the number of male and female MDs were so different, the relative size of the ES correlations cannot be compared between the sexes.

a = $p < .001$; b = $p \leq .01 > .001$; c = $p \leq .05 > .01$; d = $p > .05 \leq .10$.

differentially is more complicated. The scores of the middle-aged doctors of both sexes were substantially lower in all areas than those of the MDs under 45. The pattern of decline among male and female subjects was similar. All areas of ability (except number recall) lost ground between young and middle age in both genders. The trend toward lower scores among the older male MDs broadened and accelerated at Comparison II. Not only was every subtest score lower, but the magnitude of the ES correlations grew substantially (with the exception of Math). Again, the areas of greatest loss were the familiar trio of visuospatial facility, reasoning, and verbal recall. The more numerous males in the MD sample may have produced significant levels even though the actual differences in the scores between the younger and older doctors were often quite small. With one exception, the pattern of declining in average scores for females followed the same trend as for males. Attentional skills declined but only trended toward significance ($p = .11$ for Wordlist 1 and .103 for Wordlist 2). The exception was visuospatial facility. The oldest female doctors did not score much lower than the middle-aged MDs, whereas among the oldest male physicians the means were much lower on the Tictac and Clocks subtests than among those in the 45–64 group. Though the small number of females makes any generalizations hazardous, it is possible to conclude that the decline in visuospatial abilities is less dramatic in the older adult years among women than men.

The extent to which these findings can be generalized is limited by the characteristics of the samples of subjects tested and by the cross-sectional nature of this research. The first limitation has been discussed previously: our samples of subjects lack balance by gender (the MD group could have used more females, and the Normal group had a scarcity of males in certain decades). The second limitation is that this is not a longitudinal study of individuals over time. With cross-sectional data we need to remind ourselves that these curves reflect age-related *differences* in aptitudes, but not age-related *changes*. Our findings show how groups of individuals tested one time compare with one another. They do not tell us how the abilities of a sample of women and men tested at intervals over their adult years would change with advancing age. We cannot be certain that a group of adults tested every decade or so would produce similar findings. Nevertheless, in spite of the limitations in this work, we believe that both age and years of education are strongly associated with decline in mental skills and gender far less so. These correlations present challenging hypotheses to be tested by larger-scale longitudinal studies.

7

Mild Cognitive Impairment

The condition known as mild cognitive impairment (MCI) is receiving increasing attention in the literature. There are various definitions of MCI, ranging from benign senescent forgetfulness and age-associated memory impairment to mild and limited forms of dementia. Because different investigators have used different sets of criteria for defining MCI, the estimates of the frequency of this condition within a given population vary widely. In this chapter we will discuss the criteria that define MCI and will note how these characteristics manifest themselves in our own data. We will also turn our attention to issues of reversibility in MCI. Educational training interventions have been shown to improve early stage losses of certain abilities such as memory, visuospatial orientation, and reasoning. We will objectively review these studies and pinpoint the approaches that seem most promising.

The Importance of Early Diagnosis

Some readers may wonder, "Why do I want to learn something about the early stage of a mental condition that is likely to be irreversible? Since I can't do anything about it, perhaps I'd rather not know." The answer is that just as it is crucial to be able to diagnose a physical disease in its earliest manifestations, it is equally important to be able to diagnose MCI in its initial stages. Several similarities are immediately apparent. The sooner a diagnosis is made, the greater is the likelihood that the condition can be reversed. In addition, a well-defined MCI population could be essential for the testing of new pharmacological agents or other forms of treatment. And even if the cures for AD may be generations away, early diagnosis of MCI enables researchers to gain greater understanding of the overall course of the condition, which will help in the social planning and health care of these growing numbers of individuals. It could also provide clinicians with predictive data, enabling them to counsel the afflicted and their families more effectively. Finally, we know that not everyone who exhibits signs of MCI declines. Some remain stable for a long period of time, and a small proportion apparently regain normal function. It may be that early diagnosis will help us discover factors such as diet, physical/mental exercises, or agents that might slow or even reverse the downward trends of these disorders.

Cognitive Impairment and Longevity

Alzheimer's disease, even in its mildest forms, shortens a life span. Nearly 1,000 women and men living in a rural community on an island off the Danish coast were examined when they were between ages 65 and 85. They were followed up 15 years later.[1] Their case histories showed that the average survival rates of subjects classified as having severe and mild dementia were 2.7 and 4.8 years respectively, compared to 7.8 years for those classified as normal. A problem in interpreting the results of this study is that the criteria used to diagnose dementia when the project was begun in 1961 were less reliable and accurate than those used today. Moreover, the subjects were not matched for two factors known to influence the diagnosis and course of AD—namely, socioeconomic status and years of education.

Berg and his colleagues remedied those deficiencies. Subjects who were part of the Washington University medical school's Memory and Aging Project were first carefully diagnosed as having AD or being normal. They were then matched for socioeconomic status and education. The researchers followed 43 individuals diagnosed as having AD (average age 71.4) and 58 healthy control subjects (average age 71.7) for a seven-year period. Their data show that the diagnosis of AD strongly correlates with a shorter life expectancy, confirming the findings of Nielsen and his coworkers. At 15 months into the study, 24% of the AD subjects had died, compared to only 3% of the normal subjects; at 34 months the proportions were 35% and 7%; and at 66 months the death rates were 60% and 26%.[2]

Systems for Classifying Cognitive Impairment

The primary systems for classifying cognitive impairment are the American Psychiatric Association's *Diagnostic and Statistical Manual: Third Edition—*

Revised (DSM-III-R), the World Health Organization's tenth revision of the *International Classification of Disease* (ICD-10), and the criteria specified by the Joint Workgroup of the National Institute of Neurological and Communicative Diseases and Stroke (NINCDS) and by the Alzheimer's Disease and Related Disorders Association (ADRDA). None lists MCI as a separate diagnostic category. Nonetheless, most experts agree that the condition exists. Efforts to define this disorder have been hindered by the fact that various investigators have applied their own unique sets of criteria to demarcate MCI, as shown by the different terms that have been used to describe the disorder: "benign senescent forgetfulness,"[3] "age-associated memory impairment,"[4] "very mild senile dementia,"[5] "very mild Alzheimer's disease,"[6] "limited dementia,"[7] and "mild dementia."[8]

"Benign senescent forgetfulness" is characterized by intermittent inability to recall unimportant words, numbers, or names that had previously been memorized. The person with this condition is usually aware of this trouble. Later, the individual is usually able to recall this momentarily forgotten material. This condition worsens with age, and while troublesome and occasionally embarrassing, does not usually lead to AD. Clinicians contrast "benign senescent forgetfulness" with "malignant memory dysfunction." As the term suggests, the second condition is more severe, manifesting itself in loss of memory for important data. An example might be an elderly man who can recall neither the city in which he attended his granddaughter's wedding a week ago, nor the fact that she had been married. This condition is also accompanied by spatial disorientation and by the incapacity to store new information in memory. Reminded by his wife that they attended their granddaughter's wedding, the man does not recall this event an hour later. Some aspects of memory storage remain unaffected, however, especially details of childhood and adolescence. The same man easily recalls the make and model of his first car, the name of the family dog, and the dress his wife wore fifty years ago on their honeymoon.

Memory problems are an early cognitive marker of potential MCI. It has been argued that memory impairment may occur in older people as an isolated symptom. The National Institutes of Health sponsored a workgroup to determine whether memory impairment would differ from mild forms of AD. This group devised the term "age-associated memory impairment" (AAMI) and defined criteria that characterize this condition,[9] as shown in Table 7.1. According to these standards, AAMI includes those 50 years and over with normal intellectual ability who have problems with immediate recall and memory after delay and distraction. A key criterion is the gradual loss of memory. Finally, people with this condition should score below one

Table 7.1 Proposed criteria for age-associated memory impairment

Inclusion Criteria

1. Males and females at least 50 years of age.
2. Complaints of memory loss reflected in such everyday problems as difficulty remembering names of individuals following introduction, misplacing objects, difficulty remembering multiple items to be purchased or multiple tasks to be performed, problems remembering telephone numbers or mailing codes, and difficulty recalling information quickly or after distraction.
3. Onset of memory loss must be described as gradual, without sudden worsening in recent months.
4. Memory test performance that is at least one standard deviation below the mean established for young adults on a standardized test of secondary (recent) memory for which adequate normative data are available.
5. Evidence of adequate intellectual functioning.

Exclusion Criteria

1. Evidence of delirium, confusion, or other disturbances of consciousness.
2. Any neurological disorder that could produce cognitive deterioration as determined by history, clinical neurological examination, and, if indicated, neuroradiological examination.
3. History of any infective or inflammatory brain disease, including those of viral, fungal, or syphilitic etiologies.
4. Evidence of significant cerebral vascular pathology.
5. History of repeated minor head injury (as in boxing) or a single injury resulting in a period of unconsciousness for 1 hour or more.
6. Current psychiatric diagnosis of depression, mania, or any other major psychiatric disorder.
7. Current diagnosis or history of alcoholism or drug dependence.
8. Any medical disorder that could produce cognitive deterioration, including renal, respiratory, cardiac, and hepatic disease; diabetes mellitus unless well controlled by diet or oral hypoglycemics; endocrine, metabolic, or hematological disturbances; and malignancy not in remission for more than 2 years. Determination should be based on complete medical history, clinical examination (including electrocardiogram), and appropriate laboratory tests.
9. Use of any psychotropic drug or any other drug that may significantly affect cognitive function during the month prior to testing.

Source: T. Crook and C. J. Larrabee, "Age-Associated Memory Impairment: Diagnostic Criteria and Treatment Strategies," *Psychopharmacology Bulletin,* 24 (1988): 509–514.

standard deviation or about the 15th percentile on established neuropsychological measures of memory. To further circumscribe this condition, AAMI excludes individuals who have a history of medical problems that could compromise memory, such as stroke or tumor, head injuries, medications, alcoholism, drug dependence, depression, and other psychiatric disorders. In addition, those who have evidence of Alzheimer's disease confirmed by clinical examination or test score findings are excluded.

Evidence that AAMI exists as a discrete entity has come from a longitudinal study by Lane and Snowden.[10] They report a much higher prevalence and yearly new occurrences of AAMI than of AD. Another study compared neuropsychological test data on 56 subjects who met criteria for AAMI with the same number of subjects who had been diagnosed as having mild AD. They were matched for age, gender, and educational background.[11] The investigators were able to distinguish women and men with AAMI from those with AD 88% of the time. A majority of the misclassifications were false positives, that is, classifying someone categorized as having AAMI as mildly impaired.

The committee who described AAMI may object to the inclusion of this condition in the category of mild cognitive impairment. They might see it instead as a form of normal cognitive aging, which will be described in the next chapter. There are two reasons for our decision to categorize AAMI among the forms of MCI. First, the inclusionary criteria do not specify normal functioning in domains such as visuospatial functions, reasoning, calculation skills, or attention; nor do the exclusionary criteria rule out individuals who also may be declining in these areas along with memory functions. It seems reasonable to think that the case for AAMI as a discrete disorder would be enhanced by this type of evidence. The second reason we believe that AAMI is not an independent condition comes from our own cross-sectional data of MD and Normal subjects reported in Chapter 4. With both groups, mean scores on memory functions decline apace with other cognitive functions such as visuospatial facility and reasoning by decade.

Although the notion that AAMI can appear in older people as a distinct disorder while other mental aptitudes remain unimpaired is an attractive idea, it may be premature to conclude that the condition is distinct from milder forms of dementia because it is possible that AAMI is merely the early expression of MCI. With time, older people with AAMI may begin to exhibit the other characteristic intellectual deficits of MCI. To test this question, it would be necessary to follow a well-defined group of AAMI subjects over a decade or more to determine whether this is a separable entity or merely an early stage of AD.[12]

The other terms—"very mild senile dementia," "very mild AD," "limited dementia," and "mild dementia"—all refer to forms of MCI. While most of these terms are meant to describe a less severe form of AD, it is appropriate to note that AD is not the only form of cognitive impairment afflicting older people that can result in a subtle and gradual decline. In fact, a worldwide survey by Jorm and colleagues found that multi-infarct dementia (MID) was more prominent than AD among older males in four out of five countries, while the opposite pattern occurred with females—more older women were afflicted with AD than MID.[13] Surveys such as this are useful in reminding us that there may be many reasons for the decline of a person's intellectual functions. When we use the term MCI, we have all of these causal agents in mind, not just AD.

Distinguishing individuals with MCI from those with normal cognitive aging (NCA) is a most challenging task for the medical and psychological sciences. As with many physical and mental disorders, the more severe forms of AD are diagnosed with a high degree of reliability. Far more complex is the detection of such an illness in its earliest stages. Experts have been saying for more than a decade that valid criteria have yet to be developed to differentiate MCI from NCA. For the most part they have focused on the lack of standards for MCI. Jonker and Hooyer phrased it this way: "No valid instruments exist to diagnose dementia, nor do valid criteria exist to distinguish between age related cognitive deterioration and mild dementia at an early stage."[14] Berg concurred, commenting: "Criteria for mild dementia are still problematic."[15] In arguing for more comprehensive assessment processes for elderly people who may be suffering from MCI, O'Connor and his research team said: "The border between normal aging and mild dementia is so poorly understood that simple demarcations cannot adequately encapsulate the wealth of clinical material that needs to be taken into account in assigning diagnostic labels."[16]

The lack of standards for MCI has led to vast differences in the reported rates of mild dementia. As an example, Mowry and Burvill (1988) applied five different criteria for MCI to 100 elderly women and men to see what proportion might be classified as impaired using each set of standards.[17] As can be seen from Table 7.2, the standards for MCI determine the frequency of diagnosis in this population. The proportions for all ages range from 3% to 64%. The DSM-III characteristics yielded by far the smallest proportion of individuals assessed as suffering from mild dementia (3%), while the MMSE, along with two cognitive measures (the Smith Simple Digit Design Test and the Ravens Matrices Subtest B) produced the highest number of positives (64%). This is not surprising since the two tests added to the MMSE tap visuospatial functions. The latter are known to decay far more rapidly with age than do information and short-term memory, the primary cognitive components of the DSM-III standards for mild dementia.

Table 7.2 Prevalence rates of mild dementia according to five differing criteria

Criteria	Percentage Rated Impaired		
	All Ages	70–79	80+
DSM-III: Mild Dementia			
With impaired social performance	3	3	4
Without impaired social performance	15	12	22
Mini-Mental State Examination (MMSE)	9	5	19
MMSE with symbol digit and matrices tests	64	63	67
Gurland: Limited Dementia	29	17	71
N	100	73	27

Source: B. J. Mowry and P. W. Burvill, "A Study of Mild Dementia in the Community Using a Wide Range of Diagnostic Criteria," *British Journal of Psychiatry*, 153 (1988): 331.

A seven-country review of the literature on the incidence of MCI by Shibayama, Kasahara, Kobayashi, and colleagues confirmed the vast range of positive diagnoses found in Mowry and Burvill's British study.[18] The Japanese researchers found that reports of mild dementia ranged from 52.7% to 1.9%. Both extremes were studies carried out in Japan. They concluded that there were five reasons for the enormous variation in incidence rates: differences in standards for positive diagnosis; differences in the methods of data collection (for example, an intensive personal interview by clinicians versus a questionnaire); differences in the age of the subjects; differences in sampling procedure (for example, subjects living independently in the community versus those who are institutionalized); and cultural biases (for example, Japan in contrast to the United States and Europe has more patients with multi-infarct dementia and cerebrovascular dementia than Alzheimer's disease).

If one problem in distinguishing mild cognitive impairment from normal cognitive aging is the lack of agreement on criteria for MCI, surely a difficulty of equal magnitude is the absence of guidelines for NCA. Paging through recent scholarly works on cognitive aging, we looked in vain for references to normal aging. While most indices list cognitive impairment as associated with getting older, almost no mention is made of NCA. Recently some researchers have begun to write about the need to identify the markers of NCA, but little has yet been offered. NCA is defined only by exclusion as an absence of pathology, as light might be said to be the absence of darkness. Hope for identifying normative criteria for NCA comes from research published in the past decade on healthy, normal older subjects. Summaries of these and other studies are contained in Salthouse.[19]

Because normal age-related declines in intellectual functions are similar to the changes associated with MCI, performing a differential diagnosis can be more an art form than a science. Partial endorsement of this statement comes from the work of Storandt and Hill.[20] These researchers gave a brief battery of neuropsychological tests to groups of subjects who were documented by another comprehensive evaluation to be normal, or to have either very mild or mild AD. They found that the normal subjects could be differentiated from the individuals with mild AD on the basis of their higher scores on memory, speeded visuomotor performance, and object naming. However, they also discovered that there was considerable overlap between the scores of the subjects in the very mild AD category and those of both the normal and mild AD groups. The overlap was so great that no single cutoff point was found which allowed accurate discrimination of this middle group from either extreme.

These results led Storandt and Hill to conclude that NCA and mild AD are not separate categories, but are a matter of degree. This conclusion is supported by Bryne and Calloway, who carried the argument a step further,[21] stating that NCA and AD (not just mild AD) lie on the same continuum. It used to be thought that AD and NCA were distinct conditions, much like the situation where one either has cancer or does not have cancer. Present thinking is that the two cognitive states are distributed unimodally, from normal to demented, in much the same way that unmedicated blood pressure measures among a group of 75-year-olds will range from normal limits through marginally elevated to hypertensive.

If NCA and MCI are indeed distributed on a continuum among older individuals, like blood pressure, then we are still left with the question of where to draw the line separating NCA from MCI. Some have thrown up their hands in frustration. Describing the problem of differentiating AD from NCA, the noted Oxford physician and gerontologist J. Grimley Evans said, "In fact, to draw a distinction between disease and normal aging is an attempt to separate the undefined from the undefinable."[22]

This may be far too pessimistic a view. We can be relatively certain of the extremes of NCA and AD. Where the problem becomes more difficult is in the border between NCA and very mildly compromised cognition. Several promising criteria are shown in Table 7.3. Several of the indicators of MCI

Table 7.3 Promising criteria for mild cognitive impairment

1. Decline in memory.
2. Impairment of at least one other domain, such as attention, orientation, judgment, and problem solving.
3. Impaired functioning in community affairs, home and hobbies, and personal care.
4. Occasional potentially dangerous memory or other cognitive lapses.
5. Onset must be gradual over at least a six-month period.
6. Other disorders (medical, neurological, and psychiatric) are excluded that could be responsible for cognitive impairment.
7. These findings are based on reports by the individual and confirmed by an informant.

Source: Adapted from L. Berg et al., "Mild Senile Dementia of the Alzheimer Type: 2. Longitudinal Assessment," *Archives of Neurology,* 23 (1988): 466–484; C. Jonker and C. Hooyer, "The Amstel Project: Design and First Findings. The Course of Mild Cognitive Impairment of the Aged: A Longitudinal Four Year Study," *The Psychiatric Journal of the University of Ottawa,* 15 (1990): 207–211; and A. S. Henderson and F. A. Huppert, "Editorial: The Problem of Mild Dementia," *Psychological Medicine,* 14 (1984): 5–11.

listed in this table are taken from the DSM-III-R; others were developed by investigators working in the United States and England. All agree that there is a gradual decline in memory, with at least one other cognitive domain compromised. In addition, there is impaired functioning in day-to-day life. Henderson and Huppert have added the diagnostic criterion that the person may have occasional (about once a month), potentially destructive memory lapses, such as setting fire to food being cooked, forgetting that the water in the bathtub is running, or wandering off.[23] These criteria must be confirmed by someone close to the individual and must not be caused by physical or psychological factors. When we speak of MCI, we have these criteria in mind.

Even when these criteria become more refined, other problems will need to be resolved before they can be validly applied to a heterogeneous population. One problem is the confounding effects of premorbid IQ, education level, socioeconomic status, race, and primary language. Our own data suggest that the intelligence level of people in their prime gives them an edge on most cognitive tasks as they grow older. Those individuals with higher levels of ability, education, and social status may appear to be normal when in fact they have lost a great deal of ground mentally. By the same token, other people who are normal but with lower measured ability in their prime and from lower socioeconomic origins may appear to be impaired because they have never scored particularly well on tests. We also know that minority group status and a primary language other than English (presuming the test was given in that language) can cause older subjects to score substantially lower on cognitive screening tests even though they may be, in fact, unimpaired.

All of this adds up to the recognition that when we are attempting to determine how well an individual is functioning mentally, we need to ask the question, "compared to whom?" We should make sure that the reference or standardization group we have in mind is adequately balanced for the factors appropriate to the individual in question. If the person's first language was English, he is well educated, and he is socially advantaged, we want to examine the test data in the context of validity studies with subjects who share similar demographics. It follows that if the subject in question has an eighth grade education and grew up in a barrio speaking Spanish, we would want to know that the individual's test results would be considered in the context of normally functioning people from a similar background.

The Frequency of MCI

What is a reasonable estimate of the frequency of MCI, and how do these proportions compare to the percentage of individuals with more severe AD in an older population? The worldwide studies we reviewed earlier gave estimates of the incidence of MCI that varied hugely.

More agreement exists concerning the incidence of moderate and severe forms of AD in later adulthood. A comprehensive survey of 47 studies from 1945 to 1985 on the prevalence of dementia was reported by Jorm and colleagues.[24] They limited their focus to studies of larger samples of representative community-dwelling subjects, and they did not include studies of mild dementia in their investigation because of the problems in defining this condition. Their findings, giving the prevalence rates for moderate and severe forms of AD, are shown in Table 7.4. A glance at this table reveals a remarkably consistent relationship between the prevalence of AD and age. For every half-decade, the percentage is about twice the rate of the previous five-year interval: at ages 65–69, the incidence is 1.4%; at 70–74, it is 2.8%; and at 75–79, the percentage is 5.6.

Assuming that it is possible to assess MCI, what might the percentage of that group be relative to the incidence of moderate and severe AD? Would it be lower or higher? Perhaps the answer is "lower" because those studies that separate subjects into mild, moderate, and severe AD would distribute those we might label as MCI into one of the more severe categories. Or per-

Table 7.4 Estimated prevalence rates for moderate and severe dementia
by 5-year age intervals

Age Group	Estimated Prevalence (%)
60–64	0.7
65–69	1.4
70–74	2.8
75–79	5.6
80–84	10.5
85–89	20.8
90–95	38.6

Source: A. F. Jorm, A. E. Korten, and A. S. Henderson, "The Prevalence of Dementia: A
Quantitative Integration of the Literature," *Acta Psychiatrica Scandinavica*, 76 (1987): 465–479.

haps it is "higher" because a more refined diagnostic system would recognize a number of subjects as impaired who did not meet the criteria for probable AD.

One approach to assessing the relative frequency of MCI in an older population is to pull together studies that have classified their subjects into groups of normals and of mild, moderate, and severe AD by age group. We located three studies in three different countries of large samples of community-dwelling subjects.[25] In each case, considerable effort was invested in evaluating each of the participants. The percentages of individuals in these studies with mild, moderate, and severe dementia are presented in Table 7.5.

We can see right away that these studies have different designs, which makes comparisons slightly difficult. First, the researchers divided their subjects into age groups that are not exactly comparable: two used five-year intervals, while the Swedish study by Hagnell and colleagues separated their subjects by decade. Second, Nielsen and colleagues in the Danish study rated their subjects as either "mildly" or "severely" demented and did not have a moderate group. Though not strictly comparable, these studies nevertheless provide useful evidence to address the question of the incidence of MCI relative to more severe forms of AD.

Looking at the total frequency of dementia by age group, we note that the two most recent studies, those from Sweden and England, produced figures for subjects in their seventies that look much like those in Table 7.4. The percentages of Nielsen and colleagues, 16.8% and 28.5% for the 70–74 and

Table 7.5 Percentage estimates of incidence of AD by severity level
among community-dwelling subjects

| Investigators | Age Group | Level of Dementia | | | |
		Mild	Moderate	Severe	All
Nielsen et al., 1977	65–69	5.0	x	0.0	5.0
(Samso, Denmark)	70–74	15.2	x	1.6	16.8
N = 994	75–79	26.1	x	2.4	28.5
	80+	36.3	x	11.9	48.2
	ALL				23.0
Hagnell et al., 1983	60–69	0.3	0.4	0.7	1.4
(Lundby, Sweden)	70–79	0.2	2.4	4.5	7.1
N = 481	80–89	4.0	6.7	15.2	25.9
	ALL				9.4
O'Connor et al., 1989	75–79	2.2	1.5	0.3	4.1
(Cambridge, England)	80–84	5.7	4.2	1.4	11.3
N = 2,311	85–89	9.3	7.9	2.0	19.1
	90+	13.6	11.4	7.6	32.6
	ALL				10.5

Notes: (1) x = no ratings in this group. (2) Row percentages may not sum exactly because of
rounding.

the 75–79 age groups, are much higher than in the other two reports. In
fact, it may be that their incidence rates are inflated generally, since the
overall population of those found to be impaired in their study (23.0%) is
more than two times what is usually found in a post-65 population.[26]

Estimates for the total incidence of cognitive impairment depart most
dramatically at the extremes. For instance, the percentage of dementia
among the 69 and under set in Table 7.4 would average about 2.0%. While
we may think that the Danish estimate of 5.0% is too high for their 65–69
year old subjects, note that the Swedish subjects aged 60–69 had a 1.4%
incidence of AD. This is about 40% larger than the estimate from Jorm and
colleagues in Table 7.4 for that age group. Beyond age 80, the frequency of
AD from the two Scandinavian investigations provides a more pessimistic
view than Table 7.4. About half of the Danish subjects and a quarter of the
Swedish subjects were rated as demented, as compared with about 15% in
Table 7.4.

Why so much difference? The answer may be that the two Scandinavian studies reported mild dementia, while Table 7.4 includes only the percent-ages of those with moderate and severe dementia. If we subtract the per-centage of subjects with mild dementia from the Danish and Swedish 80+ year olds, we come out with estimates of 11.9% and 21.9% respectively, well within the range predicted by Jorm and colleagues.[27]

These reports suggest that the incidence of MCI may be higher in the 60–69 and 80+ decades than has been previously recognized. They may explain why many studies that include subjects with mild dementia come up with higher incidence rates of impaired subjects than those that do not.[28] Other data indicate that the one-to-one ratio of MCI to moderate and severe de-mentia follows the pattern in the English study.[29] That is, whatever the pro-portion of AD found for an age group, the percentage of those with MCI is likely to be equal to those with moderate and severe dementia.

A dissenting voice comes from the Swedish study by Hagnell and col-leagues.[30] Among their subjects, a far larger number would be rated as mod-erately or severely demented than as mildly impaired. However, it should be noted that the Swedish study was carried out in the interval 1957–1972 using the diagnostic techniques of that period, and it may be that the ad-vances made in assessment techniques since then would yield a more accu-rate discrimination of mild impairment from the more advanced condi-tions. Perhaps new investigations using these more sophisticated techniques will confirm or reject these speculations.

Distinguishing MCI from NCA: The Atlanta Validation Study

In Chapter 3 we discovered that a cutoff score of about 60% correct on MicroCog discriminated the NCA from the MCI subjects 89% of the time. We also noted that the variability among the two groups in the Atlanta Val-idation Study was substantial. What is interesting to look at are those sub-tests for which the MCI subjects were not only lower in average scores than the NCA individuals, but also where the standard deviations were less. The lower standard deviations indicate a tighter clustering of scores, so the range of MCI and NCA scores overlap less than if the variance were greater. This may give us a clue as to what specific aptitudes were significantly com-promised among these impaired subjects.

Table 7.6 shows those subtests that had lower standard deviations as well as the overall subtest scores for two comparison groups—the Atlanta Vali-dation Study subjects and 268 normal volunteers aged 65–74 from the Flor-ida Geriatric Research Program. As we can see, several subtests meet the

Table 7.6 MicroCog subtests with both lower mean scores and standard deviations: Subjects with documented MCI compared to two normal groups

MicroCog Subtests	Atlanta Validation Study Normals (N = 50)	Florida Volunteers (N = 268)
Alphabet		*
Numbers Forward		*
Stories: Immediate Recall	*	*
Stories: Delayed Recall		*
Address	*	*
Tictac	*	*
Clocks	*	*
Analogies	*	*

criterion of having significantly lower average scores and being more tightly clustered for the subjects with MCI than for either of the two normal groups. We immediately recognize the familiar faces of the visuospatial functions (Tictac and Clocks), memory after delay (Address and Stories: Immediate and Delayed Recall) and reasoning (Analogies). Also meeting the same two criteria of lower average scores and tighter standard deviations in the Florida study were subtests measuring attention (Alphabet and Numbers Forward). The MCI subjects from the Atlanta Validation Study can be distinguished from the Florida Normal subjects by another empirical standard. In addition to substantially lower performance in three cognitive areas known to decline with normal aging—visuospatial facility, verbal memory, and reasoning—the MCI subjects also exhibited lower scores than the Florida volunteer Normals on attentional tasks.

Assuming these results are representative of the true differences between the cognitive patterns of MCI and NCA, it looks as though the differences are those of degree and not of type. That is, our data confirm the reports of others who see the intellectual functioning of the elderly on a continuum. Those diagnosed as having MCI in the Atlanta study showed greater losses in three domains already demonstrated in our groups of Normals and MDs in Chapter 4 to decline early and steeply with age—namely, visuospatial facility, reasoning, and verbal memory.

The exception to the typical pattern of age-related cognitive decline among the MCI subjects was the substantially lower scores on subtests measuring attention. It has been said that the absence of a distinctive marker variable is a handicap in identifying MCI. On the basis of these findings, it could be that significantly lower scores on measures of attention, along with other particular skills known to deteriorate with age, would be a promising place to look for the first, faint signals of MCI.

Spontaneous Reversibility of MCI

Not everyone with the early signs of diminished cognition characteristic of MCI will inevitably decline rapidly into the more severe stages of AD. Consider, for instance, the results of three different longitudinal studies of groups of subjects whose initial assessment classified them as having MCI. In New York City, 72 individuals (average age = 69.8) were diagnosed as having very mild or mild cognitive decline on the basis of the Global Deterioration Scale. When they were followed up approximately 3½ years later, three (4.1%) had improved while 62 remained unchanged.[31] The Washington University research team found that five of sixteen subjects from the Memory and Aging Project (average age = 71.7) classified as having very mild AD on the basis of a complete diagnostic process, the Clinical Dementia Rating (CDR) scale, did not deteriorate over a three- to seven-year follow-up period.[32] Of these nonprogressive subjects, two (12%) were assessed as normal at one or more occasions during follow-up.

The relative youth of the subjects is a limitation of these studies. Since we know that the incidence of AD rises rapidly after age 75, the argument that MCI may reverse in some cases would be more convincing with an older population. Here the work of a British research team is relevant.[33] They examined a group of elderly (average age 84.6) residents of Cambridge, England, using the comprehensive CAMDEX. They divided their subjects into three groups—normal, minimal dementia, and mild dementia—and then reexamined them 12 months later. Of 29 subjects who were initially diagnosed in the minimal dementia category, 13 (44.8%) were reclassified as normal in the year 2 evaluation. Of 67 subjects diagnosed as having mild dementia initially, 4 (6.0%) were classified as normal or minimal dementia at follow-up. 38 (56.7%) did not worsen. However, their data do show that the more severe the degree of initial impairment, the more rapid was the progression to the later stages of dementia.

It is clear from these studies that once an individual enters the early stages of cognitive impairment, the decline may not be as predictable and steep as has been suggested. We note that a large proportion of cases did not deteriorate rapidly over a period of several years to more severe dementia. What is not known at this point is why there is so much individual variability among subjects in the early stages of MCI. Accumulating knowledge about the qualities, habits, or other patterns that characterize those whose decline is more gradual compared to their contemporaries whose descent to AD is more rapid is a challenging and exciting area of research still to be explored.

These findings—that many individuals diagnosed as having MCI do not progress rapidly to more severe stages of AD, and that a small number may actually return to normalcy—have led to spirited debate among gerontological specialists. Some argue that a large number of patients assessed as having MCI may have been misdiagnosed just because the patients were elderly and the doctors presumed that failing cognition was likely caused by AD rather than merely by having a bad day. Others suggest that older individuals may have treatable medical or psychological conditions rather than AD that would account for lower levels of intellectual functioning. If this were the case, then the proper therapeutic interventions could reverse the cognitive decline. In a review of studies on dementia, Besdine estimated that 10 to 25% of all people over age 65 with cognitive impairment have unrecognized, potentially treatable diseases.[34] A report from the National Institute on Aging (NIA) Task Force on mental impairment included a list of many medical conditions that could give rise to dementia, delirium, or both.[35] All of these are reversible by medical treatment. Table 7.7 shows 20 major categories of illness that are potential sources of mental status alterations in older individuals.

Clarfield, however, states that one must exercise caution before assuming that a large minority of individuals diagnosed initially as being demented have a reversible condition.[36] He examined 32 studies on reversible dementias involving 2,889 subjects and found that only 11 of the reports provided adequate follow-up. In 11% of these studies the dementias resolved, either partially (8%) or fully (3%). The most common reversible causes were drug abuse (28%), depression (26%), and metabolic problems (for example, thyroid) (16%).

On the basis of a careful analysis of the research methodologies employed in the studies purporting to show high percentages of reversible dementias, Clarfield points to a number of design flaws which lead him to conclude that the incidence of these conditions may be far less than initially estimated. His primary reservations include questions of bias in subject selection and a lack of independent confirmation of reversibility.

What this may add up to is that older people need to be aware that MCI can be caused by conditions other than progressive AD. In a few cases,

Table 7.7 Reversible causes of organic mental disorders in the elderly

Causes	Dementia	Delirium	Either/Both
Therapeutic drug intoxication			x
Depression	x		
Metabolic factors			
Axotemia/renal failure (dehydration, diuretics, obstruction, hypokalemia)			x
Hyponatremia (diuretics, excess ADH, salt wasting, intravenous fluids)			x
Hypernatremia (dehydration, intravenous saline)		x	
Volume depletion (diuretics, bleeding, inadequate fluids)			x
Acid-base disturbance		x	
Hypoglycemia (insulin, oral hypoglycemics, starvation)			x
Hyperglycemia (diabetic ketoacidosis or hyperosmolar coma)		x	
Hepatic failure			x
Hypothyroidism	x		
Hyperthyroidism (especially apathetic)	x		
Hypercalcemia	x		
Cushing's syndrome	x		
Infection and/or fever			
Viral respiratory or gastrointestinal		x	
Bacterial		x	
Pneumonia		x	
Pyslonephritis		x	
Cholecystitis		x	
Diverticulitis		x	
Tuberculosis (TB)			x
Endocarditis			x
Cardiovascular			
Acute myocardial infarction		x	
Congestive heart failure			x
Arrhythmia		x	
Vascular occlusion		x	
Pulmonary embolus		x	
Brain disorders			
Vascular insufficiency		x	
Transient ischemia			x
Stroke			x
Trauma			
Subdural hematoma			x
Concussion/contusion		x	

Table 7.7 (continued)

Causes	Dementia	Delirium	Either/Both
Trauma (*cont.*)			
Intracerebral hemorrhage	x		
Epidural hematoma		x	
Infection			
Acute meningitis (pyrogenic, viral)		x	
Chronic meningitis (TB, fungal)			x
Neurosyphilis	x		
Subdural empyema			x
Brain abscess			x
Tumors			
Metastatic to brain			x
Primary in brain			x
Pain			
Fecal impaction			x
Urinary retention		x	
Fracture	x		
Surgical abdomen	x		
Sensory deprivation states such as blindness or deafness	x		
Hospitalization			
Anesthesia or surgery			x
Environmental change and isolation		x	
Alcohol toxicities			
Lifetime alcoholism	x		
Alcoholism new in old age			x
Decreased tolerance with age producing increasing intoxication		x	
Acute hallucinosis		x	
Delirium tremens		x	
Anemia			x
Tumor: systemic effects of nonmetastatic malignancy			x
Chronic lung disease with hypoxia or hypercapnia			x
Deficiency states such as vitamin B12, folic acid, or niacin	x		
Normal pressure hydrocephalus	x		
Accidental hypothermia		x	
Chemical intoxications			
Heavy metals such as arsenic, lead, or mercury			x
Consciousness-altering agents			x
Carbon monoxide			x

Source: National Institute on Aging Task Force, "Senility Reconsidered: Treatment Possibilities for Mental Impairment in the Elderly," *Journal of the American Medical Association,* 244 (1980): 261.

perhaps between 5% and 15%, these conditions may be truly reversible with adequate medical and diagnostic treatment.

The Question of Reversibility through Training

The question of whether age-related cognitive decline can be reversed by training has been exciting the interest of gerontological specialists for the past decade. Simply put, do aging individuals have the intellectual plasticity or reserve capacity to improve their intellectual functioning with training? Is it possible to reverse the normal decline in specific aptitudes, such as memory, reasoning, and visuospatial ability, with practice? If it is possible to improve certain cognitive aptitudes, would the benefits apply to those with MCI as well as those with NCA?

The investigative team that first produced convincing results that aptitudes could be improved among older adults was Schaie and Willis and their colleagues. More than a decade ago, they reported improvement among 109 older subjects living in central Pennsylvania on reasoning, spatial ability, and attention tasks following five one-hour training sessions in small groups. Their gains were maintained at a six-month follow-up. These findings were confirmed by their later research with subjects from the Seattle Longitudinal Study.[37]

An early colleague from this team confirmed Schaie and Willis's findings with respect to these particular aptitudes.[38] This researcher divided 204 subjects (average age = 72) into experimental and control groups. The experimental subjects were given 10 one-hour cognitive training sessions. The results of pre-testing and post-testing showed that the experimental group improved significantly more than the control subjects.

It is more convincing when other investigators not connected with the original research team produce confirmatory findings. Hill, Storandt, and Simeone instructed a group of older subjects (average age = 70.33) to memorize a 30-item list of things they might pack for a trip (for example, a passport, a gray sweatshirt). After studying the list for up to fifteen minutes and following five minutes of distracting activity, the subjects were asked to recall as many of the items as possible. One group was given two hours of classroom instruction along with one night of homework using a memory training manual. Their post-test recall was substantially stronger than that of subjects who received no instruction.[39]

Rebok and Balcerak compared a group of older women and men given five hours of memory training and feedback with a matched sample who were not. The trained subjects had on average a greater recall of one-syllable nouns from a word list than did a control group. These investigators also discovered that abilities *not* targeted for instruction (digit recall in this case) were not improved.[40]

Others have found that memory can be enhanced either by following a how-to manual[41] or by participating in a group discussion focusing on interpersonal and emotional issues without specific training in memory enhancement.[42] To explore this question more closely, researchers tested female and male subjects (average age = 68.12) on several measures of verbal memory. They then were placed in one of three groups: no treatment; bibliotherapy in the form of reading a training manual on memory improvement; or bibliotherapy and supplemental discussions. After four 90-minute training sessions it was found that subjects given a training manual to read had significantly higher scores at post-test on measures of immediate and delayed recall than did the controls. The scores of those who had both bibliotherapy and discussion exceeded the training manual group.[43]

Recently, a meta-analysis of the literature on memory training was carried out.[44] This analysis looked at 33 studies that included 1,539 subjects with a mean age of 69.1 years. The defining factors for inclusion in this study were the following: healthy normal subjects over the age of 60, without evidence of disease-related cognitive impairment; use of some type of mnemonic training to improve memory performance; and a pre- and post-treatment measure of recall. Because many of the studies did not include control group comparisons, the procedure of control-treatment comparisons was abandoned for a focus on treatment gain. The study found that the effect size correlations for memory-trained groups were greater than for groups receiving no training apart from testing. Their scores were also higher than those of groups receiving a variety of non-memory-related treatments, such as concentration, feedback, information about aging, and relaxation training. The study did not find significant differences between the effectiveness of the different types of mnemonics used. Finally, these researchers confirmed the findings of Schaie and Willis that training was effective only for specifically targeted cognitive areas and not for non-targeted domains. Their analysis showed that four variables affected performance gains following training: a negative correlation of age to increased performance, and increased gains when pretraining was provided, when training was conducted in groups, and when the sessions were relatively short.

While these studies show that cognitive training can be beneficial, especially memory training, we are left with two nagging questions: Will these techniques work with an older group of subjects, and will they be effective with individuals who have MCI? We note that in several of the studies cited earlier, the subjects were clearly in what has been called the "young-old" group. Would these training techniques be effective with those in the eighth and ninth decades of life, or with those who may be cognitively impaired?

Willis and Schaie examined the differences in improvement through cognitive training among cohorts of 67, 74, and 81 year olds,[45] comparing the subjects' performance on spatial and reasoning skills. Following a short period of training, they found that the two youngest groups improved to a level above their initial testing on the Primary Mental Abilities (PMA) test 14 years previously in both spatial ability and reasoning. For the 81-year-olds, the cognitive training remediated their decline.

Willis and Schaie then examined this problem from the point of view of subjects who had either remained stable or declined in particular aptitudes over the 14-year interval. The criteria for change were scores on the reasoning and spatial components of the PMA tests. Those whose later test scores fell slightly below their scores at the first testing (equal to or less than -1 standard error of the means) were classified as "decliners" and the remainder as "stable." Both groups were divided into experimental and control conditions. Experimental subjects were given five one-hour training sessions over a two-week period in areas of weakness. Both groups improved with training specific to their pre-test scores compared with the controls. Abilities in the areas not targeted did not improve.

A major problem with these results, however, is that these subjects were *relative* decliners in comparison to previous testing. For many, the amount of decline would have been relatively small. There were no independent measures as to whether they were, in fact, suffering from early cognitive decline. Hill and co-workers took on this problem with a group of 102 older female and male subjects (average age = 75.4).[46] The subjects were pretested with the Mini-Mental State Examination[47] and were then given ten hours of group instruction in how to improve their ability to match names with faces and recall a list of words. Improvement was judged on the basis of pre- and post-test scores. Individuals who scored below 26 on the MMSE (indicating mild or more severe cognitive impairment) showed virtually no improvement in either recall of name/face or words. There was a stepwise gain in name/face recall by MMSE score: those with the highest scores of 29 or 30 nearly doubled the improvement of those with scores of 26 or 27. Few differences occurred in word list recall. The authors concluded that the relative degree of preexisting impairment governs the amount of improvement that is possible through training.

A difficulty with this conclusion is that although the MMSE is highly sensitive to more severe forms of dementia, it is a poor measure of MCI. For example, scores of 26 and greater are generally considered to be in the normal range, even for well-educated individuals.[48] Still, these results suggest that a lower level of intellectual functioning prior to training may limit the potential positive effects.

To our knowledge, only one study has compared documented elderly normals with individuals diagnosed as having AD.[49] These investigators studied three groups of patients with dementia of the Alzheimer type (DAT, a synonym for Alzheimer's disease) of varying degrees (mild, moderate, severe) and two groups of normal healthy adults averaging 73 and 82 years old. The objectives of the research were to determine three things: whether the recall of a word list could be improved by motor activity during the encoding phase; whether normals and DAT patients differed in their ability to utilize this motor encoding as an aid to memory; and whether the level of severity of these DAT patients affected their capacity to use motor encoding.

The motor encoding process, which was called Subject Performed Task (SPT), involved instructing the subject to carry out a physical activity when a particular word to be memorized was presented—for example, "lift a CUP," "put on a GLOVE." There were 25 words divided into five semantic categories (kitchen utensils, clothes, toys, drawing materials, and body parts) to be memorized while carrying out the SPT recall enhancement. Following the presentation of the words, the subjects were given five minutes to remember as many as possible during what was called a free recall (FR) period. After the subjects exhausted their memory, they were given the five semantic categories and asked to recall as many words as they could. This was called the cued recall (CR) phase.

Another group of subjects, consisting of two normal and three DAT categories, matched for age and gender, were given the same 25 words to recall in the form of sentences to be read aloud without the SPT enhancement. They were later asked to remember the words in exactly the same FR and CR conditions. The results of the experiment are shown in Figure 7.1. Three patterns immediately stand out in this figure. First, the use of motor acts accompanying the memorization task clearly improves the recall of all subjects, even those with severe DAT. Encoding using SPT made a dramatic

Mean number of items recalled

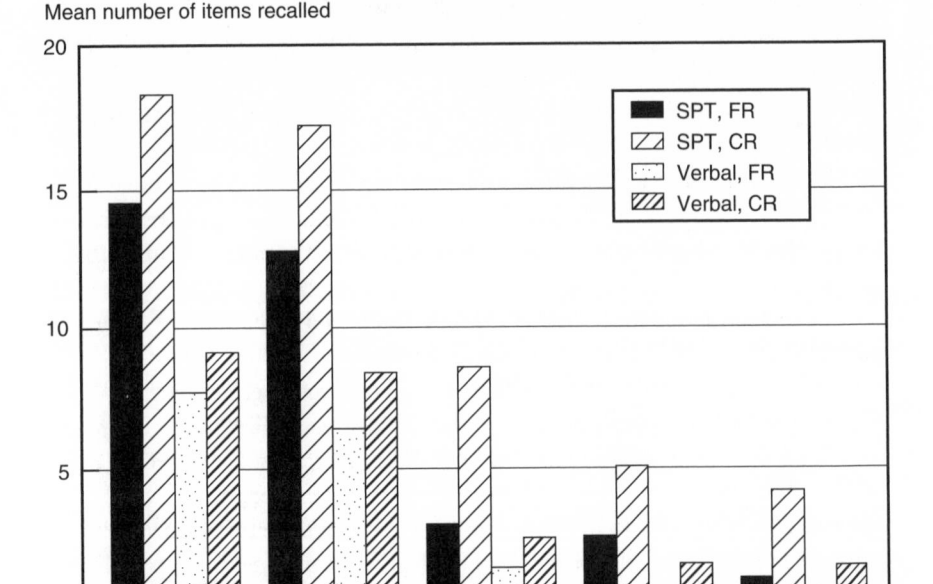

Figure 7.1 Mean number of items recalled by two groups of normal older adults (73- and 82-year-olds) and three groups of AD patients (mildly, moderately, and severely demented) in free (FR) and cued (CR) recall of subject performed tasks (SPT) and verbal commands. *Source:* Adapted from T. Karlsson et al., "Memory Improvement at Different Stages of Alzheimer's Disease," *Neuropsychologia,* 27 (1989): 737–742.

difference in the free recall of the word list among normal older subjects. The 73- and 82-year-olds given SPT remembered about twice as many words in the FR period as did those who merely read sentences aloud containing the words. The same relative differences were noted in the mildly and moderately impaired patients, though not in those with the more severe cases of SDAT.

The second pattern is that the cued recall of motor-enhanced memory made considerably more difference to the DAT patients than it did for the normal subjects. For example, 73-year-olds given CR following SPT improved their memory about 29% compared to the free recall phase. By contrast, the three DAT groups more than doubled their memory for motor task encoded words with cued recall. Indeed, the cued recall of SPT-reinforced memory among the mildly impaired and moderately impaired demented patients yielded scores that were in the same range as the free recall of sentences of the two normal groups.

A third pattern is that encoding with SPT is far more effective in absolute terms with the normal elderly than with those afflicted with DAT. SPT-enhanced memory among normals enabled them to remember well over two-thirds of the word list, whereas none of the DAT groups were able to bring back more than two words in the free recall condition.

How impressive it is to see how much improvement in mental skills can be achieved with relatively little intervention—in most cases fewer than 10 sessions. It is also remarkable that aptitudes *not* targeted for intervention remain unimproved. Certainly this argues for a much higher degree of plasticity in the cognition of seniors than has previously been imagined.

Yet despite these impressive results in improving cognitive functioning in older individuals, several questions remain unanswered. Some of these have been stated concisely by Park.[50] First, there is the question of generalizability. Do the improvements demonstrated in the laboratory setting extend to the real world? Notable, too, by their absence are nonpsychometric criteria by which the training effects could have been verified. Can a 76-year-old whose spatial relations skills were shown to be enhanced by training through improved pre-test and post-test scores find her car in a mall's parking lot more reliably than before? Can an older man better remember the names of his son and daughter-in-law's friends upon first meeting them more accurately than he did in the past? Also among the missing ingredients in these studies are pre- and post-training reports by the subjects themselves, or by informants who know the individuals well, concerning cognitive changes. It seems reasonable to want to know whether higher scores on tests of word list memory are reflected in a subjective sense of improvement in everyday life, such as recalling where certain things are around the house, memory for magazine or newspaper article contents, or remembering what the TV newscaster said a few moments ago, the names of new neighbors, or whether certain items from a grocery list have already been put into the shopping cart. Ideally, this information would be provided by the subjects themselves and by someone close to the subject prior to and following the intervention.

The second question concerns individual differences. It has been pointed out that the relationship between individual differences and training outcomes is a neglected area of research and merits considerable further study.[51] Though large numbers of subjects have benefited from cognitive training, many have not. In the study mentioned earlier by Willis and Schaie, about a quarter of the subjects rated as cognitive decliners and a third of the "stables" did not improve in reasoning.[52] In spatial areas, 37.3% of the decliners and more than half (52.9%) of the stables failed to show significant improvement. A number of differences among individuals might explain the disparity in training outcomes. Certainly, one possibility is the age of the subjects: older individuals seem to need more intervention to improve. Another is the cognitive status of the subjects prior to training. We learned from the studies of Hill and colleagues,[53] Karlsson and associates,[54] and others that lower levels of functioning are correlated with lower rates of improvement. There is also the matter of the effect of certain personality traits. Consider, for example, the characteristics of compliance and motivation. If subjects are matched for cognitive status, are those with more desire to please the examiners or a greater need for achievement more likely to improve with training than are those with lower scores on a scale of compliance and motivation? Physical energy is another factor that may influence outcome: more vigorous individuals may outperform those with less energy. Finally, socioeconomic status may be a factor in who improves and who does not with training.

As an example of how individual differences can influence training, consider a study carried out with active and inactive elderly subjects in southern California.[55] Half of them were from lower income levels and half were not. The investigators divided these subjects into three groups to determine whether different types of instruction would result in higher levels of training-related cognitive improvement. The gains of the three elderly samples were then compared with the improvement of a group of undergraduates at the University of California at Irvine. All subjects were given a free and cued word recall test under four graduated levels of support from the examiner: (1) Free-Free recall (subjects were presented with a list of 10 words to memorize with no mnemonic aids and then asked to recall as many as possible); (2) Free-Cued (same as above with the addition of the subject being given a short description of the word to be retrieved prior to recall—"a type of bird," or "part of a tree"); (3) Cued-Free (the mnemonic aid given during the presentation only—"used in schools, BOOK"); (4) Cued-Cued (mnemonic aids given at both the representation and retrieval phases). The results of this study are shown in Table 7.8.

Two interesting findings emerge from these results which do not bear directly on the experiment but are nonetheless of interest. First, the amount

Table 7.8 Mean scores on three experimental tasks

Task and Condition	Group			
	Old 3	Old 2	Old 1	Young
Word Generation				
Letter	8.5	12.1	20.6	21.0
Category	9.3	10.8	15.2	17.5
Paired Associates				
High	3.9	5.1	6.3	6.9
Low	0.5	2.0	2.4	3.6
Word Recall				
Cued-Cued	5.5	7.3	8.1	7.8
Cued-Free	2.2	5.4	5.8	5.6
Free-Cued	2.2	4.5	5.3	5.8
Free-Free	2.4	4.6	4.7	6.0

Source: F. I. M. Craik, M. Byrd, and J. M. Swanson, "Patterns of Memory Loss in Three Elderly Samples," *Psychology and Aging,* 2 (1987): 82.

of improvement from the Free-Free to the Cued-Cued conditions is greater among the three older groups than in the young subjects. This would suggest that there is significant plasticity in older individuals in terms of their capacity to improve with assistance. Second, the Old 1 subjects performed nearly as well as the college students half a century younger on most recall tasks. This reminds us that the differences in mental functioning between older and younger individuals can be relatively small.

The experimenters interpreted these results as showing that cognitive gains among older subjects should be viewed as a complex function of the particular tasks, the type of instruction, and subject characteristics. In this case, the more active older subjects (Old 1 and Old 2) improved in graduated increments from the Free-Free to the Cued-Free and then again to the Cued-Cued conditions. The less active Old 3 subjects improved only with substantially greater mnemonic instruction. The authors pointed out that the more affluent subjects in the Old 1 group also differed from the others in years of education and initial vocabulary, both of which are highly correlated with intellectual ability. However, the more active subjects and the less active Old 1 subjects did not differ on either of these dimensions. This suggests that the level of physical and intellectual activity may be strongly associated with the type of training intervention required to enhance cognitive functioning.

A third question is "what causes the improvement?" It has been shown that group support and training, both individually and together, are associated with enhanced intellectual performance. It also has been shown by Willis and Schaie that merely the act of testing and retesting individuals whose aptitudes had declined over a 14-year period resulted in the restoration of test performance to the pre-decline level. For instance, in spatial abilities, testing alone reversed the 14-year decline in subjects averaging 67 and 74 years of age. Retesting had the same positive effect for 67-year-olds in reasoning. The 81-year-olds did not improve with retesting only.[56]

The durability of the cognitive remediation programs is the fourth question. How long might we expect someone's improved memory to endure after the training program ends? A review of more than a decade of research on maintenance by Willis points out that most investigations have not included an assessment of the stability of the gains several months afterward.[57] Those studies which have assessed the maintenance progress at six- or twelve-month intervals have found that the initial gains were maintained for one to twelve months.[58] Factors other than training may affect cognitive performance on retest. For instance, could it be that subjects' merely knowing that they will be followed up in one, six, or twelve months raises the probability that their improvement will be maintained? An analogy is the man who attended a weight loss clinic and shed 20 pounds. His motivation to keep the weight off is likely to be increased by the knowledge that he is part of a research project that will follow up on him at regular intervals. By contrast, those in a class who lost the same amount may be less motivated to control their eating habits if no provision is made for follow-up. Some confirmation for this theory comes from the research of Blieszner and colleagues, who noted that control subjects retested six months after the completion of cognitive training showed as much test score improvement as did experimental subjects.[59]

A final question concerns the independent verification of the stability of the cognitive improvement due to training. Certainly, results showing that higher levels of intellectual functioning are maintained at six months and beyond are impressive. There is always the possibility, however, of examiner bias effect.[60] Sometimes subjects perform better because they feel the examiner wants them to or because the latter provides encouragement, reassurance, or other subtle cues that result in improved test scores. A notable gap in the training literature is the blind assessment of the experimental and control subjects by independent investigators.

Overall, then, there is reason to be optimistic about the improvement in cognitive functioning due to training. Thus far, the relative changes have been measured and not manipulated. In order to understand what kinds of training work best with what types of subjects, we will need to work with much larger groups, subdivided by individual qualities such as social class, with experimental groups being given different types of training interventions ranging from test-retest to more comprehensive approaches. Different approaches to maintenance also need to be evaluated. Finally, training needs to be judged by independent investigators who are blind to the experimental or control status of the subjects.

8

Normal Cognitive Aging

Many people are interested in finding out about the specific characteristics of normal cognitive aging (NCA), perhaps because they are wondering whether they themselves or someone they know is cognitively normal. This chapter will focus on the problem of how to define normal cognitive aging from an empirical perspective. Using several different statistical criteria, we will demarcate four subtypes of NCA using a cognitive test instrument such as MicroCog. We will apply these four standards for normalcy to both the MDs and Normals over 65. Then we will calculate the percentage in each group that would be classified as NCA using these criteria. These statistical alternatives will be explored from the point of view of the trade-offs each involves with respect to false positives and false negatives. Finally, we will address practical issues related to screening for NCA.

Defining NCA

Hearing of our research on cognitive aging in physicians, a 65-year-old surgeon affiliated with a large teaching hospital came to see one of us because he was not sure how long he should continue to practice. Now that the age ceiling at his university for mandatory retirement (66) had been lifted, he was not certain whether he should continue his work as an active surgeon. He still took difficult cases and worked a demanding schedule beginning at 6 A.M. As far as he could tell, he was as able in his surgery as he had ever been, but lately he had noticed he was having difficulty recalling the names of new residents. The previous week, on returning from a professional meeting, he had difficulty remembering where he had left his car in a large multi-level airport parking lot. And just this morning, he had opened the refrigerator door and could not remember why he had done it.

The surgeon went on to say that he had consulted an internist, who, after an examinination, told him that he was "just fine." The surgeon was not reassured. He pressed the internist about the criteria being used to assess his mental status and received a reply to the effect that he was a great deal sharper than most 65-year-olds he knew, and besides he didn't exhibit any of the classical signs of Alzheimer's disease.

The surgeon realized that one of the reasons he was not reassured was that the doctor and the patient had very different frames of reference. The internist had in mind the criteria for AD and his extensive experience examining other post-60-year-olds when he said the surgeon was functioning normally. The surgeon's frame of reference was himself at age 40 or 50; in those years he prided himself on his memory and had never had the lapses he recently experienced. Thus, his frame of reference indicated that he was not functioning as before. But was he still normal? He wanted to continue his surgical practice and teaching, but if his symptoms foreshadowed AD, or something equally ominous, then he would have to begin to make other plans.

The surgeon's concerns mirror the anxieties of thousands of older individuals at every level of employment and every walk of life who observe in themselves word/number/name-finding problems or difficulties with memory, orientation, or calculation skills. They want to know, "Am I normal?" This question illustrates the importance of providing ways of defining the boundaries separating normal cognitive aging from mild cognitive impairment.

The emphasis in this chapter will be on statistical models for characterizing NCA, while recognizing that this is only one perspective, one way of thinking about cognitive normalcy. Although we strongly believe that an empirical means of delimiting the normal condition is necessary as well as quite useful to clinicians and concerned patients alike, these are not stand-alone criteria. The assessment of an individual's cognitive status would normally include a careful history, information from collateral sources, and medical and other tests. It is from this comprehensive assessment that the most valid judgment can be made as to whether or not a person is functioning normally. We believe, however, that well-validated cognitive tests can be an important part of the response when questions of normal functioning arise.

Four Empirical Criteria for NCA

In an article on normal aging of the central nervous system, the Canadian neurologists Calne, Eisen, and Meneilly point to the need to define the normal elderly so that we can more fully understand those changes in cognition which occur in individuals free of diagnosable diseases of the nervous system.[1] They believe that the concept of NCA can be defined by statistical means. For instance, NCA might be represented by an overall test score falling within two standard errors of the mean of the average for a given population, as suggested by Calne and Calne.[2] Though we would disagree with the arbitrary setting of the normal range as being within the relatively small span of two standard errors of the mean, we do concur that a well-validated cognitive test can provide findings that can be a valid statistical basis for setting score thresholds for NCA.

Let us now return to the surgeon with the question of whether he is functioning normally. The value of having a test such as MicroCog with adequate sensitivity to cognitive impairment and specificity for NCA is that it enables us to apply a descriptive statistical model to define distinct types of "normal" cognition. This model can be used with scores generated by MicroCog or similar cognitive screening instruments. We should keep in mind that such comparisons presume the existence of a normative group who share characteristics in common with the individuals being tested. These include demographics well known to be associated with scores on ability tests, such as years of education, race, socioeconomic status, and gender.

The four statistical criteria for NCA are listed in Table 8.1. The table shows that no matter what standards we apply, we are defining as normal a much larger group than Calne and Calne suggest. The reason is that their definition of normalcy restricts the range to those who are within two standard errors of the average score on a cognitive test. To illustrate the problem with this definition, we can use the 112 subjects aged 65–69 from our MD sample. The average total MicroCog score for this group is about 81% correct, and the standard deviation is 7%. Calne and Calne's definition of normal would embrace those with a total MicroCog score of 79.7% to 82.6%. This would include only about 16 of the 112 MDs, which seems too small a group. We believe that statistical criteria that include a larger share of the individuals in the older age groups would be more useful in defining NCA.

The first empirical definition of NCA, Age Group Normative, is based on

Table 8.1   Four statistical criteria for normal cognitive aging*

1. *Age Group Normative*
   Based on overall test battery score placing the individual in the percentage of his or her age cohort thought not likely to be cognitively impaired on the basis of re-search reports of the incidence of AD (for example, the top 97.2% of 65–69 year olds).

2. *Probably Not Impaired*
   Based on a test battery cutting score validly identifying the presence or absence of cognitive impairment with at least 85% sensitivity and specificity (for example, MicroCog total test score higher than 60%).

3. *Reference Group Normative*
   Based on an overall test battery score placing the individual in the top 99% of a healthy reference group (for example, doctors aged 45–64).

4. *Reference Group Plus*
   Same as No. 3 with the additional criterion that no more than one component abil-ity score (for example, attention, memory, visuospatial ability, reasoning, or calcu-lation) can be lower than the 15th percentile.

*Based on a standardization group balanced for education, SES, race, and gender.

an overall test battery score placing the individual at that percentage thought to be normal on the basis of research estimating the incidence of AD within each age group. For instance, if we think that the percentage of AD is about 2.8% for those aged 65–69 and 11.2% for women and men aged 75–79, we then adjust the cutoff percentile thresholds so that the top 97.2% of the 65–69 year olds (100% minus 2.8% likely to have AD) and the upper 88.8% of 75–79 year olds (100% minus 11.2% likely to have AD) would fall into the NCA category. Actually, the 80+ estimate is an average of the proportions found among those in three age categories: ages 80–84, 85–89, and 90+. The actual percentages estimated for these age groups are 15%, 25%, and 35%, respectively. Using the percentage estimates of AD by age group given in Chapter 7, we can calculate the percentage of NCA for each group. The percentage in each five-year age category who would be classified as NCA by the Age Group Normative criterion is shown in Table 8.2.

A limitation of this statistical approach to demarcating NCA is that it is dependent on highly variable estimates of the proportion of the population with AD, especially below age 70 and beyond 85. As the criteria for AD be-come more accurate and are applied to the youngest-old and the elderly, these percentages will stabilize.

Table 8.2 Percentage of MDs and Normals meeting four different empirical criteria for normal cognition by age group

Age Group	N		1 Age Group Normative	2 Probably Not Impaired		3 Reference Group Normative		4 Reference Group Plus	
	MDs	Normals		MDs	Normals	MDs	Normals	MDs	Normals
65–69	112	155	97.2	99.1	94.8	98.2	96.1	76.8	74.8
70–74	98	192	94.4	96.9	86.5	94.9	88.5	57.1	49.5
75–79	100	47	88.8	88.0	76.6	83.0	70.2	39.0	42.5
80+	46	12	68.5	69.5	66.7	65.2	66.7	23.9	33.3

Notes: (1) Age Group Normative criteria are calculated by doubling the percentages in Table 7.4 so as to include mild as well as moderate and severe AD. (2) Percentage of cognitive impairment in 80+ age group is estimated from the median percentage of AD for subjects aged 80 and over from Table 7.5. (3) The Reference Group Normative standard for the MD subjects is a MicroCog total of 69% correct. For the Normals, it is 60%.

Now let us return to the surgeon's problem. The advantage of applying this criterion to him is that he can compare himself with a cohort who shared similar cultural, historical, and educational experiences. The disadvantages of this criterion are equally apparent. For this surgeon's purpose, being above the lowest 2.8% for his age group, or even in the top half of a sample of doctors, is not particularly reassuring because he has always believed that he was far more capable than average.

The second criterion, Probably Not Impaired, is based on the valid identification of cognitive impairment by a test battery cutoff score. This threshold is based on a high degree of demonstrated sensitivity to AD and specificity for NCA. In this case, the total MicroCog threshold score for NCA is set at 60% correct. It is based on the accurate identification of individuals documented to be cognitively normal and impaired by the Atlanta validity study, as described in Chapter 3. This metric for NCA may be somewhat more reassuring for our surgeon, since it tells him that he is not likely to be in the early stages of dementia. It does not, however, relieve him of the anxiety as to whether he is losing ground in comparison to his prime. Here criteria 3 and 4 are more useful.

Ideally, the best way to tell if we are "losing it" mentally is to compare present measurements of intellectual functioning with previous test scores. Presuming that a person was not assessed in his or her prime, the second best way of judging someone's capability is by comparing that person with a reference group, in this case doctors aged 45–64. This criterion assumes that only those in the bottom 1% of a group of community-dwelling, responsibly employed physicians are vulnerable to impairment. This means that the other 99% are likely to be functioning normally. This also presumes an overall score on our cognitive screening test above the cutoff threshold for cognitive impairment. In this case that is exactly what happens, as the top 99% of a group of 45–64 year old doctors score above 85% correct on MicroCog. This is 25 percentage points higher than the boundary for Alzheimer's disease.

"But wait," the surgeon says. "You really can't judge me on the basis of an overall score." He correctly surmises that one problem with using a total score to differentiate NCA from dementia is that strong aptitudes in some areas may compensate for diminishing skills in other domains, giving a false impression of normalcy. Therefore, the total score is misleading. This problem can be overcome by applying the Reference Group Plus criteria, which involves what might be called a "global-specific" approach. To be appraised as being within normal limits on MicroCog, an individual must meet two conditions: having a total score in the top 99% of the Reference Group; and having no more than one aptitude component score (for example, attention, memory, visuospatial ability, reasoning, or calculation) below one standard deviation or the 15th percentile for that same population. The second condition is based on the standards for AD shown in Table 1.1, which stipulate that for the diagnosis to be made, more than one cognitive domain must be compromised.

Applying the Four Standards to Our Samples

If we were to graph the percentage of those defined as cognitively normal in our data sets, we could examine these four different standards for NCA from the point of view of both scientific findings and common sense. From a scientific perspective, do the proportions of individuals who would be assessed as NCA on the basis of their test scores follow the ratios described by others? Do the numbers of individuals in our samples assessed as normal conform to the findings of those who have reported on the percentage of elderly subjects who continue to function at the same level as adults in their prime?

Table 8.2 shows the percentages of physicians and Normals aged 65 and older who meet three standards for NCA on MicroCog. Criterion 1, Age Group Normative, is provided in this table as a frame of reference for the other percentages. The curves tracing the percentages of those defined as statistically NCA on the basis of the increasingly rigorous criteria 2, 3, and 4 show slopes familiar to clinicians and researchers alike in the field of gerontology. This is especially true of the MD sample, whose percentages for Probably Not Impaired conform closely to Age Group Normative statistics. Using the Probably Not Impaired criterion, we see that relatively little decline occurs prior to age 70. Just one of the MDs aged 65–69 would fail to be classified as NCA according to criterion 2. Only 3.1% of those 70–74 and only 12% of the 75–79 MDs fall short of criterion 2. But beyond age 80, the percentage of those functioning normally drops to 69.5%.

The proportion of both samples meeting the standards for NCA diminishes as the criteria become more rigorous, especially among the older subjects. Among the 75–79 year old MDs, for example, approximately nine out of ten function normally according to criterion 2, but only 39.0% meet the Reference Group Plus standards. The Reference Group Plus criteria drastically thin out the ranks of both the MDs and Normals. At ages 65–69, criterion 4 finds just over three-quarters of the MDs functioning normally; at 70–74, the proportion of physicians measuring up dips to 57.1. In the 75–79 half-decade, fewer than four doctors in ten would be classified as normal using this standard, while at 80+, 23.9% of the physicians would be called NCA by Reference Group Plus criteria.

For the most part, the percentages of Normal subjects meeting the three different standards for NCA follow the same pattern as for the MDs. In comparing the Normals and MDs on criteria 3 and 4, we need to keep in mind that the two groups must meet different standards to be judged as NCA. Each group of post–65 year old subjects is being compared with its own reference group of 45–64 year olds. In order to be classified as NCA according to criterion 3, the total score to be exceeded for the Normal reference group is 60%, whereas the physicians must exceed a total MicroCog score of 69%.

Slightly smaller numbers of Normals conform to the Probably Not Impaired criteria for NCA. The proportional differences are greatest in the 70–74 and 75–79 age groups. It is possible that the physicians in these age groups were a more select population. A large number of the MDs in their seventies were continuing to work, while the majority of the Normals were retired. Perhaps some of those who were retired left the work force because of cognitive problems. Indirect support for this hypothesis comes from interviews conducted by the University of Michigan's Institute for Social Research with 12,600 persons aged 51–61 as they approached or entered retirement.[3] The investigators found that about 20% of those individuals reported health conditions (such as heart problems, strokes, or lung disease) that either limited their work (6.5%) or forced them to retire on disability (13.5%). Although we know from the data presented in Chapter 5 that we must be cautious in assuming that poorer health is directly associated with lower levels of intellectual functioning, it may well be that a minority of our retired older Normal subjects left their jobs because of physical problems that may have adversely affected their mental processes.

A second possible hypothesis explaining the difference between the MDs and the Normals is that higher levels of education do provide some degree of cushioning against the onset of cognitive impairment in the decade of the seventies. Though mental decline clearly occurs among the better educated MDs just as with the Normals, the proportion of physicians rated as NCA by criterion 2 is about 10% greater than for those with fewer years of education. After age 80, the differences between the groups are not significant and look very much like the estimates for the general population.

We do not mean to take too pessimistic a tone in commenting on the decreasing proportions of those who would be categorized as NCA among the older MDs or Normals. It is surely heartening to find that, among these volunteers, two-thirds of the combined MD and Normal subjects under age 80 were functioning on MicroCog at a level comparable to those in their prime of life (criterion 3). Moreover, a third of the Normals aged 80+ measured up to the most stringent criterion 4 standards for NCA. These proportions, incidentally, are remarkably similar to those found by Benton, Eslinger, and Damasio a decade ago. They reported that one in three of their 80-year-olds functioned as well as subjects aged 16–65 in 11 cognitive tasks.[4]

We do not imagine that NCA can be identified solely by using computerized screening batteries such as MicroCog or any other individual test. We take seriously the reservations of others[5] about any single criterion for NCA being used as a standard by which this condition could be judged. Moreover, a test score or a battery of scores should not be independent of the subject's history, the observations of others, and clinical judgment.

Still, we must begin somewhere if we wish to define NCA by some standard other than the absence of Alzheimer's disease. We propose that scores on reliable and valid screening tests such as MicroCog could be used as a first step in defining NCA. The virtues of using empirical criteria rather than clinical guidelines (presuming, for the moment, that standards for NCA do indeed exist) are at least two: greater reliability and greater flexibility. There is little doubt of the first advantage. Computerized and other types of cognitive tests provide a consistent picture of a person's level of intellectual functioning, and scores from such testing can be compared against a particular threshold for NCA. The second virtue is that the empirical standards for NCA can be adjusted depending upon how rigorous the definition of NCA needs to be.

Problems of False Positives and False Negatives

As the citizens of the United States and elsewhere grow older, many will want to continue employment, and when the baby boomers begin retiring, many more will continue to be needed in their jobs. This brings us back to the question we have raised on several occasions: Can a cognitive test such as MicroCog help make the distinction between those older individuals who are impaired and those who are not? This larger question can be divided into three separate but related smaller questions. First, can a screening test accurately tell the difference between the NCAs and those with dementia? Second, can a screening test distinguish between the NCAs and the MCIs without a large number of those in either group being misclassified as false positives or false negatives? Finally, what should happen to someone in his prime who fails the screening test?

We addressed the first question at some length in Chapter 3, where the results of the Atlanta and other validation studies were discussed. There we found that MicroCog accurately identified both NCA and MCI subjects with 81% to 90% accuracy. Although these results require confirmation by others before a test like this could be used for screening purposes, no doubt exists in our minds that in a short time this test, or better ones, will be refined to the point where they could be used for this task.

The second question is far more complex. Picking out accurately those who are NCA from those subjects who are impaired in an older population while avoiding large numbers of false positives and false negatives is a remarkably challenging problem. The reader may recall that false positives are those normally functioning individuals who are inaccurately said to be impaired because their score falls below the cutoff threshold on a test. False negatives are individuals called normal on the basis of a test score when in fact they are impaired. An extreme example illustrates the difference between false positives and false negatives: If we set the cutoff score for NCA at the 99th percentile on a test and label anyone below that boundary as impaired, we are sure to have identified all those with AD, but we also will have screened out a huge proportion of those who are normal. If, on the other hand, we set the cutoff score at the 10th percentile, we have avoided the false positive problem because we call nearly everyone normal. This is at the cost, however, of labeling as normal a large number of those who are in fact cognitively impaired.

Overall, the rarer the condition, the greater will be the number of false positives relative to true positives. This causes significant problems when screening for normal cognitive aging. Imagine that we have three well-educated people consulting us about whether they are NCA. The first is the 65-year-old surgeon described earlier; the second is a 78-year-old widow with the question of whether she is functioning well enough intellectually to continue to live on her own; and the third is a 60-year-old airline pilot who wants to know whether he is mentally sharp enough to continue to fly. Imagine further that the only way we have as the first step in assessing the cognitive skills of these three individuals is to give them a test such as MicroCog.

From our Atlanta validation study, described in Chapter 3, we know that MicroCog will actually identify NCA and MCI about nine times out of ten using a threshold score of 60% correct. In the Atlanta study, however, we knew in advance that about 50% of the subjects were normal and 50% impaired. But suppose the incidence rate for dementia is not 50% but much lower. Looking at Table 8.2, we see that for the 65-year-old surgeon, the incidence rate is 2.8%; for the widow, the proportion of people in her age group likely to be cognitively impaired is 11.2%; and for the pilot, we estimate that about 1.4% of those aged 60 to 64 will be compromised intellectually.

These incidence rates result in very different probabilities for both false positives and false negatives as well as for true positives and true negatives. Table 8.3 summarizes these theoretical frequencies for 1,000 individuals. As we can see, the test does a pretty good job of picking out those who are impaired. At a 1% incidence rate, only one cognitively impaired person slips through the net; and at 10%, only 10 of the 100 positives escape detection. By far the biggest problem with these various incidence rates is the true positive to false positive ratio. At an incidence rate of 10%, the widow has about a 50-50 chance of a positive reading on MicroCog being a false alarm. At a 3% frequency of cognitive impairment in the population, a positive reading on our test for the surgeon is likely to be erroneous 3.6 times more often than it is correct. The 60-year-old pilot has the most difficult problem of all: 11 times out of 12, a positive finding is likely to be a false

Table 8.3 Hypothetical number of true positives and false positives, true negatives and false negatives in 1,000 subjects assuming four different percentages of the true incidence of cognitive impairment

True Incidence of Impairment (%)	Number in 1,000 individuals who will be:				
	True Positive	False Positive	True Negative	False Negative	TOTAL
1.0	9	99	891	1	1,000
3.0	27	97	873	3	1,000
5.0	45	95	855	5	1,000
10.0	90	90	810	10	1,000

Note: Calculations based on a test with 90% sensitivity and specificity.

positive. We should emphasize, however, that this is merely a statistical model and that the true positive to false positive ratio may be different in reality than in statistical extrapolations.

Where we set the cutoff score separating NCA from dementia can also influence the ratio of true positives to false positives. A numerical picture of the false positive/false negative trade-offs when different threshold scores are used is shown in Table 8.4, drawn from the Atlanta validation study.[6] From this table we can quickly confirm that the highest threshold score yields the highest number of false positives (34 out of 50), while the lowest cutoff score carries with it the largest share of false negatives. In the middle, between 68% and 63% correct, the number of each is relatively low, 10 at the former threshold and 11 at the latter. The types of errors are quite different. At the higher cutoff score, the proportion of false positives and false negatives is about equal (6 and 4). At the lower threshold, however, 9 of the misclassifications are false negatives, misidentifying someone who is impaired as normal.

We might wish to apply the lower cutoff score in situations where the consequences of a false negative are relatively benign. For example, if the task were to use a test such as MicroCog to advise the otherwise healthy elderly community-dwelling widow as to whether she is cognitively capable of living independently, the 63% cutoff score might be appropriate because we might wish to err on the side of maintaining individuals with MCI in the community rather than putting them in nursing homes. We might use the lower threshold because at this level the screening test still has adequate sensitivity to diminished cognition. Over 80% of the subjects scoring lower than the threshold are likely to be impaired, though we will miss 17 out of

Table 8.4 Atlanta Validation Study: Number of false negatives and false positives
for different choices of threshold scores

MicroCog Total Threshold Score for NCA (% correct)	Number of False Positives (N = 50)	Number of False Negatives (N = 52)
82	34	0
77	24	1
73	13	2
68	6	4
63	2	9
60	2	11
58	0	16

the 100 who are false negatives. However, because occurrences such as occasional lapses of memory or mild disorientation have relatively minor consequences for someone living in a community, we might be willing to accept this type of error for this group.

Now, suppose the consequences of a false negative were not benign. Imagine that our task is to screen those individuals wishing to continue into their seventh, eighth, and ninth decade who hold down intellectually demanding positions where the impact of a failing memory, disorientation, or reduced analytical skills could have lethal consequences for others—physicians and other health care workers, pilots, ship captains, and nuclear reactor operators. In these cases we might wish to use a high cutoff score, which greatly lowers the probability of a false positive. Studying Table 8.4, we can immediately anticipate a massive false-positive problem if we apply either of the Reference Group cutoff scores. Imagine for the moment that the 50 Normal subjects in the Atlanta Validation Study were older pilots who wished to continue to fly. Let us also assume that 77% correct is the Reference Group cutoff score for active pilots. That threshold would accurately screen out all but one of the impaired flyers, but it would call into question the intellectual capacity of 24 out of 50 pilots who were certifiably normal.

It is likely that refinements in the scoring of computerized cognitive screening tests can further reduce the incidence of both false negatives and false positives. If we go back and study the false negatives in the Atlanta validation study, we would find that applying the Reference Group Plus criteria enables us to pick out 4 of the 10 impaired subjects who scored above the 68% threshold. Another way to improve the sensitivity of tests such as MicroCog without producing a dramatic increase in false positives or false negatives is to use overall response time (RT). Performance on many cognitive tests is characterized by the trade-offs between speed and accuracy. By slowing down and double-checking, a subject can buy accuracy at the expense of speed. Thus, someone who scores 68% correct on MicroCog in an hour has, in an important sense, accomplished more than a person who takes two hours. These differences in overall RT can help detect those borderline individuals whose accuracy scores provide a misleading picture of their cognitive status. Although this work is still in the developmental phase, we are optimistic that a combination of the use of component scores and awarding bonus points for RT can play an important role in distinguishing true positives from false positives and true negatives from false negatives.

A Provisional Screening Protocol

Our third question with respect to screening for NCA was what happens if an individual scores below the threshold? In our view, a three-step procedure should be followed if the person being assessed wishes to proceed. First, an immediate retest should be scheduled, unless the individual has found the testing aversive and wants to move directly to a more comprehensive assessment. If another low score is obtained, the second step would be to carry out a complete medical, neurological, and neuropsychological workup. We recall from Chapter 7 that approximately 10% of those initially diagnosed with AD turned out to have reversible conditions. It is possible that a more comprehensive evaluation would find the individual functioning within normal limits, contravening the results of the short screening battery.

For those individuals requiring a full evaluation, the testing process should be done by a skilled full-service team recognized for its expertise in the diagnosis and management of dementia. There are excellent comprehensive diagnostic services in nearly every large city hospital or medical school setting in this country and elsewhere. Each has a slightly different protocol. Examples are the Cambridge Mental Disease of the Elderly Examination (CAMDEX) reported by O'Connor and colleagues[7] and the Clinical Dementia Rating (CDR) system described by Morris and associates.[8] Another approach was designed by our colleague Dr. Sandra Weintraub of

Harvard Medical School.[9] This clinical protocol can be summarized in the following steps:

1. *Neurological Examination:* The initial evaluation takes approximately 1.5 hours and consists of a careful medical, neurological, and psychiatric history (personal and family), a brief physical examination, elementary neurological examination, and mental status review. In the case of Alzheimer's disease, the elementary neurological exam is usually unremarkable. However, entities such as Parkinson's disease, supranuclear ophthalmoplegia, and stroke syndromes are all accompanied by recognizable neurological symptoms and signs.

2. *Neuropsychological Examination:* A full battery of standard neuropsychological tests is administered in a test session that may take from four to six hours depending on the speed with which the client works. This is typically done over the course of a day with breaks to prevent fatigue. The neuropsychological examination explores the patient's level of ability in attention and concentration functions, learning and memory, language, reasoning, visuospatial abilities, and motor skills. Patterns of performance are identified and combined with information from the neurological examination and the imaging studies to arrive at a diagnosis. In AD, it is very often the neuropsychological examination that is the only sign of abnormality. Certain patterns can appear on testing that are suggestive of reversible dementias rather than AD. For example, in AD the classical pattern is one in which attention tests may be performed normally but memory tests are failed. In contrast, in patients with normal pressure hydrocephalus, the reverse pattern may prevail. Finally, the neuropsychological examination provides valuable information that can be used to counsel the client and family with respect to management. For example, if the major problem is one of attention (as it often is in individuals with depression), then strategies such as oral repetition of instructions or written reminders can help to compensate for forgetfulness. If, on the other hand, the testing reveals an amnestic syndrome with intact attention, these strategies will not work and the client will likely need to have greater supervision of activities. The clinician also evaluates the available support systems and the need for services so that appropriate referrals can be made for community-based resources.

3. *Psychiatric Examination:* In the psychiatric evaluation, the patient's history and current affective state are highlighted in an hour-long interview. The presence of psychosocial stressors is explored, and the use of medications with psychoactive properties that might affect test performance is reviewed.

4. *Imaging Studies:* There are many illnesses that cannot be distinguished

on clinical grounds from AD. The magnetic resonance (MR) and computerized tomography (CT) scans are used not to confirm AD but to rule out "look-alikes" such as tumors, strokes, hydrocephalus, and subdural hematoma. There is some debate about which imaging study to use, since there are pros and cons for each. The MR has higher resolution and demonstrates brain anatomy with remarkable clarity, but there are often features that are uninterpretable (the so-called "UBOs" or "Unidentified Bright Objects" that are seen in the scans of many elderly patients). The EEG is used to look for evidence of seizures, toxic/metabolic encephalopathy, and waveforms that are characteristic of rare dementing illnesses such as Jakob-Creutzfeldt disease.

5. *Laboratory Tests:* A routine battery of tests includes electrolytes, glucose, creatinine, blood urea nitrogen (BUN), liver and thyroid function tests, B12 and folate levels, syphilis screening, and complete blood count. Special tests (for example, rheumatoid factor, Lyme and HIV titers) are ordered as deemed appropriate in the individual case.

If the results of the more comprehensive study also return the verdict that the individual is functioning well below normal limits, the third step is to help the person and his or her family begin to plan for the future, depending on the individual and the situation. For the pilot and, perhaps, for the surgeon, the question is what to do when flying or medicine is no longer a career option. For the elderly widow, the question is more likely to revolve around ways to remain as independent as possible while obtaining necessary support.

When the diagnosis is clarified, the client and family (or significant others) may benefit from meeting with a trained clinical social worker to discuss needs for support and counseling services as well as recommendations for community resources and services to which the client is entitled. In the case of a dementing illness, the social worker can help the client and family to prepare and plan for the future. A referral network should be available for channeling the client to the appropriate health provider (for example, rheumatologist, cardiologist, endocrinologist). Speech pathology, audiology, or occupational and physical therapy services may also be appropriate.

The team approach has a number of advantages. First, one member of the team is identified as the coordinator for the case, so the complete workup is synthesized for the client. The evaluation process allows the client and family to come to grips slowly with what is often a devastating diagnosis. Finally, the evaluation method outlined here is thorough, leaving no stone unturned.

9

Optimal Cognitive Aging

In their article on successful aging, Rowe and Kahn make the crucial point that research in this field has been too much concerned with documenting losses associated with growing older *between* age groups and has not focused enough on the growing differences *within* age groups.[1] We know from the data presented in Chapter 4 that the variability among our subjects within the decades rose far more rapidly than overall ability declined. A large proportion of the MD and Normal subjects in our samples continued to perform at a high level on MicroCog well into their seventies and eighties in spite of the declining average performance of their age groups.

It is these people, the optimal cognitive aging group, who are the focus of this chapter. The optimal cognitive agers—who have been called "successful," "supernormal," "productive," or just "the elite"—have been a much-neglected population in gerontology. Yet it seems important to study these individuals for a number of reasons. First, the study of those in the optimal cognitive aging (OCA) group compared with the NCA or MCI populations may enable us to identify cognitive patterns characteristic of this group. Second, we may be able to understand the ways in which these physical, social, and psychological factors may be linked to OCA. Finally, these understandings are likely to lead to recommendations about things that can be done to enhance the possibility of OCA.

These outcomes depend upon the ability to define an OCA segment in the population. We saw in the previous chapter how difficult it is to demarcate an NCA subset within our samples, and establishing criteria for OCA is no less challenging. In this chapter we will present three different empirical views of OCA and, by applying these three standards to the data sets, will form a picture of how the cognitively elite age intellectually. We will also consider extrinsic variables that may be associated with OCA and will present data from a pilot study of the nongenetic factors associated with high levels of cognitive functioning among older doctors. We will end the chapter with a discussion of another quality often associated with OCA, wisdom.

Empirical Views of OCA

Though many have pointed to the need to define an OCA population, no system for identifying this group has been reported to our knowledge. In this section we offer three ways of delineating OCA. Table 9.1 shows the criteria we used in this chapter to identify an OCA subset within our samples. The first criterion, Reference Group Plus, is carried over from the previous chapter. While it does have an application to NCA, it seems to us to work quite well in defining OCA because it sets a standard of being able to function overall at the level of those in the prime of life with no more than one component score being compromised.

If we are seeking to distill out a superior population among a group of elders, criterion A may not be rigorous enough. Certainly being in the top 99% of a physician reference group with only one component score compromised is impressive for an 80-year-old doctor. But for those who have had a long history of being in the top percentage of their contemporaries in terms of intellectual functioning, this yardstick for OCA may be seen as insufficient. Here criterion B may be more useful. Criterion B, Reference Group Superior, sets the standard for OCA as being at or above the mean (minus two standard errors of the mean) for the reference group of those 45–64 with no component score below the 15th percentile. This standard

Table 9.1   Three criteria for optimal cognitive aging

Criterion A: Reference Group Plus
A total score on MicroCog in the top 99 percent of subjects aged 45–64 with no more than one component score below the 15th percentile.

Criterion B: Reference Group Superior
At or above the mean total score for those 45–64 on MicroCog with no component score below the 15th percentile.

Criterion C: Age Group Elite
The top scorers in an age group, for example, top 5 percent.

---

requires a score of 85% correct on MicroCog for physicians and 81% correct for the Normal subjects. This is an exceptionally demanding standard: more than half of the reference group will fail to measure up because they necessarily fall in the bottom 50% of the distribution.

Criterion C, Age Group Elite, is a gauge of how someone is doing compared with his or her contemporaries. It is for those who only want to know if they are in the top small percentage of their age group. Their frame of reference is not those aged 45–64, but rather people their own age. Some may want to know if they are among the top 25 subjects in their half-decade, or in the highest 5%. Though this approach in defining OCA is informative with respect to the cohort with whom someone is aging, it is not particularly useful in helping people who may wish to know whether they should continue to practice medicine, fly an airplane, or work in a similarly demanding job. Here criteria A and B are far more useful.

If we apply these three different empirical criteria to our samples, we find that they produce an interesting picture of OCA. Table 9.2 provides a quantitative view of the proportion of the MD population by half-decade whose total MicroCog score is above the level required for OCA. We have already seen the dramatically decreasing percentage of the subjects who measure up to the Reference Group Plus criteria in the years after 65, namely, from about three-quarters of the Normals at 65–69 to one-third at 80+. The extraordinarily rigorous Reference Group Superior standards identify many

Table 9.2   Proportion of MDs and Normals by age group meeting two different criteria for optimal cognitive aging

| | Criteria for OCA | | | |
| | A Reference Group Plus | | B Reference Group Superior | |
Age Group	MDs	Normals	MDs	Normals
65–69	76.8	74.8	26.8	26.5
70–74	57.1	49.5	20.4	19.8
75–79	39.0	42.5	4.0	6.4
80+	23.9	33.3	6.5	8.3

Notes: (1) The Reference Group Plus standards require a total MicroCog score of 69% for the MD sample and 60% for the Normals. (2) The Reference Group Superior standards require a total MicroCog score of 85% correct for MDs and 81% for Normals.

Attention

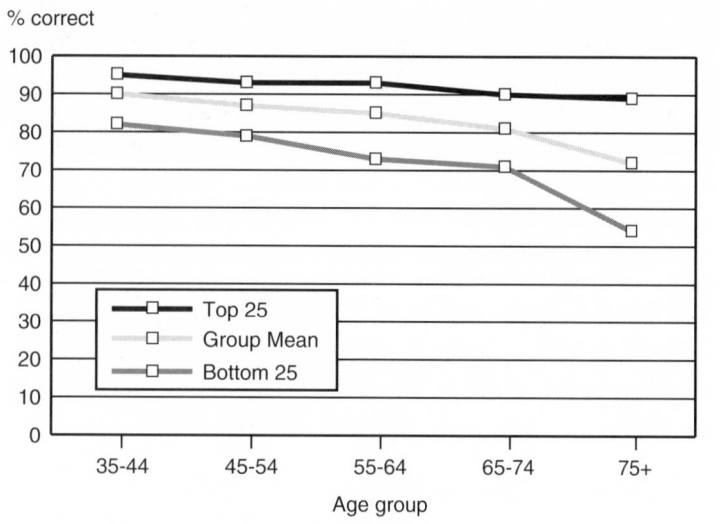

Verbal Memory

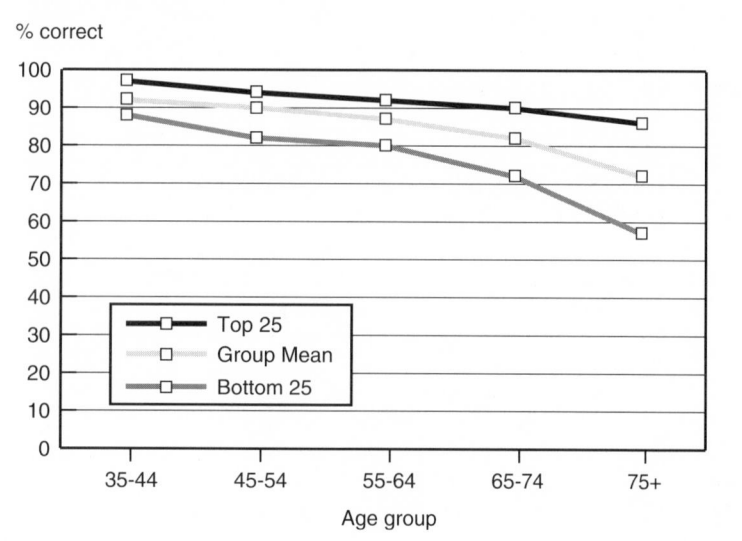

Figure 9.1 Average scores of top and bottom 25 MDs compared with age group means.

Visuospatial

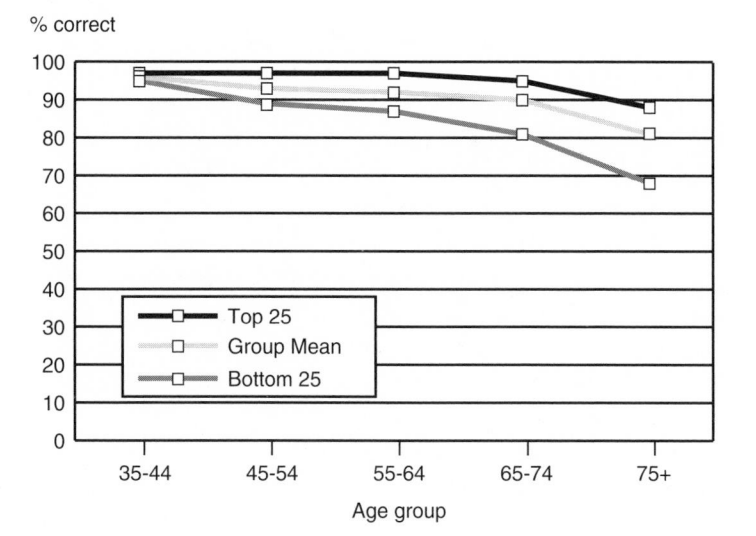

Reasoning

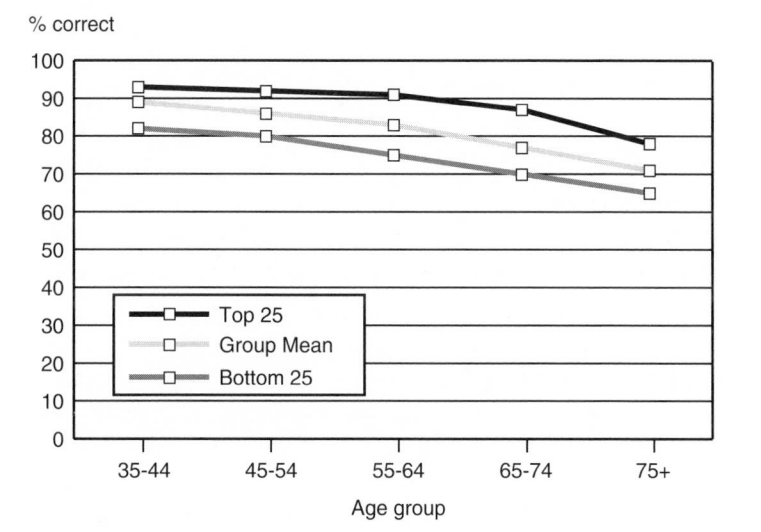

Figure 9.1 *(continued)*

fewer subjects in both groups as OCA. The MD and Normal groups track nearly parallel declines in percentages from 26.8% and 26.5% in the youngest age group to 6.5% and 8.3% in the 80+ subjects.

Though the proportion of individuals passing through this very fine filter for OCA is small beyond age 75, it is impressive to find that this significant minority does indeed exist. They represent a population who can be identified using these empirical criteria for studies of the factors associated with this highest level of intellectual functioning.

This exploration caused us to wonder whether the patterns of cognitive aging might be different for those who score in the top echelons of their age group compared to the rest. Specifically, we were interested in the question of whether the curves of declining aptitudes among the cognitively elite parallel those of the rest, but at a higher level, or whether certain abilities are preserved while others drop off normally.

To carry out this substudy, we applied criterion C and selected the top 25 physicians in each decade on the basis of their total MicroCog score. Then we compared their scores on four aptitudes (attention, verbal memory, visuospatial facility, and reasoning) with the lowest 25 scorers and the means for each decade from age 35 onward. The curves connecting the average aptitude scores of the 25 top and bottom MDs, as well as the means for each age group, are shown in Figure 9.1. A comparison of these curves reveals that the MDs in the elite group distinguish themselves from the average and lower-scoring physicians in the retention of their attentional abilities and verbal memory. While the mean of the average MDs dips about 20% from age 40 to age 75+ in attention and 22% in verbal memory, the differences are about 6% and 11% respectively for the highest scorers. The falloff is far greater for the lowest scorers: they move downward about 35% in both attentional skills and verbal memory. It is likely that these two abilities are highly related, since one must be able to focus attention in order to encode information as well as retrieve it from memory.

The differences in aptitude scores on visuospatial facility are the smallest to begin with. But the difference between the Tictac scores of the oldest and youngest subjects is only 11% among the top 25 compared to a 28% decline in the bottom 25 between 40 and 75+.

The lines of the three MD groups are more nearly parallel in reasoning. The distance between the means of the elite and average physicians remains about the same across the decades. The difference in reasoning between the two groups is 11 percentile points at ages 35–44 and about 17 points at 75+, a slight widening. The gap between the highest and lowest scorers, however, remains stable.

All in all, these data suggest that the difference between the highest and lowest scorers on overall cognitive ability is made up of a general factor and the contribution of specific skills. The data for the elite doctors suggest that all abilities contribute to the retention of superior intellectual functioning. Some areas, however, seem particularly important to higher levels of cognition, namely attention and verbal memory.

Optimizing Development through the Life Cycle

Earlier we discussed the dramatic increase in life expectancy during the twentieth century. It is also true, however, that living longer is not the same as living a healthier life. In fact, although mortality rates declined among the elderly through the 1970s, disability due to chronic and acute conditions increased. The result has been little growth in the productive life span.[2] The most recent report from the Secretary of Health and Human Services, *Healthy People 2000,* emphasizes as one of its major goals the increase of a healthy life span for Americans.[3] Figure 9.2 shows the difference between life expectancy and years of healthy life on the basis of 1980 census data. This figure was created by subtracting from the life expectancy in 1980 (73.7 years) the number of years during which major mental, physical, or social handicaps would limit a person's ability to function normally. This is estimated to be 11.7 years, or about 16% of total life expectancy. For example, the early onset of chronic emphysema because of smoking may result in numerous limitations on a man's life: he would be unable to continue working, would be forced to give up golf, and would require the watchful care of others.

Another way to think about the data in Figure 9.2 is to view the years of dysfunctional life as territory to be gained by improved health care. Consider Figure 9.3, which is Rabbitt's model of a more optimal life span.[4] If we apply this concept to the cognitive area, we might argue that Rabbitt overestimates the amount of age-related decline from maximal performance and may be slightly overly optimistic about how much territory can be gained. This proactive view of the life cycle, however, makes the assumption that the years beyond age 40 need not involve a decline in mental and physical functions. Rather, a more "rectangular" slope is possible, with mental and physical capabilities being optimized through the utilization of quality of life–enhancing practices.

Our present knowledge of the factors that may raise the probability of aging optimally in the cognitive domain remains extremely limited. The greatly increased interest in this topic as the population ages is likely to re-

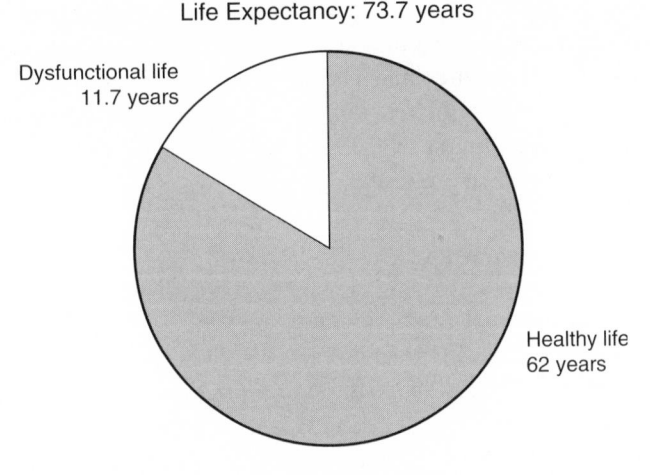

Life Expectancy: 73.7 years

Dysfunctional life
11.7 years

Healthy life
62 years

Figure 9.2 Years of healthy life as a proportion of life expectancy, U.S. population (1980). *Source:* National Vital Statistics System and National Health Interview Survey (CDC).

sult in a far greater understanding of those variables within our control that may extend the years of optimal cognitive functioning.

Correlates of OCA

How are we to gain the territory demarcated in Figure 9.3? In the last 25 years we have learned a great deal about what we can do physically to prolong both the quality and quantity of life—eating foods that are low in fat and cholesterol, controlling blood pressure, moderating alcohol intake, and stopping smoking. It may be possible to identify things we can do that would have a similar effect on maintaining our intellectual vigor in the years beyond 55. If activities or ways of living could be identified that are associated with maintaining intellectual vigor during the "late prime" of life, this could enable older citizens to live richer lives. Otherwise, what good does it do to remain physically vigorous if the possibility of cognitive impairment remains the same because of inexorable natural causes?

Heredity plays a major role in the acquisition, development, and maintenance of most human characteristics. It is also true, however, that genetic factors are not the sole influence on many individual qualities. Consider, for instance, the results of the study of twins raised together and apart conducted by the Minnesota Center for Twins and Adoptive Research.[5] In the

% max performance

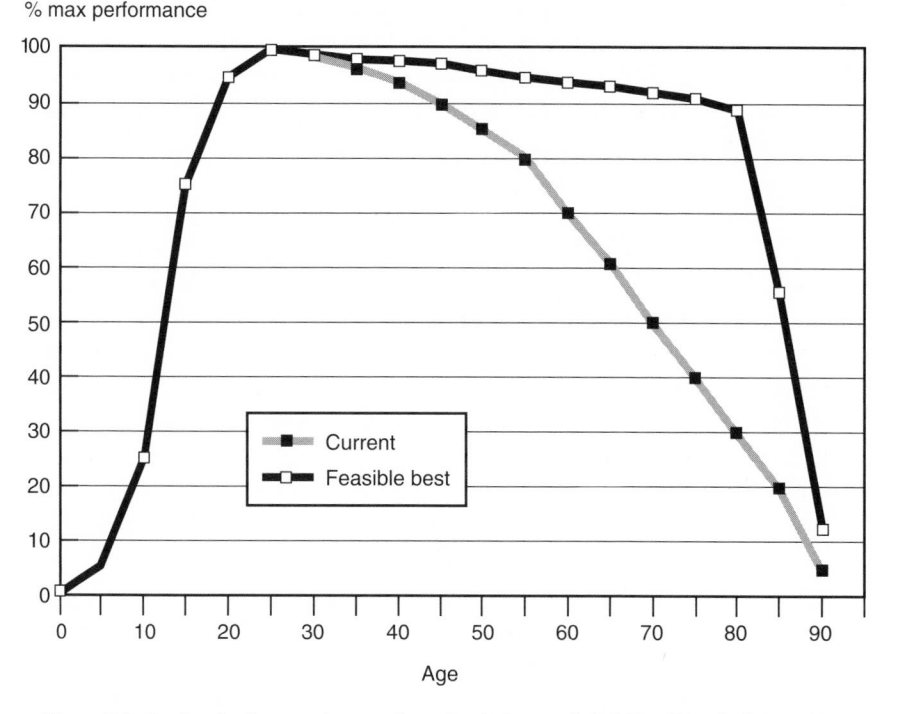

Age

Figure 9.3 Optimal aging: territory to be gained. *Source:* P. Rabbitt, "Applied Cognitive Gerontology: Some Problems, Methodologies, and Data," *Applied Cognitive Psychology,* 4 (1990): 229. Reprinted by permission of John Wiley & Sons, Ltd.

past decade, these researchers have tested extensively more than one hundred sets of identical or monozygotic twins separated at birth and reared apart (MZA). The similarity of their scores then was compared with the scores of twins raised together (MZT). This comparison of the similarities between MZA and MZT twins provides a natural and powerful method for differentiating the influence of heredity from that of environment upon certain human qualities.

Controlling for the education of the foster parents by whom each of the twins was raised, the Minnesota researchers correlated the scores of these twins on six physical, intellectual, and personality variables. The cognitive domain is of greatest interest to this research. They discovered that the WAIS Full Scale IQs correlated less strongly among the MZA pairs (.69) than with the MZT twins (.88). If one looks more closely at the households in which the MZA pairs were raised, it appears that IQ was significantly correlated with the cultural and educational resources available in the home. This could account for the lower association between the IQs of the MZA pairs. Still, a correlation of .69 means that about 70% of the variance in IQ is accounted for by heredity. To put it differently, 30% of the contribution to intellectual functioning comes from environmental causes.

One of the reasons the data on twins are of interest is that these correlations between IQ and other variables among identical twins are similar to the findings on the contribution of genetic factors to AD. No doubt exists that heredity contributes heavily to vulnerability to AD. However, just as with the twins research, factors other than genetic ones play a significant role in cognitive aging. For example, a longitudinal study of 20 aging twins with an average age of 84.3 (range 77.7 to 93.5) found only about a 50% concordance in their cognitive functioning.[6] Identical twins can have different histories with respect to AD. A clinical report of the onset of AD in twin sisters found that they led lives that were similar in terms of social status, health care, diet, marriage, and reproductive history, yet one sister developed AD in her sixties while the other twin did not develop AD until she was 83. Nearly two decades passed between the onset of AD in the first twin and the beginning of dementia in the other.[7]

Larger-scale investigations of relatives of those afflicted with AD have found a substantial number of cases in which the disease occurs with no family history. In another study in Minnesota, the relatives of 125 individuals who died in state-run institutions and had AD documented by autopsy were screened for cognitive impairment. These researchers discovered that 60% of the individuals with AD did not have a first- or second-degree relative with the disease.[8]

Retrospective studies such as these have a number of design flaws, such as difficulty in verifying subjective reports of AD and the large number of potential AD subjects for whom no follow-up was obtained. They do, however, provide additional support for the idea that qualities other than inherited ones play a role in the quality of cognition in the later years.

Nongenetic Theories

Few of the nongenetic theories about cognitive aging have much in the way of scientific foundation, but a number seem promising on the basis of animal research, clinical observation, case studies, small group investigations, or hunch. We do not mean to minimize the significance of these speculations, but merely to state that most suffer from lack of objective empirical validation with humans. These nongenetic theories can be grouped into four general categories: physical, intellectual, social, and psychological. In each of these domains we will review the theories that seem to have a reasonable probability of influencing the retention of cognitive capability.

Physical Factors. The data we reviewed in Chapter 5 showed little relationship between overall physical health and continued high-level intellectual vigor. This corresponds to the findings of others. For example, many of those afflicted with AD are free of other disease.[9] Yet there are at least three physical areas that may be related to the quality of thinking as we grow older: energy level, exercise, and diet. A common observation about men and women who rise to leadership positions in politics, business, or professional organizations is that they seem to have physical vitality. This *élan vital* is basic to preserving high-level mental operations. From another perspective, psychiatrists and other mental health workers point out that overall libido seems higher in more successful older people. A legitimate question can be raised, however, as to whether energy and libido are truly nongenetic factors. A strong argument can be made for these being inherited characteristics.

Activities that contribute to physical vitality play a role in higher-level cognition. It seems reasonable to speculate that proper diet as well as moderation in the intake of other substances is associated with maintaining high-quality intellectual functioning. To our knowledge, no substantive studies have been carried out on the relationship between cognition and lifelong eating habits. This is an area worthy of exploration.

By contrast, a large database about the role of exercise in intellectual fitness has accumulated. Theories postulating the beneficial impact of exercise on physical health are well established. For example, subjects who exercised regularly and were exposed to psychological stress showed smaller increases in systolic and diastolic blood pressure than those who were less physically active.[10] Clinicians have also noted the positive influence of exercise on emotional adjustment. Raised spirits, diminished anxiety, and improved self-confidence have been repeatedly shown to be positive outcomes of regular moderate exercise.[11] In addition, physically fit people compared with their less active counterparts exhibit higher scores on certain cognitive tests measuring visual sensitivity, reaction time, memory, and shifting of cognitive set.[12]

Intellectual Factors. The "use it or lose it" theory is widely espoused in the intellectual domain. Basically the notion is that if we keep our mind working as we grow older, through engaging in intellectually challenging activities, the probability of our maintaining our intellectual faculties will be enhanced.[13] Thus, a number of older people read regularly, take courses, and solve the daily and Sunday crossword puzzles. One doctor we met took the LSAT each year to check his mental acuity. The most compelling evidence for environmental enrichment being correlated with brain functions comes from research on both animals and humans. Diamond was one of the first to report data showing that an enriched environment improved the plasticity and thickness of the cerebral cortex of old rats just as it does with younger ones.[14] "Enriched" environments had more things in them to interest and amuse the rats—toys, tunnels, and exercise wheels. Her findings have been confirmed by a number of others, including, more recently, Renner and Rosenzweig.[15] Support for the notion that the findings in the rat studies may apply to humans as well comes from other research. Jacobs, Schall, and Scheibel found greater dendritic length correlated with richer personal experiences among humans.[16]

Not everyone agrees that regular intellectual exercise will keep us from "losing it" cognitively. As one expert put it, "To use it, you can't have lost it." Support for this viewpoint comes from the work of Salthouse,[17] who reviewed evidence from two decades of research on the "disuse" hypothesis and concluded that the cognitive skills of older people tend to decline whether they use their abilities on a regular basis or not.

Social Factors. Strong empirical evidence shows the causal impact of social relationships on physical health. A review by House, Landis, and Umberson notes that longitudinal studies consistently discover an increased risk of poor health among individuals whose social relationships are limited.[18] Evidence linking quantity of social relationships with mortality comes from six separate long-term research projects in the United States and Europe. In each of the studies the subjects were asked to describe their social networks. In one study, for example, subjects answered questions about marriage, contacts with extended family and friends, religious memberships, and other formal and informal involvement with clubs or groups. The subjects were then followed and their mortality rates examined in light of their social ties. All six studies discovered a positive correlation between the extent of social relationships and longevity. Each of these was controlled for age, race, gender, and physical condition. The results for all six studies point in the same direction whether the subjects were midwestern, Californian, or Scandinavian, or whether they were white or black: there was a higher probability of living longer when the quality of social contacts was greater.

Considerable data also show the positive impact of social relationships on mental health throughout the life cycle. Kansas researchers noted that the presence of loved ones made a difference in how children coped with stressful situations.[19] Having positive relationships with a family member is highly correlated with mental health in Vaillant's study of college graduates now in their seventies.[20] The subjects who exhibited higher scores on overall adjustment had rich friendship patterns and were in stable and satisfying relationships.

A study of nearly 300 respondents aged 55 and older in Louisville, Kentucky, examined the relationship between social supports and health.[21] Overall, strong social ties were found to be beneficial in coping with difficult stress. For instance, women with strong social relationships who were suddenly widowed managed the difficulties associated with their loss much more effectively than those widows who were isolated.

Psychological Factors. Just as it may be reasonable to assume that factors associated with physical health may positively benefit cognition, it also may be true that psychological factors that positively influence physical health may in turn enhance intellectual vitality. Several psychological theories bear indirectly on cognition. One of the most influential is Bandura's notion of self-efficacy.[22] Theories closely related to self-efficiency include White's "competence,"[23] Weinstein's "optimistic bias,"[24] Lawton's "self-regulation,"[25] and Langer's "mindfulness."[26] Although research based on these theories has yielded mixed results,[27] further testing is warranted.

One indirect influence is how we cope with stress. Vaillant has found a relationship between the "maturity" of ego defenses used to manage stress and both psychological and physical health.[28] Kobasa and Maddi's work on the "hardy personality" similarly discovered a positive relationship between well-being and those who respond to stress by feeling challenged, committed, and in control.[29]

Some emotions are more often linked to negative physical outcomes than others. Anger and anxiety especially have been identified as being associated with physical problems.[30] In a well-controlled study of 126 former college students, Russek discovered that severe anxiety was a reliable marker of coronary heart disease and other illnesses.[31]

Some psychological theories stress the connection between finding plea-

sure and health. The previously cited work by Vaillant, for instance, reported a positive correlation between the length of vacations and regular
pleasurable activities, on the one hand, and psychological and medical
health, on the other.[32] Zuckerman's research on sensation-seeking suggests
that those individuals who are higher in the desire for sensory input, adven-
ture, disinhibition, and intolerance for boredom are more likely to be open
to cognitive as well as affective experience.[33]

To our knowledge, none of the authors of these psychological theories has
produced research showing a connection to cognition. But indirect evidence linking certain psychological mechanisms to physical and mental
health suggests that they may bear upon intellectual functioning.

Pilot Study of 40 Physicians

In order to explore empirically the question of whether nongenetic factors
might be associated with level of cognition, a pilot study was carried out by
Anderson.[34] The subjects were 40 older working male physicians (mean age
= 62.3) who were part of our research pool. Twenty were selected from
among the highest scorers in their age group on MicroCog. The remaining
20, who all met criterion 2 for NCA, were picked from the bottom half of
their decade. The first group will be referred to as the OCA (Optimal Cognitive Aging) group, and the second as the NCA (Normal Cognitive Aging)
group. The physicians were interviewed individually and asked to complete
a questionnaire. The interview and questionnaire data surveyed four nongenetic domains: physical, intellectual, social, and psychological. The questions in each of the areas were drawn from the theories reviewed in the previous section.

Statistical analyses of the questionnaire data compared the 20 OCA subjects with the 20 NCA MDs to determine whether some of the nongenetic
factors might be significantly associated with level of cognition. When correlation coefficients were calculated between 122 questionnaire items and
level of cognition, 27 significant correlations resulted. They can be summarized in 16 characteristics as shown in Table 9.3. From these questionnaire
data it appears that there is reason to believe that nongenetic factors are
associated with higher levels of cognition among these subjects. These factors include high levels of energy, physical fitness as exhibited by exercise
and weight control, satisfying relationships of a social and sexual nature,
reading both for challenge and fun, and a sense of joy and competence.

Results that might be considered contrary to theory were also illuminat-

Table 9.3 Characteristics of high-scoring physicians: Significantly high correlations*

Consistent with Theory

Physical
  High physical energy
  Exercise moderately
  Strong sexual energy
Intellectual
  Read challenging books
  Read challenging magazines
  Read books for fun
  Read magazines for fun
Social
  Regular close contact with children
Psychological
  Feel joy in some aspect of life
  Feel a sense of competence regularly
  Under stress, respond step by step
  Under stress, think of future consequences of actions

Contrary to Theory

Physical
  Under stress, develop headaches
  Under stress, develop cold hands
Psychological
  Under stress, feel initially intimidated

* $p \leq .05$ (2-tailed).

ing. They portray subjects who, under stress, do not usually feel optimistic or challenged, but rather feel intimidated. Qualities that were found to be associated with this trait were feelings of loss of control and self-blame when under stress. In other words, these subjects felt anxiety and worry appropriately. They did not "hope for the best," but tried to solve problems in a sequential, step-by-step manner. Interestingly, these high-scoring physicians tended to be internalizers, developing headaches and cold hands under stress.

The personal interviews with each subject produced results that enriched the statistical findings. Anderson found that the OCA physicians had more professional opportunities during their lives than did the NCA doctors. The OCA group exerted an active control over their professional and personal lives: they learned to reduce tedium and stress by leaving more of the routine activities to the office staff or younger physicians, and they also created opportunities to be with their families and to have more frequent vacations. In contrast, the NCA physicians reported fewer professional opportunities. They found themselves being phased out early both professionally and financially, and often described how they had to struggle to preserve the gains they had made during early decades of hard work. They resigned themselves to their routines, giving evidence of having less physical energy and, in turn, concentrating their efforts on fewer avocational activities than did the OCA physicians.

A fascinating aspect of Anderson's study was the contrast she found between the quantitative and qualitative information. The statistical results seemed to her to "mask their anxiety and bravado and masked their feelings of helplessness" that came out during the interview with respect to retirement. For many of those in the OCA group whose lives had been so successful and so full of control, retirement was not easy to imagine. It was a challenge for them to let go of the control they had always enjoyed. They tried to remain active in the medical community by serving on boards and working with schools. They were full of vitality and seemed unready to give up the pleasures derived from their profession. In contrast, the NCA physicians seemed to be adjusting more easily to the prospect of giving up working. These physicians at a much earlier age had made realistic assessments of their limits and made necessary adaptations as they slowed down. There was a certain grace and dignity with which they accepted and adapted to impending retirement. This leaves us with a major puzzling question: Does a successful midlife and young-old career life preclude graceful older aging? Does less success earlier in life lead to an easier transition to the older years?

Although this pilot study is intriguing, considerable caution is appropriate in interpreting these results. One hundred and twenty-two separate correlations were computed, which means that about a half-dozen could have occurred by chance. In addition, the significant correlations imply only association, not causality. Moreover, it is not clear that some of the independent variables could not, just as easily, be seen as dependent variables. Physical energy is an example. Finally, the study suffers from four additional limitations: an all-male population, an all-physician population, limited dispersion of MicroCog scores, and small numbers. In order to explore these findings further and to generalize them to a normal population, a larger sample of more representative females and males is required. At this point in our knowledge, we must conclude that the search is just beginning for the correlates of OCA.

OCA and Wisdom

Another way of thinking about the model of OCA shown in Figure 9.3 is to view the territory to be gained in a quest for optimal intellectual functioning in the later years as consisting of new evolving qualities particular to older age rather than the maintenance of abilities that flowered in the prime of life. Wisdom is an example. Wisdom has always been thought to be the special province of the old. It stands unique among the declining life-span curves of physical and intellectual capabilities as a power that actually may increase with age. Indeed, scholars in various corners of the behavioral sciences have agreed that wisdom is far more likely to be found among the old than the young.

The growth of wisdom may be the other side of the story that aging is all about going downhill intellectually. It may be, as the book of Psalms (90:10) suggests, that the age of four score years brings with it special strength. What are these special strengths? Are the wise simply just a lot smarter than the rest of us? Or is wisdom a special type of intellectual power, such as the ability to use reasoning skills to solve complex problems? Could wisdom be accumulated knowledge or experience, so that someone could appear wise because he or she has seen most human difficulties before and knows what is likely to be the best course of action? Or perhaps wisdom is not so much a matter of intellect or experience but rather a frame of mind, a kind of style of helping others address difficulties inherent in the human condition.

The Dimensions of Wisdom

What criteria would we use to judge whether a person is wise or lacking in wisdom? Unlike IQ, no psychometric scale exists to measure wisdom. Though the term has been part of the vocabulary of humankind since the beginning of recorded history, and the word is regularly used by scientists and lay people alike, wisdom has resisted precise definition. Consider the two primary definitions in the Oxford English Dictionary. The first meaning it gives wisdom is the "capacity of judging rightly in matters relating to life and conduct; soundness of judgment in the choice of means and ends." The second definition is "knowledge (especially of a high or abstruse kind); enlightenment, learning, erudition."[35] These definitions suggest two somewhat different meanings of wisdom. The first is organized around the concept of judgment, especially in relationships with others where choices must be made. The second has to do with the possession of expert knowledge.

The concept of wisdom has been seen by ancient scholars in the Eastern and Western traditions as essential both to the development of the individual and to the stability of society. It has been said that the Eastern and Western traditions disagree somewhat on the meaning of wisdom. The Western heritage has stressed the value of the second meaning of wisdom: expert knowledge as it is manifested in intellect and reason. Eastern culture, by contrast, focuses more on contemplation and compassion, which is more in keeping with the first meaning of the term.[36] However, an inspection of the qualities associated with wisdom as conveyed in the literature of the Western world since the time of the Greeks suggests that the notion that the Western tradition stresses only the intellect may oversimplify matters. We looked through *Bartlett's Familiar Quotations* and the *Dictionary of Quotations* and found a long list of fragments from poems, stories, and other works employing the word "wisdom."[37] Among the positive qualities mentioned in the same breath as wisdom in these quotations are self-knowledge, kindness, caution, silence, patience, humility, hope, judgment, and knowing the cost of choices that are to be made. What wisdom is *not* is also of interest. It is not associated with money, power, strength, passion, excess, impulsiveness, or even knowledge. For the most part, agreement exists that wisdom comes with age. Several writers feel that wisdom comes from a life fully lived. The book of James identifies its antecedents as "earthly, sensual and devilish." In a similar vein, the nineteenth-century writer Adela Nicholson wrote that living, loving, and accepting what fate has to offer are essential to wisdom. Some writers feel that passions must be quieted by age before wisdom develops. These quotations also suggest that wisdom is hard won, coming out of defeat (Housman), grief (Ecclesiastes), and suffering (Aeschylus).

The intellect is not totally ignored among these writers. Prescience is included among the traits of the wise: it is the ability to predict what lies ahead (Milton) and involves being able to pick the least dangerous course of action (Machiavelli and Fielding). Knowledge of the tendencies of nature, especially human nature, is found among those possessing wisdom. This is suggested in a quote by Florio, "Wisdom sails with the wind and the tide." The wise have a sense of what is possible and what is impossible; they know the difference and can accept whatever happens.

Reading these quotations led us to think that wisdom is something other than intellectual brilliance. Being wise is not the same as being quick and clever; rather, it is about knowledge—of the self, of others, of the culture, and of history and context. These skills are not the same as memory, numeric ability, and visuospatial facility but involve gentleness, reflection, empathy, and tolerance.

Research Findings

Two research reports shed some empirical light on the question of whether forms of high intelligence may be associated with wisdom. The first study investigated the belief that older well-functioning individuals excel on complex rather than simple tasks compared to their younger counterparts. Researchers presented four different styles of cognitive tasks at three levels of complexity in an investigation of 431 subjects who were between ages 18 and 80. On each of these four styles of tasks, as complexity increased, the older subjects performed significantly worse than the younger ones. The conclusion was that the reason for the decline was that "more complex cognitive tasks place greater demand on working memory, a resource that declines with age."[38] Earlier studies by Hertzog and Schaie supported this more extensive investigation.[39]

An earlier study on the qualities associated with wisdom was reported by Clayton and Birren.[40] They found that the words used to describe someone who is wise include "intelligent," "knowledgeable," "observant," "intuitive," "pragmatic," "introspective," "experienced," "understanding," "gentle," "empathic," and "having a sense of humor." These researchers were interested in whether people of different ages would have different views of wisdom. They carried out a factor analysis for these terms with young (average age 21.3), middle-aged (49.2), and older (70.1) subjects. For all three groups, the first factor included the words "gentle," "peaceful," and "empathic" along with "knowledgeable." The second factor for all ages was dominated by the terms "sense of humor" and "introspective." In third place came the cognitive factors of "intelligent" and "intuitive."

An interesting difference emerged among the three age groups with respect to their views on the relationship between age and wisdom. In keeping with the long-held assumption that age brings with it wisdom, the younger and middle-aged subjects viewed age and wisdom as highly correlated. Those in the oldest group, in contrast, were less likely to see the two as related. The older subjects did not see themselves as being particularly wise. They did, however, characterize the qualities of understanding and empathy as far more important to wisdom than knowledge.

Table 9.4 Reports by 445 MDs of things they do better today than
when they were younger

	Age Group				
	≤ 44	45–54	55–64	65–74	75+
More Patient/Tolerant	9	3	12	25	13
%	12	4	14	20	14
More Thorough	3	6	4	1	6
%	4	8	5	1	7
More Empathic	3	4	7	12	3
%	4	5	8	10	3
Profit from Experience	12	7	8	8	8
%	16	9	10	7	9
Reasoning Better	2	13	16	20	13
%	3	17	19	16	14
N*	73	75	84	123	90

* The number of responses in each age group do not correspond to the total Ns because of multiple responses or no response.

In an effort to see for ourselves whether older individuals think of themselves as possessing qualities different from those of the younger generation, we asked the following question of the MDs in our sample: "It has been said that age brings with it special strength. Do you find in your day-to-day life that you do some things better than when you were younger?" We were able to code 445 of the 611 responses; the results are shown in Table 9.4. The primary quality that distinguished the MDs aged 65 and older from the younger doctors is not that they felt they were more capable intellectually, but that they were more patient and tolerant. Thirty-eight, or 19%, of the physicians beyond 65 gave responses classified in this category, compared to a much smaller percentage (10%) of those in the youngest decades. Of the 29 MDs who saw themselves as more empathic now than when they were younger, the greatest proportion, 12 (41.4%), were in the 65–74 decade. Otherwise the older doctors were no different from their younger counterparts.

The Berlin Model

During the past decade Paul Baltes and his colleagues at the Max Planck Institute for Human Development and Education in Berlin have been working on a model for wisdom. They have focused their efforts on three questions: What areas of behavior are likely to show instances of wisdom? How can wisdom-related knowledge and skills be measured? What groups of individuals are most likely to exhibit high levels of wisdom-related knowledge and skills?[41]

On the basis of their research on life-span theory, cognitive aging, and expert systems, Baltes and his co-workers have concluded that the type of knowledge and skills that are correlated with wisdom could be described as "cognitive pragmatics." By this they mean culture-based knowledge about the world and human affairs. More specifically, wisdom is defined as "an expert knowledge system in the fundamental pragmatics of life permitting exceptional insight, judgment, and advice involving complex and uncertain matters of the human condition."[42]

In the Berlin model, wisdom is knowledge-based. Wisdom-related behavior is expressed in the five criteria illustrated in Figure 9.4. We can see that expert knowledge is the centerpiece of this model. The top left component of wisdom, knowledge in the fundamental pragmatics of life, involves awareness of typical as well as differing pathways through the life cycle and

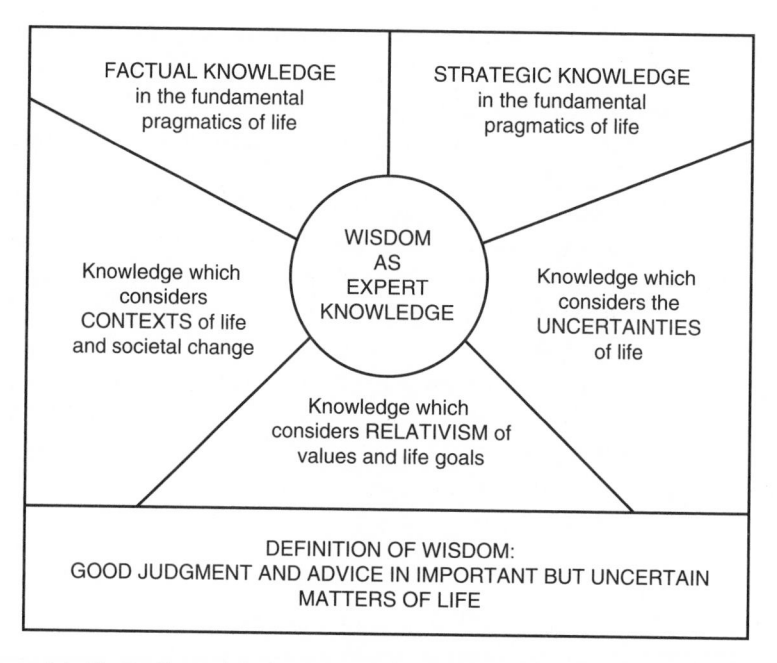

Figure 9.4 The Berlin model of wisdom. *Source:* P. B. Baltes and U. M. Staudinger, "The Search for the Psychology of Wisdom," *Current Directions in Psychological Science,* 2 (1993): fig. 1, p. 77. Reprinted with the permission of Cambridge University Press.

incorporates self-awareness. Strategic knowledge requires the understanding of others and the culture, as well as strategies for optimizing the gain/loss ratios among choices in human experiences. The remaining three constituents of wisdom involve the awareness that any knowledge is contextual and is relative to a specific culture, historical period, and personal value system. Finally, knowledge is uncertain; it offers not a perfect solution to the dilemmas of life, but a best guess about the course of action that will lead to the best possible outcome. This is not a model of black or white, yes or no, right or wrong.

The creators tested this model to see whether older people who were seen as wise would have higher scores than others. The test asked the subjects to think out loud about different life situations such as: "Imagine that a good friend calls and says that she has decided to commit suicide. How would you think about the situation and what would you do?" Baltes and Staudinger gave this question and others like it to people they thought might be wise, in this case older clinical psychologists. They compared their scores on this wisdom test with those of older controls, a younger group of clinical psychologists, and younger controls. They found that more of the older clinical psychologists (37%) had wisdom scores in the top quarter of the distribution. This percentage was much higher than that of either control group (18% each) or the younger clinical psychologists (27%). These results were in sharp contrast to the findings of the performance of these groups on standardized cognitive tests, in which none of the older subjects scored on the higher end.

The Berlin investigators reached two important conclusions from their research. The first is that the higher levels of wisdom may indeed characterize the thinking of those in the last stage of life. But it is not merely age that is the source of wisdom; life experience also matters. Their second conclusion is that wise older people are those who have "participated in a favorable, wisdom-prone set of circumstances." These researchers did not, however, say what these circumstances might be. To help us gain a more precise idea of what wisdom-enhancing life experiences might be, it is useful to look at the recent work of Erik Erikson.

Erikson's Model of Wisdom

Erik Erikson, a psychoanalytically trained psychologist, saw wisdom as the special adaptive strength of older age.[43] His stages of the life cycle, along with the developmental tasks and adaptive strengths of each, are shown in

Psychosocial stages of life

Old age								Integrity vs. Despair WISDOM
Adulthood							Generativity vs. Self Absorption CARE	
Young adulthood						Intimacy vs. Isolation LOVE		
Adolescence					Identity vs. Confusion FIDELITY			
School age				Industry vs. Inferiority COMPETENCE				
Play age			Initiative vs. Guilt PURPOSE					
Early childhood		Autonomy vs. Shame, Doubt WILL						
Infancy	Basic Trust vs. Basic Mistrust HOPE							

Figure 9.5 Erikson's stages of the life cycle. *Source:* Reprinted from *Vital Involvement in Old Age* by Erik H. Erikson, Joan M. Erikson, and Helen Q. Kivnick with the permission of W. W. Norton & Company, Inc. Copyright © 1986 by Joan M. Erikson, Erik H. Erikson, and Helen Kivnick.

Figure 9.5. Writing about the final stage of life, Erikson made the critical point that the emergence of wisdom as a special adaptive strength depends upon what might be called optimal psychological adjustment. The reason is that the formation of wisdom follows from having negotiated the earlier psychosocial stages of life, successfully confronting the particular developmental challenges associated with each stage and moving on to the next epoch of life with its own problems.

In adolescence and young adulthood the life-span challenges include forming a sense of identity in the face of role confusion and establishing an intimate bond with another person, resisting the pull toward either promiscuity or narcissism. Realized from the successful passage through these stages are the adaptive strengths of fidelity and love. The primary task of adulthood in Erikson's mind is generativity, which includes productivity and creativity in addition to procreativity.[44] The particular strength coming out of this phase of life is care, as shown in our nurturing of children, helping our own parents, being supportive of friends, and mentoring colleagues.

Successful transit through this period of the life cycle prepares the individual for moving into the final phase, where wisdom is the principal virtue. In his most recent writings Erikson regarded every stage of the life cycle as requiring "reintegrating, in new, age-appropriate ways, those psychosocial tasks that were ascendant in earlier periods."[45] In old age this means that there is a weaving back and forth between the present and the entirety of the life cycle as we re-experience the challenges to hope and will, to purpose and competence and fidelity, to love and care, that arise as we come to the last chapter of life. Ultimately it is these adaptive strengths upon which wisdom rests. Despite the inevitable biological indications placed on the body by aging, it is possible that the mind will continue to grow because it is enriched through the experiences of self-knowledge, knowledge of the human condition, knowledge of society and culture, and knowledge of the inevitable uncertainties and costs in any decision-making process. This knowledge is often called wisdom. It is these special powers of wisdom in the old that Longfellow may have recognized more than a century ago when he wrote:[46]

> For age is opportunity no less
> Than youth itself, though, in another dress,
> And as evening twilight fades away
> The sky is filled with stars, invisible by day.

10

Findings and Conclusions

In the preceding chapters we have shared with the reader our understanding of the patterns of cognitive aging through the life span based on our work with two groups of subjects. We began by pointing out the dramatic worldwide growth in the share of the population over age 65—one in five individuals by the year 2025—and the facts that these older people will be healthier physically and psychologically, will be legally entitled to work beyond age 65 if they wish, and indeed will be needed in continued employment to support the economy.

We know from our research and the studies of others that variability grows dramatically not only in the cognitive domain but in other areas as we grow older. Although it is true that the incidence of Alzheimer's disease and other disorders that affect cognition rises sharply in the years beyond 65, it is also a fact that large numbers of individuals remain intellectually vigorous into the ninth and tenth decades of their lives. Differentiating those older people who remain intellectually competent from those who are mildly impaired is a challenging task for the medical and psychological sciences.

In Chapters 2 and 3 we described our approach to developing a test, MicroCog: The Assessment of Cognitive Functioning. MicroCog measures those cognitive domains that are thought to be the most affected by aging, such as memory, visuospatial skills, reasoning, and attention. We described the characteristics of our subjects—the 1,002 physicians and 581 Normals—and discussed the limitations inherent in cross-sectional research. We believe, however, that our sample of volunteer subjects studied cross-sectionally is adequate to answer the questions we had in this investigation.

In Chapter 3 we also presented studies of the reliability and factor structure of MicroCog and looked at evidence for the validity of this test in distinguishing normal older people from those who are suffering mild cognitive impairment.

In Chapter 4 we sketched age-related cognitive changes as measured by MicroCog among both the MD and Normal subjects. We found relatively little change until about age 65, and then a steepening decline in overall ability by five-year age groups. The percentage drop in total score relative to the youngest group just about doubled in each decade after 50. This was clearest in the MD sample, but a similar pattern occurred in the Normal group. Those particular aptitudes that suffered the greatest loss associated with aging were visuospatial facility, reasoning, and verbal memory after delay. Best preserved over the years were attention-based skills and math facility. Because of the large number of subjects, we were able to detect differences between the decades relatively early. Small effect size estimates were significant when the 50-year-olds were compared with the 40-year-olds. The early small losses appeared to foreshadow greater later deterioration of age-grouped mean scores. Cognitive losses appeared to broaden and deepen by five-year intervals beyond the age of 65.

In Chapter 5 we explored qualities that might influence the trajectory of cognitive aging. We studied health, mental state, intellectual ability in one's prime, and working status among our subjects to determine the extent to which these factors correlated with scores on MicroCog. To our mild surprise, we found relatively little correlation between physical and mental health as measured by our instruments and overall intellectual functioning among the aged. Among the physician group, for example, many had serious physical illnesses and still scored in the top ranges on MicroCog. Three conditions that were negatively correlated with the quality of intellectual functioning were motor problems, cataracts, and heart conditions. Aside from anxiety, which attended lower intellectual efficiency in both MD and Normal subjects, other emotional states such as mood and anger showed no significant association with overall performance. We did find indirect evidence that overall IQ in one's prime may be correlated with higher scores on an independent measure of neuropsychological status. Retiring or continuing to work was not associated with substantial differences in overall intellectual functioning in the physician group until age 75. At that point, the working doctors were widely stronger than those who had retired. These differences were across the board—visuospatial facility, reasoning, verbal memory, attention, and calculation. The most likely explanation for these differences was that those who were most cognitively vigorous were the ones who had continued working.

In Chapter 6 we investigated two variables thought to be highly correlated with differences in intellectual performance: gender and education. We were interested in how well these factors correlated with overall intellectual performance and their interaction with cognitive aging. For the most part, we found no significant differences among either our MD or Normal subjects. Where differences did occur, they tended to favor younger females and older males. For instance, women were stronger on attention and reasoning prior to age 65 among the Normals and prior to 45 in the physician group. In middle age and beyond, males were widely superior especially in the visuospatial and numeric domains. Women maintained their superiority in attention in the later years.

By far the strongest effects upon differences in cognitive aging came from years of education. Among the Normal subjects aged 65–74, those with some college experience had substantially higher scores than those with only a high school education or less. The differences were far greater for females than for males. This may be because women who attended college in the 1930s were a far more select group than their male counterparts.

In Chapter 7 we examined the concept of mild cognitive impairment (MCI). We came to recognize that Alzheimer's disease and normal cognitive aging (NCA) lie on a continuum. Where one decides to draw the line between MCI and NCA is a matter of both clinical judgment and research-based criteria. We defined criteria that separated MCI from NCA and found that various criteria that have been applied to define MCI yield very different estimates of those who would be judged as afflicted with cognitive impairment.We also looked at the question of spontaneous reversibility of MCI. It appears that estimates of spontaneous improvement in the range of 8 to 10 percent are accurate. Far more heartening are the results of the reversal of cognitive losses in the normal elderly through training. Although these interventions have focused more on efforts to help people than to systematically evaluate their effectiveness, no doubt exists that normal older individuals can reverse age-related declines in memory, visuospatial ability, and reasoning through a small number of cognitive training sessions.

In Chapter 8 we attempted to define normal cognitive aging using four different empirical criteria. The four increasingly rigorous criteria were the following: Age Group Normative, based on an overall test battery score placing the individual in that percentage of his age cohort thought not likely to be cognitively impaired; Probably Not Impaired, based on a cutoff score validly differentiating cognitive impairment from NCA; Reference Group Normative, based on an overall score placing an individual in the top 99% of the healthy reference group; and Reference Group Plus, the same as Reference Group Normative with the additional criterion that no more than one component ability score can be lower than the 15th percentile. We stressed that these are not "stand-alone" standards for normalcy, but they provide a first step in thinking about how to define NCA. The Probably Not Impaired and Reference Group Normative criteria worked quite well in distinguishing those in the NCA category. The last, Reference Group Plus, might be useful for screening purposes if the task were to identify those individuals in highly demanding positions who may wish to continue to work beyond the normal retirement age. We explored the false positive/false negative trade-offs associated with various cutoff scores and considered the question of how one might go about screening for NCA in the decades ahead.

Chapter 9 examined the characteristics of optimal cognitive aging (OCA). We began by considering three separate definitions of OCA: Reference Group Plus, Reference Group Superior (at or above the mean score for people in their prime with no component score below the 15th percentile), and Age Group Elite. About one in five MDs and one in three Normal subjects over 80 had MicroCog scores that would meet the criteria for OCA using Reference Group Plus standards. Less than 10% of either group would meet the exceptionally rigorous Reference Group Superior criteria. We carried out a substudy of the top and bottom 25 MDs and compared their mean scores with one another as well as with the average for the age group. We found that the elite group maintained particular skills (attention and verbal memory) longer than the average doctor did, while other abilities declined apace with the others. We then turned our attention to nongenetic factors associated with higher levels of intellectual functioning among older people. Several findings from a small pilot study differentiated the higher- and lower-scoring older MDs; these factors included energy level, moderate exercise, and reading for challenge and fun. Finally, we explored the dimension of wisdom. Several paradigms were considered including the Berlin and the Erikson models. In essence, wisdom seems to be a characteristic composed of judgment, knowledge, and interpersonal skills rooted in a sound psychological adjustment.

Convergence and Divergence

In this section we will present the key points from our investigations which are consistent with current theory, those which raise questions about current theory, and those ideas which are somewhat apart from present thinking.

Points of Agreement

We find ourselves in general agreement with the following points: that computerized testing does indeed have significant advantages; that growing age-grouped variability occurs in cognitive functioning; that the "young-old" and the "old-old" differentiation is valid; that it is important to control for years of education when carrying out cross-sectional research on cognitive aging; that normal cognitive aging and AD very likely exist on a continuum; and that groups of normal cognitive agers and optimal cognitive agers can be identified using statistical criteria.

Advantages of Computerized Cognitive Testing. Our experience with computerized cognitive testing in the form of MicroCog was positive, confirming the literature cited in Chapter 2 and more recent studies.[1] Computerization provided a ready platform for our research team, few of whom were experienced with automated testing, to create the software for MicroCog. Once the test was developed, we administered it on dozens of different IBM-compatible computers in more than a score of different locations in all quadrants of the United States and Canada.

In the course of this research the test was administered successfully by more than fifty different examiners with varying amounts of testing experience to approximately 2,000 subjects. For those of us trained in an earlier era of hard copies and computation by hand, the ease with which the data from a project of this magnitude was managed and analyzed was truly impressive.

We also found this computerized test to be user-friendly from the point of view of both the administrator and the subject. We did not find it difficult to train examiners even though some did not possess word-processing skills. While a large number of the younger subjects and many of the older volunteers were computer-literate, the majority of those over 60 had no hands-on experience with computers. We were surprised and pleased to observe how easily the subjects, especially those in the "old-old" group, adjusted to taking MicroCog. We also noticed that once a brief period of instruction was given, the vast majority of subjects were able to continue on their own with no additional help from the examiners.

We were not surprised to find it more labor-intensive to give MicroCog to cognitively impaired individuals. Much more attention was necessary to be certain that the instructions were understood. A major problem for cognitively impaired subjects was that once the directions left the screen, it was impossible to bring them back for review. Often it was necessary for the examiner to repeat them. Encouragement also was required when, inevitably, the cognitively impaired subjects had difficulty answering questions correctly. We discovered that MicroCog could be given to most individuals with mild cognitive impairment (MMSE scores in the 24–27 range) without unusual difficulty and that we could obtain reliable estimates of the quality of their intellectual functions.

The enthusiasm we have expressed for computerized testing is based on our experience with MicroCog. Our feeling, however, is that these comments could apply equally to other computerized tests which have been developed for the same purposes as this research.

Variability. Time and time again in our data analyses, we were just as impressed by the growing variability among our subjects as they grew older as we were with the decline in average cognitive functions. Most of the time the percentage change in variability by decade was greater than the percentage of global cognitive loss. The growing dispersion occurred also at the level of specific abilities in both the MD and Normal samples. We found that knowing the variance helped us understand the cognitive aging process in ways that were obscured by looking only at mean scores. Although on average intellectual performance dropped off with advancing decades, the growing variability around the age-grouped means told us that there remained a group of individuals in every decade who were continuing to function at a high level. It was understanding this dispersion of scores, not the averages, that told us what someone's potential might be. It was the recognition of this group that led us to a definition of optimal cognitive aging.

Identification of Optimal Cognitive Agers. Our data confirm the observations of others that an elite group of cognitive agers does exist and can be identified using empirical criteria.[2] As many as a third of the octogenarians in one of our samples, and one out of five in another, functioned as well cognitively as those in their prime. Even the most rigorous standards found about 6–8% of those aged 80+ in the OCA group. Being able to identify this population using statistical criteria such as these, or better ones, gives us the opportunity to study them in order to learn more about the factors contributing to OCA.

The Importance of Years of Education. Of all the moderating variables that we examined, years of education seemed to be the most important. We found dramatic differences among age-matched groups on MicroCog between those who had some college education and those who had only high school degrees or less. Years of education is highly correlated with intellectual ability. Present evidence suggests, however, that years of education influences IQ scores. We have discovered that intellectual ability has a moderate correlation with the quality of cognition throughout the life cycle. Therefore, we should not be surprised to find that people with high levels of education outscore those with less. This finding is also useful in practical terms. When one is carrying out a research project and attempting to eliminate potential confounds, it is unlikely that one will have the resources to carry out individual IQ tests on each of the subjects or have access to records that will give this type of cognitive information. Years of education is almost always easily obtained and is an adequate surrogate for measured IQ.

Normal Cognitive Aging and Alzheimer's Disease as a Continuum. Our findings indicate that NCA and AD reside on a continuum. This work supports the findings of a number of others. Specifically, we found that older people, impaired or normal, distributed themselves along a continuum and that there was considerable overlap. We believe it is possible to use empirical criteria to define normal cognitive aging. Just using a threshold score can produce accurate classifications 80–90% of the time. A problem occurs when one is screening a population where the incidence of impairment is likely to be relatively small—such as screening airline pilots in the 60–64 year old age group. It may be possible to refine a screening test such as MicroCog in such a way that by using a combination of speed bonus points and component analyses, one could reduce the high number of false positives without substantially increasing the proportion of false negatives that would occur by using a single cutoff score to distinguish normal functioning. This is an area that should attract a good deal of interest in the decades ahead as older individuals continue to work in responsible positions.

The "Young-Old" and the "Old-Old." Bernice Neugarten's contribution to our understanding of the qualitative differences among seniors, the young-old (60–75) and the old-old (75+),[3] was largely supported by our studies. In our data the young-old could be distinguished by their higher scores on

MicroCog compared to those in their prime. The differences in mean scores on MicroCog were relatively small until the early part of the eighth decade of life. After ages 70–74, the downward slope in intellectual functioning steepened sharply for age groups in the old-old category. In addition, the percentage of those judged as NCA by the statistical criteria in Chapter 8 were much larger prior to age 75 than afterward.

Points of Partial Support

Our investigations lead us to partially support a number of issues in the cognitive aging field. However, we would like to add some amendments to this support in each case. The areas of partial support include the "flattening in the fifties" cognitive decline curve; the "use it or lose it" theory; how early cognitive losses can be detected; the sequence of aptitude losses in cognitive aging; the importance of attentional loss as a marker of MCI; and small but detectable gender differences in older people.

Evidence for a "Flattening in the Fifties." In these cross-sectional data the mean MicroCog scores did not fall in a regular fashion. Rather, they exhibited a pattern of declining and holding, and then dropping off more steeply. The extent of decline was greater both from ages 40–50 and from ages 60–70 than from ages 50–60 among the MD subjects. Since this same shallowing in the decline trajectories did not emerge among the normal subjects in the decade of the fifties but rather ten years later, it was first thought that this pattern was a statistical artifact. But we noted subsequently that data provided by Schaie from the Seattle Longitudinal Study largely confirmed the observation from our MD data that less overall cognitive decline occurred from ages 50–60 than in the two adjacent decades.[4] The scores for overall intellectual ability in Schaie's cross-sectional samples trace the same trajectory as in our MD sample. Moreover, two (nearly three) of his four longitudinal cohorts followed suit. Those longitudinal samples which did not show the flattening in the fifties cognitive pattern exhibited the shallowing from ages 60 to 67. As more longitudinal and cross-sectional data emerge, it will be interesting to see whether or not this slowing of global cognitive decline in the fifties is supported by new evidence.

"Use It or Lose It" Theory. Present research fails to confirm the intuition that continuing to "use it" in the form of working results in older individuals functioning at the level of their younger counterparts. On the whole, these

data are in keeping with the findings of Salthouse and his colleagues,[5] who have not found support for the disuse theory as a primary factor in cognitive aging. Fragmentary evidence was found in our data for the "use it or lose it" hypothesis among the MDs who continued to work beyond age 75. This was in the form of working doctors outscoring retired MDs. Unfortunately, we do not know if this was because continuing to exercise their minds at work enabled them to remain more cognitively vigorous, or whether being more cognitively vigorous to begin with enabled them to continue to exercise their minds at work.

Early Detection of Cognitive Losses. Other research has been unable to detect reliable decrements in intellectual functions prior to the age of 60.[6] Our data found cognitive losses more than a decade earlier. With a reliable instrument and sufficient statistical power, small differences in global and specific abilities were found between 40-year-old and 50-year-old MDs. After 50, the number of cognitive domains negatively correlated with age increased by census decade through age 70. After 70, there were across-the-board significant differences by five-year intervals.

Sequences of Losses in Cognitive Aging. Memory has long been said to be an early casualty of the aging process. This was the case with memory after delay among our subjects. In addition, statistical analysis of our data led to two further conclusions. First, visuospatial facility and reasoning are also affected early by the aging process, both probably earlier than memory. It is also true, however, that since our visuospatial and reasoning tasks both require the application of memory, these distinctions may suggest greater differences than actually exist. Our data led us to a second conclusion, which was that attentional skills and math calculation seem to be best preserved.

Attentional Losses as a Marker of Impairment. The absence of a reliable early marker for MCI or AD has been noted. Much has been made of memory loss as the primary early indicator of AD. It is surely true that secondary and tertiary memory are compromised in AD. In addition, we know that some of the other reliable indicators of impairment in older individuals, such as visuospatial functions and reasoning, are early casualties of the aging process. However, losses in these abilities are associated as well with NCA. This makes the differential diagnosis between NCA and MCI or AD quite difficult. By contrast, attentional skills are maintained until much later in life.

Our data suggest that a decline in attention in the context of losses in the other domains normally declining with age may be a reliable marker of early cognitive impairment since these skills normally hold up quite well. Attentional loss may not be a factor in every case of MCI or AD. This potential marker, however, is worth further study.

Gender Differences. Although most of the calculations performed between males and females found no results, it was interesting to note that females tended to show cognitive superiority through middle age but males tended to have higher scores after age 65 in education-matched data. It could be that the reason there were so few differences through middle age and, where there were differences, the females dominated, was that younger women have had more educational opportunities in the past quarter-century and therefore scored higher on our test. By contrast, older women, especially those beyond 65, may not have had on average the educational advantages of men. Some cold water was thrown on this theory by our finding that older female physicians, who were presumably a match for the male MDs in ability as well as occupation, scored lower, on the whole, than the men. There is no doubt that the small numbers of females in the MD sample may have contributed to measurement problems there, which may have inflated the male superiority. However, since we found the same differences in our male and female subjects in the Normal sample beyond age 65, one must be cautious in assuming that years of education is the only factor differentiating males and females in older age. This seems an important area for continued investigation.

Points of Divergence

Our research and thinking about the factors that influence cognitive aging have led us to conclusions which diverge to varying degrees from some of the widely held theories in neuropsychology and gerontology. However, since this is a very large field with a great many significant contributors, we are aware that many would not find these views so divergent. These points of divergence include the following: the relative insignificance of reported health as a moderating variable among community-dwelling subjects in cognitive research; failure to find a link between depression and the intellectual functioning of elders; the lack of support for the AAMI theory; and our finding that the decline of specific abilities is nested within an overall global downward trend in normal cognitive aging.

Reported Health as a Moderating Variable. We were surprised to find a limited relationship between reported physical health and cognitive functioning. Little relationship was found between cognition and reported health in the MD sample except with individuals who had cataracts or heart conditions. At first we wondered whether these results might have occurred because of the special strengths of these volunteer MDs, or whether our medical history forms were insufficiently sensitive. But we have subsequently found evidence from other studies supporting our findings. This evidence leads us to conclude that cognitive vigor can be remarkably resilient in the face of serious physical problems among older individuals.

Depression and Cognitive Functioning. Another finding that surprised us most was the absence of a significant relationship between depression and cognitive functioning. Although we did find some mild effect of anxiety, we found no significant relationships between depression and cognitive functioning among older or younger subjects, among Normals or MDs, or with different types of instruments. Looking carefully at the research of others, we found inconclusive evidence of this association. It is possible that there was a flaw in our research design which caused us not to be able to find significant results in this area. It is also possible that one of the reasons the results of depression and cognition studies have been so mixed is that anxiety, which does impact cognition, often coexists with depression. Unless anxiety is disaggregated from depression, it is difficult to know which affect may be causing the cognitive dysfunction.

Lack of Support for the AAMI Theory. It has been hypothesized that age-associated memory impairment (AAMI) can occur in normal older people without other or global areas of cognition also declining.[7] We could find no support from our data that age-associated memory impairment exists as a separate entity. In all our analyses of differences in mean scores in aptitude by decade or five-year intervals, lower performance on memory tasks, especially verbal recall, was accompanied or preceded by declines in other skills, especially visuospatial facility and reasoning. These patterns occurred with both Normal and MD subjects, in females as well as males.

A weakness in this argument is the reliance on age-grouped data rather than individual differences. Perhaps a subgroup of older subjects exists in this sample whose aptitudes in memory decline while other skills remain stable. We were not able to identify such a population among our volunteers. Therefore, on the basis of our testing we do not find support for the AAMI thesis.

Decline in Specific Abilities Nested within a Global Downward Trend. Many well-respected theorists in gerontology and neuropsychology have maintained that normal cognitive aging does not entail general mental deterioration.[8] It has been argued that initial impairment in older adults may be relatively circumscribed. AAMI may be considered an example of such a theory. While it is undeniable that certain specific skills do fall off earlier than others (for example, visuospatial facility in our data), it is also true that after age 50 the magnitude of the negative changes in mean scores were greater for overall ability than for any specific aptitude.

This still means that the trajectory of scores of age-sensitive skills continues to fall more rapidly than global ability averages. But the percentage of decline in mean scores from one decade to another or from one five-year span to another is greater than any one aptitude score. It appears, then, from our evidence that in normal cognitive aging the loss in any particular domain is likely to be nested within a global decline of proportionally greater magnitude.

Promising Areas to be Explored

In large-scale undertakings such as this carried out over a period of years, there is the project you plan to do, the research that is actually carried out, the things you wish you had done differently, and the studies that you would like to do. In the beginning our plan was to develop a cognitive screening test that would validly differentiate individuals in higher-level occupations who were functioning normally from those who were impaired. We believe that the goal of developing a valid test was accomplished. In our minds, the content was appropriate and the choice to computerize the instrument was correct.

A decision that in retrospect we believe was a correct one was to continue to use the research version of MicroCog through all of the studies. This meant living with several weaknesses in the test which we recognized early, such as subtests with inadequate dispersion. We resisted the impulse to upgrade old subtests or create new ones because we believed that having all of the subjects tested with the same instrument would provide us with more opportunity to study changes in cognition among our subjects as well as factors other than aging that influenced cognitive patterns. On balance, we feel that the benefits of retaining the research version of the test through the entire project far outweighed the advantages of creating an updated Micro-Cog.

We did not plan in advance to obtain a group of Normal subjects, since that was not part of the original charter. Rather, we accumulated these subjects unsystematically in the beginning and more systematically toward the end of the study when we began to realize the importance of having a Normal panel. In the process of obtaining data on the potential confounds of MicroCog scores, we became interested by the failure of our data to mesh with the common wisdom about the relationship of health and mood to intellectual performance. This evolved into a major substudy, along with an examination of the mediating effects of gender and education.

If we were beginning this project today, there are definitely some things we would do differently. With respect to MicroCog itself, we would give it more ceiling so as to create greater dispersion among the subjects. We would very likely add additional subtests, perhaps dichotic attention tests, and also mental rotation problems. In addition, we would treble our efforts to balance the MD sample by gender and minority groups and to increase the range of education among the Normals. It should be said that we tried very hard over a 12-month period to incorporate more females and minorities into the MD panel, but with the exception of the younger age groups, these efforts were without notable success. We had similar difficulty recruiting men in the 45–64 age range, especially those with less than a high school education: they were either too busy or didn't like taking tests.

Another facet of our research that hindsight tells us could have been improved was the study of health and emotional state. Since we were dealing with volunteers, who were not being paid and most of whom were quite busy, we were reluctant to discourage their participation by asking them to complete too many measures other than taking MicroCog. Were we to do it again, we would ask more detailed questions about the present as well as past physical condition of the subjects. For example, a history of alcoholism for someone who has been sober for 20 years very likely doesn't have the same impact on present mental operations as a situation where an individual is two weeks out of detoxification. We would have asked far more specific questions about heart conditions, past and present, especially to obtain data on any valvular replacement or bypass surgery. In the study of depression and anxiety, we could have chosen to use more measures, including some that have been used in other projects, so that clear comparisons could have been made.

A number of interesting avenues remain to be explored. We were not able to investigate several other potential moderating variables that could explain some of the differences in the cognitive functioning of older individuals.

Had we had an opportunity, we would like to have examined primary language. Our theory is that those who first learn a language other than English will show deficits in older age which may cause them to appear to be cognitively impaired on tests given in English when they are, in fact, normal. Laterality or handedness also interests us. Do left-handers age differently from right-handers in terms of the pattern of their cognitive decline? Finally, we would like to examine the effects of socioeconomic class on the retention of cognitive skills after controlling for education and gender.

Another challenging area is how to think about the applications of Micro-Cog or similar tests for cognitive screening. For the reasons mentioned earlier, we believe it will not be long before some type of screening procedure will be implemented to enable people to work beyond what used to be the normal retirement age. We see the beginnings of this process today in new requirements for recertification in professions such as medicine; with airline pilots going to court to challenge the FAA age-60 retirement rule; in state legislation that can require evidence of cognitive competence in order to continue to practice a profession or drive a car.

The problems surrounding the application of tests such as MicroCog to cognitive screening are both political and scientific. The political problems are substantial. Few institutions or professions are eager to confront the question of how to set fair standards which enable capable and motivated older workers to continue and weed out those with diminished capacities. Yet they know they must take this problem on and are looking to science for help—help that will not create more problems than it solves.

The scientific problems in using a test such as MicroCog or other devices for this type of screening are daunting. The first problem, that of false positives and false negatives, has been discussed earlier. A method of drastically reducing the proportion of false positives is crucial to the use of a test for cognitive screening. Otherwise, when the incidence of impairment is tiny (as in the group of pilots aged 60–64), even the best tests are likely to return eleven false positives for every true positive. This could cause severe political and legal problems among organizations or professions using a screening tool. We have made a small amount of progress in reducing the percentage of false positives by applying a combination of reaction time and component analysis, but this work is still in the preliminary stage.

A related scientific problem is the absence of a demonstrated relationship between test scores and performance in a criterion setting. While we know that having a total score below 60% on MicroCog suggests the strong possibility of cognitive impairment, does a score below this threshold indicate that a family practitioner should give up practicing medicine or that an airline pilot should retire? We do not have data available now to answer these legitimate questions. For tests to be employed as screening instruments, this correlation has to be firmly established for each occupation or setting in which it is to be used.

Finally, a source of frustration in research such as this is the inability to follow our subjects, especially the physician subjects, longitudinally. A pool of more than 700 doctors from the 1,002 who took MicroCog have volunteered to remain as research subjects. They offer investigators a remarkable opportunity to study life-span changes in cognition that are less likely to be influenced by factors such as education, average intellectual ability, socioeconomic status, or access to health care. This could enable researchers to examine how cognition might be influenced by prime-of-life ability, health, continuing to work, and factors such as exercise or intellectual stimulation that may play a role in optimal cognitive aging. We can also imagine the value of such a group in identifying early markers of mild cognitive impairment and, for those who choose to volunteer their brains after death, in studies of the relationship between test scores and brain pathology.

All of us involved in this project feel fortunate to have been part of the team invited to address the exciting area of cognitive aging. Although we are winding up with as many questions as answers, we are reasonably content with the results of our investigations. And our interest in this fascinating subject remains high. We hope that our work will be useful to other researchers and clinicians, as well as the growing number of all of us for whom cognitive aging has a personal interest.

Notes

1. Introduction: Understanding Cognitive Aging

1. Department of Health and Human Services, *Omnibus Solicitation of the Public Health Service for Small Business Innovation Research (SBIR) Grant and Cooperative Agreement Application* (Washington, D.C.: U.S. Government Printing Office, 1992), pp. 18–21.

2. G. Spencer, *Population Profile of the United States, 1989: Current Population Reports,* ser. P23, no. 159 (Washington, D.C.: Bureau of the Census, 1989).

3. L. Martin, "Population Aging Policies in East Asia and the United States," *Science,* 251 (1991): 527–531.

4. R. A. Butatao et al., *World Population Projections: Short and Long Term Estimates* (Baltimore, Md.: Johns Hopkins University Press, 1990).

5. A. Rees and S. P. Smith, "The End of Mandatory Retirement for Tenured Faculty," *Science,* 253 (1991): 838–839.

6. F. J. Landy et al., *Alternatives to Chronological Age in Determining Standards of Suitability for Public Safety Jobs: Executive Summary* (University Park, Pa.: Center for Applied Behavioral Science, Pennsylvania State University, 1992), p. 13.

7. Ibid.

8. J. W. Rowe and R. L. Kahn, "Human Aging: Usual and Successful," *Science,* 237 (1987): 143–149.

9. P. B. Hammond and H. B. Morgan, *Ending Mandatory Retirement for Tenured Faculty: The Consequences for Higher Education* (Washington, D.C.: National Academy Press, 1991), pp. 50–51.

10. Rees and Smith, "The End of Mandatory Retirement for Tenured Faculty."

11. Bernice Neugarten has differentiated the "young-old," those from ages 60 to 75, from the "old-old", those who are over 75. See B. L. Neugarten, "Time, Age, and the Life Cycle," *American Journal of Psychiatry,* 136 (1979): 887–894. See also B. L. Neugarten, "Age Groups in American Society and the Rise of the Young-old," *Annals of the American Academy of Political and Social Sciences,* 415 (1979): 187–198.

12. Figure 1.2 is drawn from *Masters Age-graded Tables,* 1990 ed. (Van Nuys, Calif.: National Masters News). It may be that the curves that are presented are somewhat

more linear by age group than occur in fact. Data collected by TACSTATS\USA suggest a more dramatically steepening curve after age 70, and greater gender differences favoring males following age 55.

13. Among his many writings on competence, see R. White, "Strategies of Adaptation: An Attempt at Systematic Description," in B. Coelho, A. Hamburg, and J. Adams, eds., *Coping and Adaptation* (New York: Basic Books, 1974).

14. S. Freud, "An Example of Psychoanalytic Work," *The Standard Edition of the Complete Psychological Works of Sigmund Freud,* vol. 21, ed. and trans. James Strachey (London: Hogarth Press, 1930).

15. A. Maslow, *Motivation and Personality,* 2nd ed. (New York: Harper and Row, 1970).

16. D. Powell and P. Driscoll, "How Middle-Class Unemployed Men Feel and Act: Four Progressive Stages," *Society,* 10 (1973): 18–26.

17. H. Morse and R. Weiss, "The Function and Meaning of Work and the Job," *American Sociological Review,* 20 (1955): 191–198. See also R. Vecchio, "The Function and Meaning of Work and the Job: Morse and Weiss Revisited," *Academy of Management Journal,* 23 (1980): 361–367.

18. J. Rosow and R. Zager, *The Future of Older Workers in America: New Options for an Extended Working Life* (Scarsdale, N.Y.: Work in America Institute, 1980).

19. L. R. Offerman and M. K. Gowing, "Organizations of the Future: Changes and Challenges," *American Psychologist,* 45 (1990): 95–108.

20. These data are based on a middle-level projection for population growth. See H. N. Fullerton, "Outlook 2000: New Labor Force Projections, Spanning 1988 to 2000," *Monthly Labor Review,* 112 (1989): 3–12.

21. R. E. Kutscher, "Outlook 2000: Projections Summary and Emerging Issues," *Monthly Labor Review,* 112 (1989): 66–74.

22. See Fullerton, "Outlook 2000: New Labor Force Projections."

23. G. Byrne, "U.S. Students Flunk Math, Science," *Science,* 24 (1989): 729.

24. N. C. Saunders, "The Aggregate Structure of the Economy," *Monthly Labor Review,* 112 (1989): 13–24.

25. Kutscher, "Outlook 2000: Projections Summary and Emerging Issues."

26. This presumes a moderate level of economic growth. Board of Trustees, *The 1993 Annual Report of the Board of Trustees of the Federal Old-age and Survivors Insurance and the Federal Disability Insurance Trust Funds, Pursuant to 42 U.S.C. 401 (c) (A) p. 25,* House Document 103-63 (Washington, D.C.: U.S. Government Printing Office, 1993).

27. A. Murray, "Retirees Pose Burden for Economy," *Wall Street Journal,* September 16, 1991, p. 1.

28. Fullerton, "Outlook 2000: New Labor Force Projections."

29. These calculations are based on transitions per unit cohort at age 55 for 1980 and 1972. As an example, there were .366 returns to work among women in 1972 compared with .582 in 1980. See M. D. Hayward, W. R. Grady, and S. D. McLaughlin, "The Retirement Process among Older Women in the United States: Changes in the

1970s," *Research on Aging,* 10 (1988): 358–382. See also M. D. Hayward, W. R. Grady, and S. D. McLaughlin, "Changes in the Retirement Process among Older Men in the United States: 1972–1980," *Demography,* 25 (1988): 371–386.

30. U.S. Department of Labor, Bureau of Labor Statistics, *Handbook of Labor Statistics,* bull. 2340 (Washington, D.C.: U.S. Government Printing Office, 1989), p. 1318.

31. Rowe and Kahn, "Human Aging: Usual and Successful."

32. A. L. Benton, P. Eslinger, and A. R. Damasio, "Normative Observations on Neuropsychological Test Performances in Old Age," *Journal of Clinical Psychology,* 3 (1981): 33–42.

33. E. A. Nelson and D. Dannefer, "Age Heterogeneity: Fact or Fiction? The Fate of Diversity in Gerontological Research," *The Gerontologist,* 32 (1992): 17–23.

34. From LEXIS/NEXIS for 1980 and 1990.

35. Committee on Nomenclature and Statistics of the American Psychiatric Association, *Diagnostic and Statistical Manual of Mental Disorders,* 2nd ed. (DSM-II) (Washington, D.C.: American Psychiatric Association, 1968), p. 24.

36. For example, J. S. Coleman, *Abnormal Psychology and Modern Life* (Chicago, Ill.: Scott, Foresman, 1955).

37. G. McKhann et al., "Clinical Diagnosis of Alzheimer's Disease: Report of the NINCDS-ADRDA Workgroup under the Auspices of the Department of Health and Human Services Task Force on Alzheimer's Disease," *Neurology,* 34 (1984): 939–944.

38. *Diagnostic and Statistical Manual of Mental Disorders,* 3rd ed., rev. (DSM-III-R) (Washington, D.C: American Psychiatric Association, 1987), pp. 103–107.

39. Ibid., pp. 119–120.

40. See H. Matsuyama, "Incidence of Neurofibrillary Change, Senile Plaques, and Granulovacuolar Degeneration in Aged Individuals," in B. Reisberg, ed., *Alzheimer's Disease: The Standard Reference* (New York: Free Press, 1983), pp. 149–154. See also F. D. Miller et al., "A Descriptive Study of Neuritic Plaques and Neurofibrillary Tangles in an Autopsy Population," *American Journal of Epidemiology,* 120 (1984): 331–341.

41. R. Katzman, "Alzheimer's Disease as an Age-dependent Disorder," in D. Evered and D. Whelan, eds., *Research and the Aging Population,* Ciba Foundation Symposium 134 (Chicester: Wiley, 1988), pp. 69–85.

42. J. C. Morris et al., "Very Mild Alzheimer's Disease: Information-based Clinical Psychometric and Pathologic Distinction from Normal Aging," *Neurology,* 41 (1991): 469–478.

43. R. Katzman and T. Saitoh, "Advances in Alzheimer's Disease," *FASEB Journal,* 5 (1991): 278–286.

44. R. Heaton, *The Wisconsin Card Sorting Test* (Odessa, Fla.: Psychological Assessment Resources, 1981); R. A. Zachary, *Shipley Institute of Living Scale, Revised Manual* (Los Angeles, Calif.: Western Psychological Services, 1986); D. Wechsler, *Wechsler Memory Scale—Revised* (San Antonio, Tex.: Psychological Corporation, 1987).

45. See P. J. Eslinger et al., "Neuropsychologic Detection of Abnormal Mental Decline in Older Persons," *Journal of the American Medical Association,* 253 (1985): 670–674. See also R. Berg, M. Franzen, and D. Wedding, *Screening for Brain Impairment: A Manual for Mental Health Practice* (New York: Springer, 1987).

46. Four references—across studies, across countries, and across diagnostic instruments—are of interest. They are M. S. Albert, "Assessment of Cognitive Dysfunction," in M. S. Albert and M. B. Moss, eds., *Geriatric Neuropsychology* (New York: Guilford, 1988); D. W. O'Connor et al., "The Influence of Education, Social Class, and Sex on Mini-Mental State Scores," *Psychological Medicine,* 19 (1989): 772–776; T. J. Heeren et al., "Reference Values for the Mini-Mental State Examination (MMSE) in Octo- and Nonagenarians," *Journal of the American Geriatric Society,* 38 (1990): 1093–1096; T. N. Tombaugh and N. J. McIntyre, "The Mini-Mental State Examination: A Comprehensive Review," *Journal of the American Gerontological Society,* 40 (1992): 922–935.

2. MicroCog and the Volunteers

1. The test formed the basis of *MicroCog: The Assessment of Cognitive Functioning,* by the Psychological Corporation, San Antonio, Tex., 1993. Its authors are D. H. Powell, E. F. Kaplan, D. K. Whitla, S. Weintraub, R. Catlin, and H. H. Funkenstein. The published version of MicroCog differs slightly in that it is shorter, integrates response speed, converts raw to standard scores, and has education-based norms.

2. See L. J. Long and M. Wagner, "Computer Applications in Neuropsychology," in D. Wedding, A. M. Horton, and J. Webster, eds., *The Neuropsychology Handbook: Behavioral and Clinical Perspective* (New York: Springer, 1986).

3. See R. A. Maulucci and R. H. Eckhouse, "The Use of Computers in the Assessment and Treatment of Cognitive Disabilities in the Elderly," *Psychopharmacology Bulletin,* 24 (1988): 557–564. See also S. E. Embretson, "Computerized Aptitude Testing: Its Potential Substantial Contributions to Psychological Research and Assessment," *Current Directions in Psychological Science,* 1 (1992): 129–131.

4. M. D. Schwartz, "Clinical Applications of Computers: An Overview," in D. Baskin, ed., *Computer Applications in Psychiatry and Psychology* (New York: Brunner/Mazel, 1991).

5. K. Watts, A. Baddeley, and M. Williams, "Automated Tailored Testing Using Raven's Progressive Matrices and the Mill Hill Vocabulary Tests: A Comparison with Manual Administration," *International Journal of Man-Machine Studies,* 17 (1982): 231–234.

6. R. L. Kane and G. G. Kay, "Computerized Assessment in Neuropsychology: A Review of Tests and Test Batteries," *Neuropsychology Review,* 3 (1992): 1–117.

7. E. L. Baker et al., "A Computer-based Neurobehavioral Evaluation System for Occupational and Environmental Epidemiology: Methodology and Validation Studies," *Neurobehavioral Toxicology and Teratology,* 7 (1985): 369–377.

8. R. J. Branconnier, "A Computerized Battery for Behavioral Assessment in Alzheimer's Disease," in L. W. Poon, ed., *Handbook for Clinical Memory Assessment of Older Adults* (Washington, D.C.: American Psychological Association, 1986).

9. T. Crook and C. J. Larrabee, "Age-associated Memory Impairment: Diagnostic Criteria and Treatment Strategies," *Psychopharmacology Bulletin,* 24 (1988): 509–514.

10. S. H. Ferris, S. Flicker, and D. Reisberg, "NYU Computerized Battery for Assessing Cognition in Aging and Dementia," *Psychopharmacology Bulletin,* 24 (1988): 699–702.

11. R. L. Horst and G. G. Kay, "COGSCREEN: Personal and Computer-based Tests of Cognitive Function for FAA Medical Certification," presented at the Sixth International Symposium on Aviation Psychology, Columbus, Ohio, 1991.

12. D. H. Powell et al., *MicroCog: The Assessment of Cognitive Functioning.*

13. Public Census Data, 1980 Decennial Census.

14. R. Rosenthal and R. L. Rosnow, *The Volunteer Subject* (New York: Wiley, 1975).

15. Ibid., pp. 198–199.

16. For a more extensive discussion, see T. A. Salthouse, *Theoretical Perspectives on Cognitive Aging* (Hillsdale, N.J.: Erlbaum, 1991), pp. 57–58.

17. K. W. Schaie, "The Hazards of Cognitive Aging," *The Gerontologist,* 29 (1989): 484–493.

18. Most longitudinal studies have tended to emphasize factors of interest to the medical and behavioral sciences at the time the study was initiated. Examples are temperament, personality, or resiliency to stress. Most have spent relatively little effort in the cognitive domain. See A. Thomas and S. Chess, *Temperament and Development* (New York: Brunner/Mazel, 1977); L. B. Murphy and A. E. Moriarty, *Vulnerability, Coping, and Growth: From Infancy to Adolescence* (New Haven, Conn.: Yale University Press, 1976); G. E. Vaillant, *Adaptation to Life* (Boston: Little, Brown, 1977).

19. An example is the attrition in the Seattle Longitudinal Study. Of the subjects in the 1963 cohort, 11.0% had 0–8 years of education and 46.8% had 13+ years. Among those remaining through the 1977 testing, only 4.2% had 0–8 years of education, while 57.2% had at least some college. See K. W. Schaie, "The Seattle Longitudinal Study: The 21-year Exploration of Psychometric Intelligence in Adulthood," in K. W. Schaie, ed., *Longitudinal Studies of Adult Psychological Development* (New York: Guilford, 1983), pp. 64–135.

20. J. W. Rowe and R. L. Kahn, "Human Aging: Usual and Successful," *Science,* 237 (1987): 143–149.

21. See K. W. Schaie, "The Seattle Longitudinal Study: A 21-Year Exploration of Psychometric Intelligence in Adulthood," pp. 64–135. See also K. W. Schaie, "The Course of Adult Intellectual Development," *American Psychologist,* 49 (1994): 304–313.

22. Salthouse, *Theoretical Perspectives on Cognitive Aging,* p. 113.

3. Psychometric Properties of MicroCog

1. A brief and comprehensive summary of what test standards should be is provided in G. Dahlstrom, "Tests: Small Samples, Large Consequences," *American Psychologist,* 48 (1993): 373–399. Another more extended view of what a test should be is in *Standards for Educational and Psychological Testing* (Washington, D.C.: American Psychological Association, 1992). This publication was prepared by the committee to develop standards for educational and psychological testing of the American Educational Research Association, the American Psychological Association, and the National Council on Measurement and Education.

2. There was a possibility that item interdependence could have produced a spuriously high reliability coefficient; to explore this possibility it was recalculated using KR 21 formulas. This calculation resulted in a coefficient of 0.930, which is a lower-bound estimate of reliability and supports the earlier finding.

3. J. D. Matarazzo, *Wechsler's Measurement and Appraisal of Adult Intelligence,* 5th ed. (Baltimore, Md.: Williams and Wilkins, 1972), p. 240.

4. D. H. Powell et al., *MicroCog: The Assessment of Cognitive Functioning* (San Antonio, Tex.: Psychological Corporation, 1993).

5. See, for example, M. Mitrushina and P. Satz, "Effects of Repeated Administration of a Neuropsychological Battery in the Elderly," *Journal of Clinical Psychology,* 47 (1991): 790–801.

6. D. Wechsler, *The Measurement and Appraisal of Adult Intelligence,* 4th ed. (Baltimore, Md.: Williams and Wilkins, 1958).

7. W. R. Cunningham and W. A. Owens, "The Iowa State Study of the Adult Development of Intellectual Abilities," in K. W. Schaie, ed., *Longitudinal Studies of Adult Development* (New York: Guilford, 1983), pp. 20–39.

8. J. Cohen, "The Factorial Structure of the WAIS between Early Adulthood and Old Age," *Journal of Consulting Psychology,* 21 (1957): 283–290.

9. J. Cohen, "A Factor-Analytically Based Rationale for the Wechsler Adult Intelligence Scale," *Journal of Consulting Psychology,* 21 (1957): 451–457.

10. W. E. Hale, R. G. Marks, and R. B. Stewart, "The Dunedin Program, a Florida Geriatric Screening Process: Design and Initial Data," *Journal of the American Geriatrics Society,* 27 (1980): 377–380.

11. D. Wechsler, *Wechsler Memory Scale-Revised* (San Antonio, Tex.: Psychological Corporation, 1987); R. Heaton, *Wisconsin Card Sorting Test* (Odessa, Fla.: Psychological Assessment Resources, 1981); E. Kaplan, H. Goodglass, and S. Weintraub, *The Boston Naming Test* (Philadelphia, Pa.: Lea and Febiger, 1983).

12. C. R. Cimino et al., "Concurrent Validity of the Assessment of Cognitive Skills (ACS)," *Journal of Clinical and Experimental Neuropsychology,* 13 (1991): 106.

13. R. C. Green et al., "Screening for Cognitive Impairment in Older Individuals: Validation of Study of Computer-based Test," *Archives of Neurology,* in press.

14. For reviews, see R. Berg, M. Franzen, and D. Wedding, *Screening for Brain Impair-*

ment: A Manual for Mental Health Practice (New York: Springer, 1987). See also C. J. Golden and M. Maruish, "The Luria-Nebraska Neuropsychological Battery," in D. Wedding, A. M. Horton, and J. Webster, eds., *The Neuropsychological Handbook: Behavioral and Clinical Perspectives* (New York: Springer, 1986).

15. M. D. Lezak, *Neuropsychological Assessment,* 2nd ed. (New York: Oxford University Press, 1983), pp. 152–153.

16. For reviews, see T. Boll, *Handbook of Clinical Neuropsychology* (New York: Wiley, 1981). See also R. M. Reitan and L. A. Davison, eds., *Clinical Neuropsychology: Current Status and Application* (Washington, D.C.: V. H. Winston and Sons, 1974); W. C. Halstead, *Brain and Intelligence* (Chicago: University of Chicago Press, 1947).

17. L. Wheeler, C. H. Burke, and R. M. Reitan, "An Application of Discriminate Functions to the Problems of Predicting Brain Damage Using Behavioral Variables," *Perceptual and Motor Skills,* 16 (1963): 681–701.

18. R. M. Reitan, "Validity of the Trail Making Test as an Indicator of Brain Damage," *Perceptual and Motor Skills,* 8 (1958): 271–276.

19. For reviews, see C. J. Golden, "A Standardization Version of Luria's Neuropsychological Tests: A Quantitative and Qualitative Approach to Neuropsychological Evaluation," in S. B. Filskov and T.J. Boll, eds., *Handbook of Clinical Neuropsychology* (New York: John Wiley and Sons, 1981). See also T. Hammeke, C. J. Golden, and A. Purisch, "A Short Comprehensive and Standardized Version of Luria's Neuropsychological Tests," *International Journal of Neuroscience,* 8 (1981): 135–141.

20. R. Berg, M. Franzen, and D. Wedding, *Screening for Brain Impairment* (New York: Springer, 1987), pp. 165–170.

4. Cognitive Changes over the Life Span

1. *VO$_2$ max* curves are based on percentage decline in maximal oxygen uptake in male distance runners, with age group mean for ages 30–39 being 100%. Data drawn from T. Fuchi et al., "Changes Associated with Decreased Aerobic Capacity and Aging in Long-distance Runners," *European Journal of Applied Physiology,* 58 (1989): 884–889. Decline curves for non-active subjects parallel those who are active, though at a lower level. See P. Astrand and K. Rodahl, *Textbook of Work Physiology: Physiological Bases of Exercise* (New York: McGraw-Hill, 1977), pp. 318–325. *SBP:* theoretical percentages for non-smokers with systolic blood pressure above 160 mm Hg and diastolic blood pressure less than 90 mm Hg. Data from J. W. Rowe and L. A. Lipsitz, "Altered Blood Pressure," in J. W. Rowe and R. W. Besdine, eds., *Gerontological Medicine,* 2nd ed. (Boston: Little, Brown, 1988), pp. 193–207. *GFR:* glomerular filtration rate curve is based on cross-sectional mean age differences in standard creatinine clearance, as a percentage of age 30. Data from J. W. Rowe, "Renal System," in Rowe and Besdine, eds., *Gerontological Medicine,* pp. 231–245. *FEV$_1$:* normal forced expiratory volume in one second among

non-smokers, as a percentage of age 30 mean. Data from D. Sparrow and S. T. Weiss, "Pulmonary System," in Rowe and Besdine, eds., *Gerontological Medicine,* pp. 266–275. *Cardiac:* percentage decline in age group means in heart rate per minute during maximal exercise in male distance runners with age group mean for ages 30–39 being 100%. Data from T. Fuchi et al., "Changes Associated with Decreased Aerobic Capacity and Aging in Long-distance Runners."

2. E. A. Nelson and D. Dannefer, "Aged Heterogeneity: Fact or Fiction? The Fate of Diversity in Gerontological Research," *The Gerontologist,* 32 (1992): 17–23.

3. A. S. Kaufman, *Assessing Adolescent and Adult Intelligence* (Boston: Allyn-Bacon), p. 185. Mean scores for age groups through age 64 were drawn from D. Wechsler, *Wechsler Adult Intelligence Scale* (New York: Psychological Corporation, 1955), p. 19. Scores for ages 65–69 through 75+ are from J. E. Doppelt and W. C. Wallace, "Standardization of the Wechsler Adult Intelligence Scale for Older Persons," *Journal of Abnormal and Social Psychology,* 51 (1955): 312–330.

4. Kaufman, Assessing Adolescent and Adult Intelligence, p. 193.

5. For an enlightening discussion of this subject see J. A. Hall, *Nonverbal Sex Differences: Communication, Accuracy, and Expressive Style* (Baltimore, Md.: Johns Hopkins University Press, 1984), pp. 9–12.

6. A summary of the virtues of the effect size correlation is contained in R. Rosenthal and R. Rosnow, *Essentials of Behavioral Research: Methods and Data Analysis* (New York: McGraw-Hill, 1991).

7. K. W. Schaie, "The Seattle Longitudinal Study: A 21-year Exploration of Psychometric Intelligence in Adulthood," in K. W. Schaie, ed., *Longitudinal Studies in Adult Development* (New York: Guilford, 1983), pp. 64–135.

8. Many have found a negative correlation between reaction time and aging. For example, see A. T. Welford, "Sensory, Perceptual and Motor Processes in Older Adults," in J. E. Birren and R. B. Sloane, eds., *Handbook of Mental Health and Aging* (New York: Prentice-Hall, 1980). See also, more recently, T. A. Salthouse, *Mechanisms of Age-Cognition Relations in Adulthood* (Hillsdale, N.J.: Erlbaum, 1992), pp. 81–116.

9. M. J. Sharps and E. S. Golin, "Speed and Accuracy of Mental Image Rotation in Young and Elderly Adults," *Journal of Gerontology,* 42 (1987): 342–344.

10. Summaries of approaches to protecting the alpha and reducing the probability of Type I errors are contained in Rosenthal and Rosnow, *Essentials of Behavioral Research,* pp. 328–329. See also S. E. Maxwell and H. B. Delaney, *Designing Experiments and Analyzing Data: A Model Comparison Perspective* (Belmont, Calif.: Wadsworth, 1989), pp. 171–206.

11. See T. A. Salthouse, *Theoretical Perspectives on Cognitive Aging* (Hillsdale, N.J.: Erlbaum, 1991).

12. P. F. Farver and T. B. Farver, "Performance of Normal Older Adults on Tests Designed to Measure Parietal Lobe Functions," *American Journal of Occupational Therapy,* 36 (1982): 444–449.

13. See G. Hochanadel and E. Kaplan, "Neuropsychology of Normal Aging," in M. L. Alpert, ed., *Clinical Neurology of Aging* (New York: Oxford University Press, 1984), pp. 231–244.

14. A. L. Benton, P. Eslinger, and A. R. Damasio, "Normative Observations on Neuropsychological Test Performances in Old Age," *Journal of Clinical Psychology,* 3 (1981): 33–42.

15. R. K. Heaton, I. Grant, and C. G. Matthews, "Differences in Neuropsychological Test Performance Associated with Age, Education and Sex," in I. Grant and K. Adams, eds., *Neuropsychological Assessment of Neuropsychiatric Disorders* (New York: Oxford University Press, 1986), pp. 100–120.

16. R. T. Kellogg, "Age Differences in Hypothesis Testing and Frequency Processing in Concept Learning," *Bulletin of the Psychonomic Society,* 21 (1983): 101–104.

17. M. D. Shelton, O. Parsons, and W. R. Lieber, "Verbal and Visuospatial Performance and Aging: A Neuropsychological Approach," *Journal of Gerontology,* 37 (1982): 336–341.

18. V. W. Inman and S. R. Parkinson, "Differences in Brown-Peterson Recall as a Function of Age and Retention Interval," *Journal of Gerontology,* 38 (1983): 58–64.

19. M. D. Lezak, *Neuropsychological Assessment* (New York: Oxford University Press, 1983), p. 464.

20. K. Haaland et al., "A Normative Study of Russell's Variant of the Wechsler Memory Scale in a Healthy Elderly Population," *Journal of Consulting and Clinical Psychology,* 51 (1983): 878–881.

21. A. Rey, *L'Examen Clinique en Psychologie* (Paris: Presses Universitaires de France, 1964).

22. T. A. Salthouse, *Adult Cognition: An Experimental Psychology of Human Aging* (New York: Springer-Verlag, 1982).

23. See S. Weintraub and M. M. Mesulam, "Mental State Assessment of Young and Elderly Adults in Behavioral Neurology," in M. M. Mesulam, *Principles of Behavioral Neurology* (Philadelphia: F. A. Davis, 1985). See also M. Williams, "Geriatric Patients," in P. Mittler, ed., *The Psychological Assessment of Mental and Physical Handicaps* (London: Methuen, 1970).

24. Benton, Eslinger, and Damasio, "Normative Observations on Neuropsychological Test Performances in Old Age."

25. M. S. Albert and R. K. Heaton, "Intelligence Testing," in M. S. Albert and M. B. Moss, eds., *Geriatric Neuropsychology* (New York: Guilford, 1988), pp. 13–32. See also Kaufman, *Assessing Adolescent and Adult Intelligence,* pp. 398–399.

26. K. W. Schaie, "The Seattle Longitudinal Study: A 21-Year Exploration of Psychometric Intelligence in Adulthood," in K. W. Schaie, ed., *Longitudinal Studies of Adult Psychological Development* (New York: The Guilford Press, 1983), pp. 64–135.

27. H. B. C. Reed and R. M. Reitan, "Changes in Psychological Test Performance Associated with the Normal Aging Process," *Journal of Gerontology,* 18 (1963): 271–274.

See also K. A. Moehle and C. J. Long, "Models of Aging and Neuropsychological Test Performance Decline with Aging," *Journal of Gerontology,* 44 (1989): 176–177.

28. In fact, some strenuously object to the phrase "statistically significant difference," calling it misleading, especially when the mean differences are small. The phrase "probable nonchance difference" has been suggested as an alternative. See S. J. Lachman, "Statistically Significant Differences or Probable Nonchance Differences," *American Psychologist,* 48 (1993): 1093.

5. Other Influences on Cognitive Aging

1. For example, see M. D. Lezak, *Neuropsychological Assessment* (New York: Oxford University Press, 1983), pp. 165–203.

2. D. Field, K. W. Schaie, and E. V. Leino, "Continuity in Intellectual Functioning: The Role of Self-reported Health," *Psychology and Aging,* 3 (1988): 385–392.

3. R. J. Ivnik, "Normative Neuropsychological Research above Age 54: General Considerations," paper presented at the Annual Meeting of the American Psychological Association, San Francisco, 1991. See also J. F. Malec, R. J. Ivnik, and G. E. Smith, "Neuropsychology and Aging: Clinician's Perspective," in R. W. Parks, R. F. Zec, and R. S. Wilson, eds., *Neuropsychology and Alzheimer's Disease and Other Dementias* (New York: Oxford University Press), in press.

4. T. A. Salthouse, *Theoretical Perspectives on Cognitive Aging* (Hillsdale, N.J.: Erlbaum, 1991), p. 66.

5. Ibid., p. 63.

6. P. D. Nussbaum and G. Goldstein, "Neuropsychological Sequelae of Heart Transplantation: A Preliminary Review," *Clinical Psychology Review,* 12 (1992): 475–483.

7. A. F. Willner et al., "Analogical Reasoning and Post-operative Outcome: Predictions for Patients Scheduled for Open Heart Surgery," *Archives of General Psychiatry,* 33 (1976): 255–259. See also C. J. Rabiner and A. F. Willner, "Differential Psychopathological and Organic Mental Disorder at Follow-up, Five Years after Coronary Bypass and Cardiac Valvular Surgery," in H. Speidel and G. Rodewald, eds., *Psychic and Neurological Dysfunctions after Open-Heart Surgery* (New York: Thieme Stratton, 1988), pp. 237–249.

8. T. A. Salthouse, *Theoretical Perspectives on Cognitive Aging,* p. 66.

9. A. W. Kaszniak, "Neuropsychological Aspects of Dementia and Depression in Older Adults," workshop presented at the Annual Meeting of the American Psychological Association, Boston, 1990. See also A. W. Kasniak, M. Sadeh, and L. Z. Stern, "Differentiating Depression from Organic Brain Syndromes in Early Age," in G. M. Chaisson-Stewart, ed., *Depression in the Elderly: An Interdisciplinary Approach* (New York: Wiley, 1985), pp. 169–189; J. Cavenar, A. Maltbie, and L. Austin, "Depression Simulating Organic Brain Disease," *American Journal of Psychiatry,* 136 (1979): 521–523.

10. C. E. Wells, "Pseudodementia," *American Journal of Psychiatry,* 136 (1979): 895–900.

11. See H. F. O'Neil, Jr., C. D. Spielberger, and D. N. Hansen, "Effects of State Anxiety and Task Difficulty on Computer-assisted Learning," *Journal of Educational Psychology,* 60 (1969): 343–350. See also C. D. Spielberger, "The Effects of Anxiety on Complex Learning and Academic Achievement," in C. D. Spielberger, ed., *Anxiety and Behavior* (New York: Academic Press, 1966); C. D. Spielberger and L. H. Smith, "Anxiety (Drive), Stress, and Serial-position Effects in Serial-verbal Learning," *Journal of Experimental Psychology,* 72 (1966): 589–595.

12. C. Hertzog and P. Blanchard-Fields, "Cognitive-affective Relationships in Adulthood," paper presented at the annual meeting of the American Psychological Association, Boston, 1990.

13. See C. Eisdorfer, J. Nowlin, and F. Wilkie, "Improvement of Learning in the Aged by Modification of the Autonomic Nervous System's Activity," *Science,* 170 (1970): 1327–1329.

14. A. Tesser et al., "Conflict: The Role of Calm and Angry Parent-Child Discussion in Adolescent Adjustments," *Journal of Social and Clinical Psychology,* 8 (1989): 317–330.

15. M. Zuckerman and B. Ruben, *Multiple Adjective Adjustment Checklist* (San Diego, Calif.: Educational and Industrial Testing Service, 1985).

16. J. C. Cavanaugh and N. Z. Murphy, "Personality and Metamemory Correlates of Memory Performance in Younger and Older Adults," *Educational Gerontology,* 12 (1986): 385–394.

17. D. H. Powell, "Cambridge Research Mood Survey" (Cambridge, Mass.: Cambridge Research Center, 1988).

18. C. D. Spielberger, "Preliminary Manual for the State-Trait Personality Inventory (STPI): Test Forms and Psychometric Data" (Tampa, Fla.: University of South Florida, 1979).

19. A. T. Beck et al., "An Inventory for Measuring Depression," *Archives of General Psychiatry,* 4 (1961): 561–571.

20. C. D. Spielberger, *Manual for the State-Trait Anger Inventory* (Odessa, Fla.: Psychological Assessment Resources, 1991). See also C. D. Spielberger, *Manual for the State-Trait Anxiety Inventory (STAI-Form Y)* (Palo Alto, Calif.: Consulting Psychologists Press, 1983).

21. See G. L. Klerman, "Problems in the Definition and Diagnosis of Depression in the Elderly," in L. D. Breslau and M. R. Haug, eds., *Depression and Aging: Causes, Care, and Consequences* (New York: Springer, 1983), pp. 1305–1319. See also A. Stenback, "Depressive and Suicidal Behavior in Old Age," in J. E. Birren and R. B. Sloane, eds., *Handbook of Mental Health and Aging* (Englewood Cliffs, N.J.: Prentice-Hall, 1980), pp. 616–652.

22. M. C. Feinson, "Aging and Mental Health: Distinguishing Myth from Reality," *Research in Aging,* 7 (1985): 155–174. See also R. Hirschfeld and C. Cross, "Epidemi-

ology of Affective Disorders: Psychosocial Risk Factors," *Archives of General Psychiatry,* 3 (1982): 35–46.

23. J. P. Newmann, "Aging and Depression," *Psychology and Aging,* 4 (1980): 150–165.
24. D. Blazer et al., "The Association of Age and Depression among the Elderly: An Epidemiologic Exploration," *Journal of Gerontology,* 46 (1991): 210–215.
25. P. A. Parmalee, M. H. Kleban, and M. P. Lawton, "Depression and Cognitive Change among Institutionalized Aged," paper presented at the Annual Meeting of the American Psychological Association, Boston, 1990.
26. J. A. Yesavage et al., "Development and Validation of a Geriatric Depression Scale," *Journal of Psychiatric Research,* 17 (1983): 31–49.
27. Parmalee, Kleban, and Lawton, "Depression and Cognitive Change among Institutionalized Aged."
28. See G. Niederehe, "Depression and Memory Impairment in the Aged," in L. W. Poon, ed., *Handbook for Clinical Memory Assessment of Older Adults* (Washington, D.C.: American Psychological Association, 1986), pp. 226–237. See also M. W. O'Hara et al., "Differential Impact of Brain Damage and Depression on Memory Test Performance," *Journal of Clinical and Consulting Psychology,* 54 (1986): 261–263.
29. J. J. Sweet, P. Newman, and B. Bell, "Significance of Depression in Clinical Neuropsychological Assessment," *Clinical Psychology Review,* 12 (1992): 21–45.
30. See V. O. B. Emery, *Pseudodementia: A Theoretical and Empirical Discussion* (Cleveland: Western Reserve Geriatric Education Center, 1988). It seems important to attempt to identify those aspects of depression that may mimic cognitive impairment. One promising approach is suggested by D. W. O'Connor et al., "A Follow-up Study of Dementia Diagnosed in the Community Using the Cambridge Mental Disorders of the Elderly Examination," *Acta Psychiatrica Scandinavica,* 81 (1990): 78–82. Their data suggest that depressed individuals can mimic mild dementia when there is psychomotor retardation. See also V. O. B. Emery and T. E. Oxman, "Update on the Dementia Spectrum of Depression," *American Journal of Psychiatry,* 149 (1992): 305–317.
31. This possibility is suggested by the work of O'Connor et al., "A Follow-up Study of Dementia Diagnosed in the Community Using the Cambridge Mental Disorders of the Elderly Examination."
32. See Lezak, *Neuropsychological Assessment,* p. 225.
33. S. Weintraub and M. M. Mesulam, "Mental State Assessment of Young and Elderly Adults in Behavioral Neurology," in M. M. Mesulam, *Principles of Behavioral Neurology* (Philadelphia: F. A. Davis, 1985).
34. R. K. Heaton, I. Grant, and C. G. Matthews, "Differences in Neuropsychological Test Performance Associated with Age, Education and Sex," in I. Grant and K. Adams, eds., *Neuropsychological Assessment of Neuropsychiatric Disorders* (New York: Oxford University Press), pp. 100–120. See also M. S. Albert and R. K.

Heaton, "Intelligence Testing," in M. S. Albert and M. B. Moss, eds., *Geriatric Neuropsychology* (New York: Guilford, 1988), pp. 13–32.

35. D. Wechsler, *Wechsler Adult Intelligence Scale-Revised* (New York: Psychological Corporation, 1955).

36. G. P. Prigatano, "Wechsler Memory Scale: A Selective Review of the Literature," *Journal of Clinical Psychology*, 34 (1978): 816–832.

37. See S. L. Willis, R. Bliezner, and P. B. Baltes, "Training, Research and Aging on the Fluid Ability of Inductive Reasoning," *Journal of Applied Developmental Psychology*, 2 (1981): 247–265. See also E. S. Schneidman, "The Indian Summer of Life," *American Psychologist*, 44 (1989): 684–694.

38. T. A. Salthouse, *Theoretical Perspectives on Cognitive Aging* (Hillsdale, N.J.: Erlbaum, 1991), pp. 150–152.

39. T. A. Salthouse et al., "Age and Experience Effects in Spatial Visualization," *Developmental Psychology*, 26 (1990): 128–136.

40. T. A. Salthouse and D. R. D. Mitchell, "Effects of Age and Naturally Occurring Experience on Spatial Visualization Performance," *Developmental Psychology*, 26 (1990): 845–854.

6. The Effects of Gender and Education

1. G. E. Vaillant, *Adaptation to Life* (Boston: Little, Brown, 1977).

2. D. J. Levinson et al., *The Seasons of a Man's Life* (New York: Knopf, 1978).

3. S. H. King, *Five Lives at Harvard* (Cambridge, Mass.: Harvard University Press, 1973). See also D. Heath, *Maturity and Competence: A Transcultural View* (New York: Gardner, 1977).

4. G. Vaillant and C. O. Vaillant, "Natural History of Male Psychological Health: Work as a Prediction of Positive Mental Health," *American Journal of Psychiatry*, 138 (1981): 1433–1440.

5. H. S. Maas and J. A. Kuypers, *From Thirty to Seventy* (San Francisco: Jossey-Bass, 1974).

6. K. W. Schaie, "The Seattle Longitudinal Study: A 21-year Exploration of Psychometric Intelligence in Adulthood," in K. W. Schaie, ed., *Longitudinal Studies of Adult Psychological Development* (New York: The Guilford Press, 1983).

7. M. Lowenthal et al., *Four Stages of Life: A Comparative Study of Women and Men Facing Transition* (San Francisco: Jossey-Bass, 1976).

8. Maas and Kuypers, *From Thirty to Seventy.*

9. E. E. Maccoby and C. N. Jacklin, *The Psychology of Sex Differences* (Stanford, Calif.: Stanford University Press, 1974).

10. Ibid., p. 61.

11. Ibid., p. 75.

12. H. J. Walberg, "Physics, Femininity, and Creativity," *Developmental Psychology*, 1 (1969): 47–54.

13. Maccoby and Jacklin, *The Psychology of Sex Differences*, pp. 92–97.

14. See R. Rosenthal, *Meta-analytic Procedures for Social Research* (Newbury Park, Calif.: Sage, 1991). See also R. J. Light and D. B. Pillemer, *Summing Up: The Science of Reviewing Research* (Cambridge, Mass.: Harvard University Press, 1984); G. V. Glass, B. McGaw, and M. L. Smith, *Meta-analysis and Social Research* (Beverly Hills, Calif.: Sage, 1981).

15. J. S. Hyde and M. C. Linn, "Gender Differences in Verbal Ability: A Meta-analysis," *Psychological Bulletin*, 104 (1988): 53–69.

16. J. S. Hyde, E. Fennema, and S. J. Lamon, "Gender Differences in Mathematics Performance: A Meta-analysis," *Psychological Bulletin*, 107 (1990): 139–155.

17. M. C. Linn and A. C. Peterson, "Emergence and Characterization of Sex Differences in Spatial Ability: A Meta-analysis," *Child Development*, 56 (1985): 1479–1498.

18. R. Rosenthal and D. B. Rubin, "Further Meta-analytic Procedures for Assessing Cognitive Gender Differences," *Journal of Educational Psychology*, 74 (1982): 708–712.

19. Maccoby and Jacklin, *The Psychology of Sex Differences*, pp. 78–83.

20. J. S. Hyde and M. C. Linn, "Gender Differences in Verbal Ability: A Meta-analysis," *Psychological Bulletin*, 104 (1988): 53–69.

21. Hyde, Fennema, and Lamon, "Gender Differences in Mathematics Performance."

22. D. W. Schwartz and S. A. Karp, "Field Dependence in a Geriatric Population," *Perceptual and Motor Skills*, 24 (1967): 495–504.

23. See J. F. Malec, R. J. Ivnik, and G. E. Smith, "Neuropsychology and Normal Aging: The Clinician's Perspective," in R. W. Parks, R. F. Zec, and R. S. Wilson, eds., *Neuropsychology of Alzheimer's Disease and Other Dementias* (New York: Oxford University Press, 1993), pp. 81–111. See also J. F. Malec, R. J. Ivnik, G. E. Smith, E. G. Tangelos, R. C. Petersen, E. Kokmen, and L. T. Kurland, "Mayo's Older Americans Normative Studies: Utility of Corrections for Age and Education for the WAIS-R," *The Clinical Neuropsychologist*, 6 (Special Supplement, 1992), pp. 31–48.

24. R. K. Heaton, I. Grant, and C. G. Matthews, "Differences in Neuropsychological Test Performance Associated with Age, Education and Sex," in I. Grant and K. Adams, eds., *Neuropsychological Assessment of Neuropsychiatric Disorders* (New York: Oxford, 1986), pp. 100–120. See also M. S. Albert and R. K. Heaton, "Intelligence Testing," in M. S. Albert and M. B. Moss, eds., *Geriatric Neuropsychology* (New York: Guilford, 1988), pp. 13–32.

25. Albert and Heaton, "Intelligence Testing," in Albert and Moss, eds., *Geriatric Neuropsychology*, p. 30.

26. S. J. Ceci, "How Much Does Schooling Influence General Intelligence and Its Cognitive Components? A Reassessment of the Evidence," *Developmental Psychology*, 27 (1991): 703–722.

27. See Malec, Ivnic, and Smith, "Neuropsychology and Normal Aging: The Clinician's Perspective," pp. 81–111.

28. In 1930 approximately 300,000 males and 367,000 females graduated from high school. Four years later 82,341 males attained a bachelor's or first professional degree, as compared to 53,815 females. This amounts to about 27% of the males and 15% of the females who graduated from high school four years earlier. U.S. Department of Commerce, Bureau of the Census, *Historical Statistics of the United States: Colonial Times to 1970* (Series H 597-6018 and H 759-765) (White Plains, N.Y.: Krause International Publications, 1989).

29. In 1988 approximately 476,842 males and 516,520 females earned a bachelor's degree. The source is National Center for Education Statistics, *Digest of Education Statistics* (Washington, D.C.: U.S. Department of Education, 1990), Table 1.56.

7. Mild Cognitive Impairment

1. J. Nielsen, A. Homma, and T. Biørn-Henriksen, "Follow-up 15 Years after a Geronto-psychiatric Prevalences Study: Conditions Concerning Death, Cause of Death, and Life Expectancy in Relation to Psychiatric Diagnosis," *Journal of Gerontology*, 32 (1977): 554–561.

2. L. Berg et al., "Mild Senile Dementia of the Alzheimer Type: 2. Longitudinal Assessment," *Archives of Neurology*, 23 (1988): 466–484.

3. V. A. Kral, "Senescent Forgetfulness: Benign and Malignant," *Journal of the Canadian Medical Association*, 86 (1962): 257–260.

4. T. Crook, "Age-associated Memory Impairment: Proposed Diagnostic Criteria and Measures of Clinical Change—Report of the National Institute of Mental Health Work Group," *Developmental Neuropsychology*, 2 (1986): 261–276.

5. M. Storandt and R. D. Hill, "Very Mild Senile Dementia of the Alzheimer Type: II. Psychometric Test Performance," *Archives of Neurology*, 46 (1989): 383–386.

6. J. C. Morris et al., "Very Mild Alzheimer's Disease: Information-based Clinical Psychometric and Pathologic Distinction from Normal Aging," *Neurology*, 41 (1991): 469–478.

7. B. J. Gurland et al., "Criteria for the Diagnosis of Dementia in the Community Elderly," *The Gerontologist*, 22 (1982): 180–186.

8. D. W. O'Connor et al., "Clinical Issues Relating to the Diagnosis of Mild Dementia in a British Community Survey," *Archives of Neurology*, 48 (1991): 530–534.

9. T. Crook and C. J. Larrabee, "Age-associated Memory Impairment: Diagnostic Criteria and Treatment Strategies," *Psychopharmacology Bulletin*, 24 (1988): 509–514.

10. F. Lane and J. Snowdon, "Memory and Dementia: A Longitudinal Survey of Suburban Elderly," in P. Lovibond and P. Wilson, eds., *Clinical and Abnormal Psychology* (Holland: Elsevier, 1989).

11. J. R. Youngjohn, C. J. Larrabee, and T. H. Crook, III, "Discriminating Age-associ-

ated Memory Impairment from Alzheimer's Disease," *Psychological Assessment: A Journal of Consulting and Clinical Psychology,* in press.

12. For further discussion, see E. H. Rubin et al., "Very Mild Senile Dementia of the Alzheimer Type: I. Clinical Assessment," *Archives of Neurology,* 46 (1989): 379–382.

13. A. F. Jorm, A. E. Korten, and A. S. Henderson, "The Prevalence of Dementia: A Quantitative Integration of the Literature," *Acta Psychiatrica Scandinavica,* 76 (1987): 465–479.

14. C. Jonker and C. Hooyer, "The Amestel Project: Design and First Findings. The Course of Mild Cognitive Impairment of the Aged: A Longitudinal Four Year Study," *Psychiatric Journal of the University of Ottawa,* 15 (1990): 207–211.

15. L. Berg, "Minor Cognitive Deficits and the Detection of Mild Dementia," *Psychiatric Journal of the University of Ottawa,* 15 (1990): 230–231.

16. D. W. O'Connor et al., "Clinical Issues Relating to the Diagnosis of Mild Dementia in a British Community Survey."

17. B. J. Mowry and P. W. Burvill, "A Study of Mild Dementia in the Community Using a Wide Range of Diagnostic Criteria," *British Journal of Psychiatry,* 153 (1988): 328–334. Actually this study used seven criteria, but two of the scales have been eliminated in Table 7.2 because they seem less relevant to the diagnosis of MCI. These categories were called "pervasive dementia" and "rational."

18. H. Shibayama, Y. Kasahara, H. Kobayashi, et al., "Prevalence of Dementia in a Japanese Elderly Population," *Acta Psychiatrica Scandinavica,* 74 (1986): 144–151.

19. Two comprehensive reviews of normative data on cognitive aging are contained in two recent works by Salthouse: T. A. Salthouse, *Theoretical Perspectives on Cognitive Aging* (Hillsdale, N.J.: Erlbaum, 1991), and T. A. Salthouse, *Mechanisms of Age-Cognition Relations in Adulthood* (Hillsdale, N.J.: Erlbaum, 1992).

20. Storandt and Hill, "Very Mild Senile Dementia of the Alzheimer Type: II."

21. C. Bryne and P. Calloway, "Normal Ageing, Impaired Cognitive Function, and Senile Dementia of the Alzheimer Type: A Continuum?" *Lancet,* 1 (1988): 1265–1267.

22. J. G. Evans, "Ageing and Disease," in D. Evered and J. Whelan, eds., *Research and the Ageing Population,* Ciba Foundation Symposium 134 (Chicester: Wiley, 1988), pp. 38–47.

23. A. S. Henderson and F. A. Huppert, "Editorial: The Problem of Mild Dementia," *Psychological Medicine,* 14 (1984): 5–11.

24. Jorm, Korten, and Henderson, "The Prevalence of Dementia"

25. The Danish study was carried out by J. Nielsen, A. Homma, and T. Biørn-Henriksen, "Follow-up 15 Years after a Geronto-psychiatric Prevalence Study: Conditions Concerning Death, Cause of Death, and Life Expectancy in Relation to Psychiatric Diagnosis," *Journal of Gerontology,* 32 (1977): 554–561. The Swedish study was conducted by O. Hagnell et al., "Current Trends in the Incidence of Senile and Multi-infarct Dementia: A Prospective Study of the Total Population Followed over 25 Years; The Lundsby Study," *Archives of Psychiatry and Neurological Sciences,* 233 (1983): 423–438. The English study was done by D. W. O'Connor,

"The Prevalence of Dementia as Measured by the Cambridge Mental Disorders of the Elderly Examination," *Acta Psychiatrica Scandinavica,* 79 (1989): 190–198.

26. D. A. Evans, "Prevalence of Alzheimer's Disease in a Community Population of Older Persons," *Journal of the American Medical Association,* 262 (1989): 2551–2556.

27. Jorm, Korten, and Henderson, "The Prevalence of Dementia"

28. For example, Evans et al., "Prevalence of Alzheimer's Disease in a Community Population of Older Persons."

29. B. Reisberg et al., "Longitudinal Course of Normal Aging and Progressive Dementia of the Alzheimer's Type: A Prospective Study of 106 Subjects over a 3.6 Year Mean Interval," *Progress in Neuro-psychopharmacology and Biological Psychiatry,* 10 (1986): 571–578. See also Shibayama, Kasahara, and Kobayashi, "Prevalence of Dementia in a Japanese Elderly Population."

30. Hagnell et al., "Current Trends in the Incidence of Senile and Multi-infarct Dementia."

31. Reisberg et al., "Longitudinal Course of Normal Aging and Progressive Dementia of the Alzheimer's Type."

32. E. H. Rubin et al., "Very Mild Senile Dementia of the Alzheimer Type: I. Clinical Assessment."

33. D. W. O'Connor et al., "A Follow-up Study of Dementia Diagnosed in the Community Using the Cambridge Mental Disorders of the Elderly Examination," *Acta Psychiatrica Scandinavica,* 81 (1990): 78–82.

34. R. W. Besdine, "Dementia," in J. W. Rowe and R. W. Besdine, eds., *Health and Disease in Old Age* (Boston: Little, Brown, 1982).

35. National Institute on Aging Task Force, "Senility Reconsidered: Treatment Possibilities for a Mental Impairment in the Elderly," *Journal of the American Medical Association,* 244 (1980): 259.

36. A. M. Clarfield, "The Reversible Dementias: Do They Reverse?" *Annals of Internal Medicine,* 109 (1988): 476–486.

37. These studies are reviewed in K. W. Schaie and S. L. Willis, "Can Decline in Adult Intellectual Functioning Be Reversed?" *Developmental Psychology,* 22 (1986): 223–232. See also S. L. Willis, "Improvement with Cognitive Training: Which Old Dogs Learn What Tricks?" in L. W. Poon, D. L. Rubin, and B. A. Wilson, eds., *Everyday Cognition in Adulthood and Later Life* (New York: Cambridge University Press), pp. 545–569.

38. P. B. Baltes and U. Lindenbergen, "On the Range of Cognitive Plasticity in Old Age as a Function of Experience: 15 Years of Intervention Research," *Behavior Therapy,* 19 (1988): 283–320.

39. R. D. Hill, M. Storandt, and C. Simeone, "The Effects of Memory Skills Training and Incentives on Free Recall in Older Learners," *Journal of Gerontology,* 45 (1990): 227–232.

40. G. W. Rebok and L. J. Balcerak, "Memory Self-efficacy and Performance Difference

in Old and Young Adults: The Effect of Mnemonic Training," *Journal of Developmental Psychology*, 25 (1989): 714–721.

41. N. J. Treat and H. W. Reese, "Age, Pacing, and Imagery in Paired-associative Learning," *Developmental Psychology*, 12 (1978): 119–124.

42. S. J. Zarit, K. P. Cole, and R. L. Guider, "Memory Training Strategies and Subjective Complaints of Memory in the Aged," *The Gerontologist*, 21 (1981): 158–164.

43. T. M. Flynn and M. Storandt, "Supplemental Group Discussions in Memory Training for Older Adults," *Journal of Psychology and Aging*, 5 (1990): 178–181.

44. P. Verhaigen, A. Marcoen, and L. Goosens, "Improving Memory Performance in the Aged through Mnenomic Training," *Journal of Psychology and Aging*, 7 (1992): 242–251.

45. S. L. Willis and K. W. Schaie, "Training the Elderly in the Ability Factors of Spatial Orientation and Inductive Reasoning," *Psychology and Aging*, 1 (1986): 239–247.

46. R. D. Hill et al., "Mental Status as a Predictor of Response to Memory Training in Older Adults," *Educational Gerontology*, 15 (1989): 633–639.

47. M. F. Folstein, S. E. Folstein, and P. R. McHugh, "Mini-Mental State: A Practical Method for Grading the Cognitive State of Patients for Clinicians," *Journal of Psychiatric Research*, 12 (1975): 189–198.

48. For a review, see T. N. Tombaugh and N. J. McIntyre, "The Mini-Mental State Examination: A Comprehensive Review," *Journal of the American Geriatric Society*, 40 (1992): 922–935.

49. T. Karlsson et al., "Memory Improvement at Different Stages of Alzheimer's Disease," *Neuropsychologia*, 27 (1989): 737–742.

50. D. C. Park, "Applied Cognitive Aging Research," in F. I. M. Craik and T. A. Salthouse, eds., *The Handbook of Aging* (Hillsdale, N.J.: Erlbaum, 1992), pp. 449–494.

51. Willis, "Improvement with Cognitive Training."

52. Willis and Schaie, "Training the Elderly in the Ability Factors of Spatial Orientation and Inductive Reasoning."

53. Hill et al., "Mental Status as a Predictor of Response to Memory Training in Older Adults."

54. Karlsson et al., "Memory Improvement at Different Stages of Alzheimer's Disease."

55. F. I. M. Craik, M. Byrd, and J. M. Swanson, "Patterns of Memory Loss in Three Elderly Samples," *Psychology and Aging*, 2 (1987): 79–86.

56. Willis and Schaie, "Training the Elderly in the Ability Factors of Spatial Orientation and Inductive Reasoning."

57. Willis, "Improvement with Cognitive Training."

58. See P. B. Baltes, F. Dittman-Kohli, and R. Kliegl, "Reserve Capacity of the Elderly in Aging-sensitive Tests of Fluid Intelligence: Replication and Extention," *Psychology and Aging*, 1 (1986): 172–177.

59. R. Blieszner, S. L. Willis, and P. B. Baltes, "Training, Research, and Aging on the Fluid Ability of Inductive Reasoning," *Journal of Applied Developmental Psychology*, 2 (1981): 247–265.

60. R. Rosenthal and L. Jacobson, *Pygmalion in the Classroom* (New York: Holt, Rinehart, and Winston, 1968).

8. Normal Cognitive Aging

1. D. B. Calne, A. Eisen, and G. Meneilly, "Normal Aging of the Nervous System," *Annals of Neurology*, 30, no. 2 (1991): 206–207.
2. D. B. Calne and J. S. Calne, "Normality and Disease," *Canadian Journal of Neurological Sciences*, 15 (1988): 3–4.
3. A preliminary report has been prepared by the Institute for Social Research, *Health and Retirement Study: Work and Retirement* (Ann Arbor, Mich., 1993), pp. 6–22.
4. A. L. Benton, P. Eslinger, and A. R. Damasio, "Normative Observations on Neuropsychological Test Performances in Old Age," *Journal of Clinical Psychology*, 3 (1981): 33–42.
5. D. W. O'Connor et al., "Clinical Issues Relating to the Diagnosis of Mild Dementia in a British Community Survey," *Archives of Neurology*, 48 (1991): 530–534.
6. R. C. Green et al., "Screening for Cognitive Impairment in Older Individuals: Validation of Study of Computer-based Test," *Archives of Neurology*, in press.
7. O'Connor et al., "Clinical Issues Relating to the Diagnosis of Mild Dementia in a British Community Survey."
8. J. C. Morris et al., "Very Mild Alzheimer's Disease: Information-based Clinical Psychometric and Pathologic Distinction from Normal Aging," *Neurology*, 41 (1991): 469–478.
9. S. Weintraub, "Outline for Implementation of Follow-up Protocol," in D. H. Powell et al., *The Assessment of Cognitive Skills: Technical Progress Report* (Cambridge, Mass.: Risk Management Foundation, 1990), pp. 160–166.

9. Optimal Cognitive Aging

1. J. W. Rowe and R. L. Kahn, "Human Aging: Usual and Successful," *Science*, 237 (1987): 143–149.
2. M. D. Hayward, W. R. Grady, and S. D. McLaughlin, "Changes in the Retirement Process among Older Men in the United States: 1972–1980," *Demography*, 25 (1988): 371–386.
3. Department of Health and Human Services, *Healthy People 2000: National Health Promotion and Disease Prevention Objectives* (Washington, D.C.: U.S. Government Printing Office, 1990).
4. P. Rabbitt, "Applied Cognitive Gerontology: Some Problems, Methodologies, and Data," *Applied Cognitive Psychology*, 4 (1990): 225–246.
5. T. J. Bouchard et al., "Sources of Human Psychological Differences: The Minnesota Study of Twins Reared Apart," *Science*, 205 (1990): 223–228.
6. L. F. Jarvik, V. Ruth, and S. S. Matsuyama, "Organic Brain Syndrome and Aging: A

6-year Follow-up of Surviving Twins," *Archives of General Psychiatry,* 37 (1980): 280–286.

7. R. H. Cook, S. A. Schneck, and D. B. Clark, "Twins with Alzheimer's Disease," *Archives of Neurology,* 38 (1981): 300–301.

8. L. L. Heston et al., "Dementia of the Alzheimer's Type: Clinical Genetics, Natural History, and Associated Conditions," *Archives of General Psychiatry,* 38 (1981): 1085–1090.

9. R. Katzman and T. Saitoh, "Advances in Alzheimer's Disease?" *FASEB Journal,* 5 (1991): 278–286.

10. K. A. Perkins et al., "Cardiovascular Reactivity in Aerobically Trained vs. Untrained Mild Hypertensives and Normotensives," *Health Psychology,* 5 (1985): 407–421.

11. For a comprehensive summary of this literature, see C. H. Folkins and W. E. Sime, "Physical Fitness Training and Mental Health," *American Psychologist,* 36 (1981): 373–389.

12. The improvement in cognitive functioning associated with improved physical fitness was based on moderate exercise. See R. E. Dustman et al., "Age and Fitness Effects on EEG, ERPs, Visual Sensitivity and Cognition," *Neurobiology of Aging,* 11 (1990): 193–200.

13. E. S. Schneidman, "The Indian Summer of Life," *American Psychologist,* 44 (1989): 684–694.

14. M. C. Diamond, *Enriching Heredity: The Impact of the Environment on the Anatomy of the Brain* (New York: Free Press, 1988).

15. M. J. Renner and M. R. Rosenzweig, *Enrichment and Impoverished Environments: Effects on Brain and Behavior* (New York: Springer-Verlag, 1987).

16. B. Jacobs, M. Schall, and A. B. Scheibel, "A Quantitative Dendritic Analysis in Humans of Wernicke's Area: II. Gender, Hemispheric, and Environmental Factors," *Journal of Comparative Neurology,* 327 (1993): 97–111.

17. T. A. Salthouse, "Age-related Changes in Basic Cognitive Processes," in M. Storandt and G. R. Vandenbos, eds., *The Adult Years: Continuity and Change* (Washington, D.C.: American Psychological Association, 1989).

18. J. S. House, K. R. Landis, and D. Umberson, "Social Relationships and Health," *Science,* 241 (1988): 540–544.

19. L. Murphy and A. Moriarty, *Vulnerability, Coping, and Growth: From Infancy to Adolescence* (New Haven, Conn.: Yale University Press, 1976).

20. G. E. Vaillant, *Adaptation to Life* (Boston: Little, Brown, 1977).

21. S. A. Murrell, "Resource Versatility and Specificity for Elder Physical and Mental Health," paper presented at the 98th Annual Convention of the American Psychological Association, Boston, 1990.

22. A. Bandura, "Self-efficacy Mechanism in Human Agency," *American Psychologist,* 37 (1982): 122–147. See also A. Bandura, *Social Foundations of Thought and Action: A Social Cognitive Theory* (Englewood Cliffs, N.J.: Prentice-Hall, 1986).

23. R. White, "Strategies of Adaptation: An Attempt at Systematic Description," in B.

Coelho, A. Hamburg, and J. Adams, eds., *Coping and Adaptation* (New York: Basic Books, 1974).

24. N. D. Weinstein, "Optimistic Bias about Personal Risks," *Science,* 276 (1989): 1232–1233.

25. M. P. Lawton and S. Albert, "Affective Self-Management across the Life Span," paper presented at the 98th Annual Convention of the American Psychological Association, Boston, 1990.

26. E. Langer, *Mindfulness: The Psychology of Control* (Boston: Addison-Wesley, 1989).

27. G. W. Rebok and L. J. Balcerak, "Memory Self-Efficacy and Performance Difference in Old and Young Adults: The Effect of Mnemonic Training," *Journal of Developmental Psychology,* 25 (1989): 714–721. See also M. E. Lachman and R. Leff, "Perceived Control and Intellectual Functioning in the Elderly: A 5-year Longitudinal Study," *Developmental Psychology,* 25 (1989): 722–728.

28. See Vaillant, *Adaptation to Life.* See also G. E. Vaillant and C. O. Vaillant, "Natural History of Male Psychological Health XII: A 45-year Study of Predictors of Successful Aging at Age 65," *American Journal of Psychiatry,* 147 (1990): 1.

29. S. C. Kobasa et al., "Effectiveness of Hardiness, Exercise, and Social Support as Resources against Illness," *Journal of Psychosomatic Research,* 29 (1985): 525–533.

30. J. Barefoot, W. Dahlstrom, and W. Williams, "Hostility, Coronary Artery Disease, Incidents and Total Mortality: A 25-year Follow-up Study of 225 Physicians," *Psychosomatic Medicine,* 45 (1983): 59–64. See also P. Costa et al., "Cynicism and Paranoid Alienation in the Cook-Medley Ho Scale," *Psychosomatic Medicine,* 53 (1991): 37–44.

31. L. G. Russek et al., "The Harvard Mastery of Stress Study 35-year Follow-up: Prognostic Significance of Patterns of Psychophysiology, Arousal and Adaptation," *Psychosomatic Medicine,* 52 (1990): 271–285.

32. Vaillant, *Adaptation to Life.*

33. M. Zuckerman, *Sensation Seeking: Beyond the Optimal Level of Arousal* (Hillsdale, N.J.: Erlbaum, 1979). See also M. Zuckerman, S. Eysenck, and H. Eysenck, "Sensation Seeking in England and America," *Journal of Consulting and Clinical Psychology,* 48 (1978): 139–149.

34. S. Anderson, "Maintaining Cognitive Vigor in Later Years: The Contribution of Non-genetic Factors," unpublished doctoral dissertation, Boston University, 1992.

35. *The Compact Edition of the Oxford English Dictionary,* vol. I (London: Oxford University Press, 1979), p. 3794.

36. For a detailed discussion, see V. P. Clayton and J. E. Birren, "The Development of Wisdom across the Lifespan: A Reexamination of an Ancient Topic," in P. B. Baltes and O. G. Brim, eds., *Life-span and Development* (New York: Academic Press, 1980), pp. 104–135.

37. J. Bartlett, *Familiar Quotations,* 13th ed. (Boston: Little, Brown, 1955); B. Evans, *Dictionary of Quotations* (New York: Avenel, 1978).

38. See T. A. Salthouse, "Why Do Adult Age Differences Increase with Task Complex-

ity?" *Developmental Psychology,* 28 (1992): 905–918. This does not mean that task complexity is the only variable associated with the decline in working memory in older adults. The speed at which even elementary operations can be successfully carried out also declines greatly with age and may be even more important than task complexity. See A. Baddeley, "Working Memory," *The Journal of Science,* 255 (1992): 556–559. See also T. A. Salthouse and R. L. Babcock, "Decomposing Adult Age Differences and Working Memory," *Developmental Psychology,* 27 (1991): 763–776.

39. See C. Hertzog and K. W. Schaie, "Stability and Change in Adult Intelligence: II. Simultaneous Analysis of Longitudinal Means in Covariance Structures," *Psychology and Aging,* 3 (1988): 122–130. See also K. W. Schaie, "Individual Difference in Rate of Cognitive Change in Adulthood," in V. L. Bengston and K. W. Schaie, eds., *The Course of Later Life: Research and Reflections* (New York: Springer, 1989), pp. 65–85.

40. Clayton and Birren, "The Development of Wisdom across the Lifespan."

41. P. B. Baltes and U. M. Staudinger, "The Search for the Psychology of Wisdom," *Current Directions in Psychological Science,* 2 (1993): 75–80.

42. Ibid., pp. 75–80.

43. E. Erikson, "Reflections on Dr. Borg's Life Cycle," *Daedalus,* 105 (1976): 1–28.

44. E. Erikson and J. Erikson, "On Generativity and Identity: From a Conversation with Erik and Joan Erikson," *Harvard Educational Review,* 51 (1991): 249–269.

45. E. Erikson, J. M. Erikson, and H. Q. Kivnick, *Vital Involvement in Old Age* (New York: W. W. Norton, 1986).

46. H. W. Longfellow, "Morituri Salutamus," stanza 24 (1875).

10.   Findings and Conclusions

1. There is reason to believe that the results of computerized and pencil-and-paper tests may be comparable. A recent meta-analysis examined 28 studies comparing test scores of normal late adolescent and adult subjects who were given computerized paper-and-pencil versions of the same cognitive test. The estimated correlation between the two modes was .91. The correlation was higher for timed power tests (.97) than for speeded tests (.72). See A. D. Mead and F. Drasgow, "Equivalence of Computerized and Paper and Pencil Cognitive Ability Tests: A Meta-Analysis," *Psychological Bulletin,* 119 (1993): 449–458.

2. A. L. Benton, P. Eslinger, and A. R. Damasio, "Normative Observations on Neuropsychological Test Performances in Old Age," *Journal of Clinical Psychology,* 3 (1981): 33–42. See also J. W. Rowe and R. L. Kahn, "Human Aging: Usual and Successful," *Science,* 237 (1987): 143–149.

3. B. L. Neugarten, "Time, Age, and the Life Cycle," *American Journal of Psychiatry,* 136 (1979): 887–894.

4. K. W. Schaie, "The Seattle Longitudinal Study: 21-year Exploration of Psychomet-

ric Intelligence in Adulthood," in K. W. Schaie, ed., *Longitudinal Studies of Adult Psychological Development* (New York: Guilford, 1982), pp. 64–135.

5. Two relevant works by Salthouse and his colleagues on the disuse theory are T. A. Salthouse et al., "Age and Experience Effects in Spatial-visualization," *Developmental Psychology,* 26 (1990): 128–136, and T. A. Salthouse et al., "Effects of Adult Age and Working Memory on Reasoning and Spatial Abilities," *Journal of Experimental Psychology: Learning, Memory and Cognition,* 15 (1989): 507–516.

6. Data collected from the first three cycles of the Seattle Longitudinal Study found that average decrements in psychometric abilities cannot be detected prior to age 60. Small significant declines for some, but not all, cohorts were found in their fifties. See K. W. Schaie, "The Seattle Longitudinal Studies of Adult Intelligence," *Current Directions in Psychological Science,* 2 (1993): 171–175.

7. T. Crook, "Age-associated Memory Impairment: Proposed Diagnostic Criteria and Measures of Clinical Change—Report of the National Institute of Mental Health Work Group," *Developmental Neuropsychology,* 2 (1986): 261–276.

8. For example, Schaie, "The Seattle Longitudinal Study: 21-year Exploration of Psychometric Intelligence in Adulthood."

Name Index

Adams, J., 218n13, 237n23
Adams, K., 225n15, 228n34, 230n24
Albert, M. S., 220n46, 225n25, 228n34,
  229n34, 230n25
Albert, S., 237n25
Alzheimer, A., 14
Anderson, S., 191, 192, 237n34
Astrand, P., 223n1
Austin, L., 226n9

Babcock, R. L., 238n38
Baddeley, A., 220n5, 238n38
Baker, E. L., 220n7
Balcerak, L. J., 152, 233n40, 237n27
Baltes, P., 196, 197, 198, 234n58, 238n41
Bandura, A., 189, 236n22
Barefoot, J., 237n30
Baskin, D., 220n4
Beck, A. T., 227n19
Bell, B., 228n29
Bengston, V. L., 238n39
Benton, A. L., 13, 86, 87, 88, 169, 219n32,
  225n14, 235n4
Berg, L., 135, 139, 142, 231n2, 232n15
Berg, R., 220n45, 222n14, 223n20
Besdine, R. W., 149, 233n34
Biørn-Henriksen, T., 231n1, 232n25
Birren, J. E., 195, 237n36
Blanchard-Fields, P., 96, 227n12
Blazer, D., 228
Bliezner, R., 160, 229n37
Boll, T., 223n16
Bouchard, T. J., 235n5
Branconnier, R. J., 221n8

Brim, O. G., 237n36
Bryne, C., 141, 232n21
Burke, C. H., 223n17
Burvill, W., 139, 140, 232n17
Butatao, R. A., 217n4
Byrd, M., 159, 234n55
Byrne, G., 218n23

Calloway, P., 141, 232n21
Calne, D. B., 164, 235nn1, 2
Calne, J. S., 164, 235n2
Catlin, R., 95, 220n1
Cavenar, J., 226n9
Cavanaugh, J. C., 227n16
Ceci, S., 121, 230n26
Chess, S., 221n18
Cimino, C. R., 57, 222n12
Clarfield, A. M., 149, 233n36
Clark, D. B., 236n7
Clayton, V. P., 195, 237n36
Coelho, B., 218n13, 236n23
Cohen, J., 54, 222n8
Cole, K. P., 234n42
Coleman, J. S., 219n36
Cook, R. H., 236n7
Costa, P., 237n30
Craik, F. I. M., 159, 234n55
Crook, T., 137, 221n9, 231n4, 239n7
Cross, C., 227n22
Cunningham, W. R., 54, 222n7

Dahlstrom, G., 39, 222n1
Dahlstrom, W., 237n30

241

Subject Index

Age and aging, 5, 107; cognitive functions, 1, 19–22, 77, 89; psychological factors, 1, 6–9, 189–190; physical factors, 6–9; issues, 20–22; patterns by decade, 29, 30, 35, 49, 54, 72, 74–75, 82, 138, 201, 208; negative influence of, 80–81; physical health and, 90–96, 107, 210–211; education and, 104–105; group means, 180; nongenetic theories of, 186–190; social factors, 188–189. *See also* Change(s); Cognition; Mild cognitive impairment; Normal cognitive aging; Optimal cognitive aging (OCA)

Age-associated memory impairment (AAMI), 136–138, 210, 211, 212

AIDS, 15

Alcohol(ism), 6, 70, 91, 137, 184

Alzheimer Disease Assessment Battery, 24

Alzheimer's disease (AD), 1, 14–19, 21, 107, 138–139, 162, 201; presenile, 15; diagnosis of, 16–17, 134–135, 139, 163, 167; misdiagnosis of, 96, 149; with depression, 102–103; cure for, 134; mild, 138, 141, 148; compared with normal cognitive aging, 141, 165, 169, 203, 207, 209–210; compared with mild cognitive impairment, 143–144; criteria for, 163; reversible conditions of, 174; identical twins and, 186

Alzheimer's Disease and Related Disorders Association (ADRDA), 14, 18, 136

American Association of Retired Persons (AARP), 12

Analysis of variance (ANOVA), 40–41, 77, 84, 85. *See also* Significance tests

Anger, 96, 97, 189

Aptitude(s), 74, 75, 77–89; tests and retests, 103, 160; gender differences, 112–120, 124–133; age differences, 133; decline in, 160. *See also* Attention; Intellect and intelligence; Math skills and tests; Memory; Mental skills and tests; Numeric recall; Reasoning; Verbal memory; Visuospatial

Atlanta Predictive Validation Study, 64–66, 146–148, 170, 171, 172, 173

Attention, 68, 95, 202; order of decline, 20, 84, 86, 202, 209–210; tests, 26, 49, 55, 58, 60, 74, 180, 182, 201; education and, 76–77; employment vs. retirement decisions and, 109–110; gender differences, 125, 129, 133; age-related decline, 147–148

Autopsies to determine Alzheimer's disease, 15, 18, 186, 215

Beck Depression Inventory (BDI), 97, 100

Benton Retention Test, 86

Berkeley Older Generation Study, 91, 112, 113

Berlin model for wisdom, 196–198, 204

Bias. *See* Tests

Blood pressure, 89, 90, 94, 184, 187

Boston Diagnostic Aphasia Examination, 87

Boston Naming Test (BNT), 57, 59, 62, 63

Brain, 15–18, 188; disease, 66, 90, 137; trauma, 103–104; pathology, 215. *See*